Satire and Romanticism

Satire and Romanticism ∿

Steven E. Jones

St. Martin's Press
New York

SATIRE AND ROMANTICISM
Copyright © Steven E. Jones, 2000. All rights reserved. Printed in the United
States of America. No part of this book may be used or reproduced in any manner
whatsoever without written permission except in the case of brief quotations
embodied in critical articles or reviews. For information, address St. Martin's Press,
175 Fifth Avenue, New York, N.Y. 10010.

ISBN 0-312-22879-1

Library of Congress Cataloging-in-Publication Data

Jones, Steven E. (Steven Edward)
   Satire and romanticism / Steven E. Jones.
     p. cm.
   Includes bibliographical references (p.) and index.
   ISBN 0-312-22879-1
   1. Satire, English—History and criticism. 2. Verse satire, English—History
and criticism. 3. English literature—19th century—History and criticism. 4.
Romanticism—Great Britain. I. Title.
PR936.J66 2000
827'.709 21—dc21

                                       99–045477
                                          CIP

Permission to cite from *John Keats: Complete Poems,* ed. Jack Stillinger. Copyright
© 1982 by the President and Fellows of Harvard College. Reprinted by permission
of the Belknap Press of Harvard University Press.

Permission to quote "A Character," in *Tennyson: A Selected Edition,* ed. Christopher
Ricks (Berkeley and Los Angeles: University of California Press, 1989), no. 88, p.
14.

Portions of "Lyrical Ballad" and "Rime of the Auncient Waggonere" are reprinted
with the permission of Associated University Presses.

Design by Letra Libre, Inc.

First edition: April, 2000
10 9 8 7 6 5 4 3 2 1

To W. E. Jones and P. M. Jones

Contents

Acknowledgments

This book emerged from the midst of a number of other projects and duties, so my debts to colleagues and supporters are widely distributed and ultimately innumerable. But one story must be told. I gave a talk at the Wordsworth Summer Conference in Grasmere, the English Lake District, in 1997 and received very helpful responses afterwards from Graeme Stones, Charles Donelan, Sally Bushell, Jonathan Wordsworth, Marilyn Gaull, and Karl Kroeber. That interchange shaped chapter 1 below, and in many ways, the book as a whole. In due time Marilyn Gaull became the most generous and encouraging of editors for this project, and to her I am especially grateful. Karl Kroeber's advice, in *that* setting (among the landscapes he first taught me to imagine through the language of Romantic poetry), was even more compelling than usual. On another day I heard Kroeber's typically direct (and sometimes cheerfully satiric) responses to a panel on *The Rime of the Ancient Mariner* just after seeing Hunt Emerson's raucous illustrations on display down the road, and the juxtaposition led me to write what became chapter 2. In many ways during my brief stay at the Red Lion Inn, during solitary walks along the fells above the lakes, strolls through the churchyard, and conversations over good pints, I was inspired and encouraged to complete the present book.

Since then, Jerome McGann and James Chandler have each offered critical advice at crucial stages of the project; Carl Woodring came to my aid (once more) as a reader—a clear case of mentoring beyond the call of duty; John Strachan helpfully answered specific queries on parody and, along with Michael Eberle-Sinatra, read a portion of chapter 2. For their daily collegiality in cyberspace, and for taking up the slack, thanks to my co-conspirators Neil Fraistat and Carl Stahmer. Maureen Dowd and Anne Irmen Close provided excellent research assistance when it was most needed, and financial support came in the form of two summer research grants from Loyola University Chicago. I am grateful to Hunt Emerson for his cordiality and the permission to reproduce images from his *Rime of the Ancient Mariner,* and to Ronald Tabeta of Loyola University's Center for Instructional Design for photographing the comic book pages; my thanks as well to the Newberry

Library in Chicago for the images from *The Black Dwarf.* Special thanks to Catherine Payling, Curator of the Keats House in Rome, for coordinating on short notice the photography of Byron's carnival mask and for permission to reproduce the result. A version of chapter 1 appeared in *The Wordsworth Circle* 29.1 (Winter 1998), a portion of chapter 2 was published in a special issue of *Romanticism on the Net* (August 1999), and an early portion of chapter 3 was included in *Romanticism, Radicalism, and the Press,* ed. Stephen Behrendt (Detroit: Wayne State University Press, 1997).

Finally, I'm grateful to my brother, Jeffrey Jones, for teaching me to really *read* comic books, starting with that first *Daredevil* and including lots of R. Crumb. My deepest gratitude goes to Heidi S. Jones for (among other acts of faith) building me an attic room with a lovely view of the treetops, where this book was written, and to Emilia and Henry for playing outside those windows almost every day. Perspective is everything.

Introduction ⌒

Satire and the Making of the Romantic

This book is not a survey of satire in the Romantic period (which I date from about 1760 to 1832), nor is it a collation of satiric passages in Romantic literature. Instead, this is a study of the constructive and ultimately canon-forming relationship between satiric and Romantic modes of writing. My focus, therefore, is on the space—contended space—between these two modes, how they mutually defined each other and were subtly interwoven during the late eighteenth and early nineteenth centuries. Each chapter concentrates through case studies either on the lines of generic demarcation at the moment they were hardening into familiar boundaries or on the interrelations of these conventionally oppositional modes. My main question is: How are satire and Romanticism implicated in one another during the Romantic period? In the end, this book is about a dynamic process in literary history: the making of the "Romantic" in relation to the "satiric."

Robert Southey once argued that a topical satirist of the late eighteenth century known as "Junius" was the most (perniciously) influential writer of his age.[1] The anonymous correspondent writing to newspapers as Junius was a Whig supporter of Wilkes who wrote scathing satiric attacks on George III and his ministers from 1769 to 1772, but to Southey his legacy was an example of insubordination and "disaffection." To most readers, Southey's estimation of Junius's power would seem a little absurd, but he was widely respected and feared in his day. However motivated by political gall (and it certainly is so motivated), Southey's claim is a useful reminder of the centrality of satire in the period, of its perceived rhetorical power. It explains the substantial passage on Junius in Byron's 1820 "The Vision of Judgment," a satiric parody of Southey's laureate poem on the death of George III. Among the witnesses called in Heaven against Southey is a "mighty shadow of a shade," the anonymous satirist who seemed to Southey to epitomize disaffection, the nemesis of the dead king.

> 75.
> The Shadow came! a tall, thin, grey-hair'd figure,
>   That look'd as it had been a shade on earth;
> Quick in it motions, with an air of vigour,
>   But nought to mark its breeding or its birth;
> Now it wax'd little, then again grew bigger,
>   With now an air of gloom, or savage mirth;
> But as you gazed upon its features, they
>   Changed every instant—to *what*, none could say.
>   76.
> The more intently the ghosts gazed, the less
>   Could they distinguish whose the features were;
> The Devil himself seem'd puzzled even to guess;
>   They varied like a dream—now here, now there;
> And several people swore from out the press,
>   They knew him perfectly; and one could swear
> He was his father; upon which another
>   Was sure he was his mother's cousin's brother:
>   77.
> Another, that he was a duke, or knight,
>   An orator, a lawyer, or a priest,
> A nabob, a man-midwife; but the wight
>   Mysterious changed his countenance at least
> As oft as they their minds; though in full sight
>   He stood, the puzzle only was increased;
> The man was a phantasmagoria in
>   Himself—he was so volatile and thin!
>   78.
> The moment that you had pronounced him *one*,
>   Presto! his face changed, and he was another;
> And when that change was hardly well put on,
>   It varied, till I don't think his own mother
> (If that he had a mother) would her son
>   Have known, he shifted so from one to t'other,
> Till guessing from a pleasure grew a task,
>   At this epistolary "iron mask."[2]

Byron interjects his own hypothesis: that Junius was "nobody at all," a teasing and scarifying suggestion of faceless conspiracy lurking behind the joke. When challenged by the Archangel about his satires against the king, Junius still refuses to reveal his identity; then Byron turns serious in this passage of defiant ventriloquism:

83.
"My charges upon record will outlast
    The brass of both his epitaph and tomb."
"Repent'st thou not," said Michael, "of some past
    Exaggeration? something which may doom
Thyself, if false, as him if true? Thou wast
    Too bitter—is it not so? in thy gloom
Of passion?" "Passion!" cried the phantom dim,
    "I loved my country, and I hated him.
        84.
"What I have written, I have written: let
    The rest be on his head or mine!" So spoke
Old "Nominis Umbra;" and while speaking yet,
    Away he melted in celestial smoke.

For Byron as for Southey, Junius represents a primary force at the headwaters of the political and moral discourse in the era—a force of satire. This example belies the common assumption that the most powerful modes of feeling in the age were identifiably Romantic, sincere, and inward-turning. Here it is the satirist who expresses sublime "passion" while being fully engaged in the public sphere.

But the opposition of satire and Romanticism is everywhere in Romantic studies, including, for example, the extremely influential *Natural Supernaturalism*. In the introduction, M. H. Abrams explains that Byron is to be omitted from the book altogether, "because in his greatest work he speaks with an ironic countervoice and deliberately opens a satirical perspective on the vatic stance of his contemporaries."[3] It is understandable that Byron—the contrarian defender of Pope and Gifford, even over and against his own Romantic writings—should be bracketed off in Abrams's argument. Subsequently, Byronists and Romantic ironists, among others, have offered alternatives to Abrams's account and Byron has retained his place in the Romantic canon, though that canon itself is now recognized as only one portion of the body of writing—much of it un-Romantic—produced during the period. But note the generic terms of Byron's exclusion: his "satirical perspective" counters the sincere "vatic stance" of the Romantics. Byron does not quite fit into Abrams's paradigm because he was a *satirist*. If Romantic poetry is defined as vatic or prophetic, inward-turning, sentimental, idealizing, sublime, and reaching for transcendence—even in its ironies— then satire, with its socially encoded, public, profane, and tendentious rhetoric, is bound to be cast in the role of generic other, as *the* un-Romantic mode. The extremely influential notion of English Romantic irony, which I discuss in detail below (chapter 6), is one way Romanticism has been depicted by criticism as reabsorbing—by Romanticizing—a medley of its traditional generic oppositions. Thus reconciled to one aspect of its darker side, to its self-parodic and satiric modes as these tend toward philosophical nihilism, Romanticism stands safely above generic threats from within as well as without.[4]

In *The Romantic Ideology* Jerome McGann questioned this Romantic ironic triumph as part of his argument for a more rigorous criticism; since then he has more than once suggested that a recovery of satire could contribute to this larger revisionist project, because satire represents a dialectical antithesis to the "paradigm mode" of Romanticism—expressive sincerity.[5] Basically reversing the values of Abrams's earlier opposition, McGann finds Byron's poetry particularly valuable for Romantic studies, precisely because it "opens itself to the horizon of its antithesis," to a kind of anti-Romantic public voice.[6] I would suggest that this dialectic must be pursued into subtler interrelations, that simply transvaluing the opposition of Romantic and satiric modes is not enough, but I share McGann's belief that satiric writing of the period offers an important revisionary perspective. Satire and polemical verse, as he observes, work through "publicly installed dialogical operations,"[7] so an attention to these "operations" provides a useful way to place the idea of Romanticism in a more varied literary and cultural context. And this must begin with recognizing what has been displaced. It is true that criticism of Romantic writing has tended, in this specific case as in general, to replicate Romantic ideological formations, to ignore or underplay the importance of satire in the period: "Romantic ideology, which privileges conventions of 'sincerity' over conventions of 'premeditation,' has all but obliterated our received sense of the satiric traditions that were being worked between 1790–1832."[8]

As Marilyn Butler (satirically) remarks, the "so-called Romantics did not know at the time that they were supposed to do without satire."[9] The Romantic period is full of satires, but their satiric traditions have proved difficult to recover. In the introduction to his study of genre in the Romantic period, Stuart Curran notes that satire must be omitted from the book for purely practical reasons, since it presents special problems and requires a more extensive treatment, although he also acknowledges that it is "an extremely vital mode in British Romanticism, one whose full dimensions have never been addressed by criticism."[10] As if in response, Gary Dyer's study of satire between 1789 and 1832 addresses these traditions on their own terms, mapping out the territory and offering readings of little-known works and authors, all fitting under a general thesis about the politicization and censorship of literature at the time.[11]

Thus the horizon of Romantic-period satire (and parody) has recently begun to open up to criticism to a new extent,[12] but detailed and nuanced readings of the specific ways satiric writings contributed to the developing literary history of the period are still needed, and that is what this book aims to provide: a study of the significance of some particular modes of satiric writing and the idea of the satiric as they participated in the shaping of the canon and its central concept of Romanticism. Something like the dialectical process that McGann envisions for historicist criticism, I would suggest, is already present in the earliest formation of the Romantic canon, and satire, later forgotten, played a role in this dialectic. This process I explore in chapter 2, in which I rediscover the gothic conventions and parodic energies at work within and without Coleridge's developing canonical oeuvre.

There are many oppositions at work in the construction of Romanticism (ideas of the feminine, for example, and the oriental), but satire is the dominant *generic* construct, the modal anvil over and against which early-nineteenth-century literature gets clustered, hammered out, formed, and hardened into a recognizable poetic movement, to be ensconced in literary history as uniquely representative of the spirit of the age. It would be absurd to claim too much self-consciousness for this process; in its historical moment, Romantic-era satirists did nothing directly or purposely to help make Romanticism, which at any rate did not exist yet as a concept. But I argue in the chapters that follow that various active frictions and influences, between on the one hand satiric and on the other sentimental or sincere modes, began subtly to rearrange reputations, aesthetic assumptions, standards of taste, and the distribution of symbolic and cultural capital in ways that paved the way for—and eventually made possible—the later Victorian and modern construction of the movement labeled "English Romanticism."

Although the term "Romantic" came to name a unified movement in England only in the later nineteenth century, the process of constructing what is now recognized as Romantic writing and the Romantic canon was already well under way before 1830. While in its fully canonized form Romanticism is a "posthumous movement," constructed after the fact of the Romantic period, some of the "more exciting and flattering connotations" of the label "Romantic" were "already attaching themselves to the most appropriate leading writers during their lifetimes and immediately after."[13] At the end of the eighteenth century, Pope, Swift, and Johnson, the vernacular "moderns," were the standards of critical excellence, and it was within the modes of satire that they reached their pinnacle of influence. By the mid-nineteenth century, a new set of moderns, Wordsworth, Coleridge, Byron, and (with greater ambivalence) Shelley and Keats, had displaced the Augustans in most measures of canonical status. These Romantics were associated with sentimental, sincere, sublime, and imaginative modes, with nature and feeling, often defined in direct opposition to the aesthetic regime of the Augustans.[14] Already in 1756 Joseph Warton had neatly codified the balanced, symmetrical terms of the opposition, though his views would only come to dominate taste later, in the next century: "For WIT and SATIRE are transitory and perishable, but NATURE and PASSION are eternal."[15]

By the mid- to late-nineteenth century those latter qualities were considered the heart of Romantic literature, the basis on which it deserved immortality in the English canon, and by the 1880s the term "Romantic" had come to cover a number of modes, schools, conventions, and thematic preoccupations, to serve as a powerful interpretive category for the practice of criticism and the teaching of literature. In the study that follows I use the term "Romantic" with full awareness of this history: as referring to emergent modes that were only later fitted under the term itself. Granted, a certain unavoidable anachronism attends upon using the term at all; but taking a strictly nominalist approach leads to setting the dates for the movement so *safely* late in the course of literary history that the heated, dynamic process of emergence—the making of Romanticism—is obscured. Movements such as Romanticism are real. But they are made artifacts of reception history and, in this case, made (and named) after the fact of their inchoate initial recognition. Their full recognition is cumulative and can date from an initial press release or manifesto by artists themselves, or, as is the case with Romanticism, come more gradually, as consensus builds and labels are assigned over the course of years or decades. The process of constructing a movement often coincides with the sorting out of individual works for canonization, and this inevitably involves acts of inclusion and exclusion.

I am aware that to some contemporary scholars of the Romantic period, especially those working with texts by women authors or with the drama, for example, who have helped to expand the field of study well beyond the traditional canon, my devoting so much attention to the construction of canonical ideas of Romanticism may seem unnecessary, even retrograde. But the canon of Romanticism retains a powerful interpretive force, even when it comes to defining what is "non-canonical." This is especially true outside the rarified circles of professional literary criticism. Besides, the term has a long critical history that in itself demands attention. The birth of Romanticism as a concept accompanied the development of the modern canon and the emergence of the concept of literature itself as an aesthetic category. It is important therefore to understand the history of these developments, to look at the process by which such categories were made and deployed, as part of the ongoing canon revision in eighteenth- and nineteenth-century studies.

Such I would argue is the conceptual framework within which to read David Perkins's writings on the history of the Romantic movement, to name just one prominent example.[16] One can assent to Perkins's documented evidence for the emergence of what will later be named as Romantic and still interpret that evidence differently than he does. For example, while it might be true that the "only important classification of contemporary poets was the Lake School" (130), one might wish to begin by questioning the term "important," and to look at the subsequent claims with special care:

> The later classifications by Lockhart of "The Cockney School of Poetry" and by Southey of "The Satanic School" were frankly modeled on Jeffrey's move, but enjoyed much less currency. These classifications were outrageously abusive, and for most readers did not organize the contemporary literary scene in a valid way. . . . But it is significant that most classifications of English poets in the period were originally made by politically conservative critics and were ideological and hostile. (130–31)

A feminist critic, say, might well raise serious questions about this account, beginning with the claim about what "most readers" means, and what these readers presumably found valid as classificatory schemes. But from the point of view of competing poetic modes, it is sufficient to recognize that literary history has in the event proved Jeffrey *and* Lockhart *and* Southey—and even Shelley—to be more or less on the same wavelength when it came to what mattered (including negatively) in contemporary poetry—at least to critics and tastemakers like themselves. Canon is consensus. By the later Victorian era the Cockney and Satanic schools had been integrated into a unifying description of canonical Romanticism.

Perkins describes one way in which even contemporary classifications were united at the time: they were "hostile," even "outrageously abusive"—which is to say, viewed in broad terms of generic stance, they were often satiric. Historically, literary reviews of almost any school or movement are hostile and abusive. This is in the nature of most reviewing, and Romantic writing is not the only victim of such criticism. But in this case and in this era, something more is going on. Some of the nastiness of nineteenth-century reviews was personal, and much was blatantly political. The field of reviewing itself was defined at the time by the pure, anonymous vitriol of *Blackwood's,* and by the polarized split of the Tory *Quarterly Review* from the Whig *Edinburgh Review.* At times it seems that nearly everyone involved at that most public level in the reviews was in the pay of one party or the other. Nevertheless, these conflicts were also part of broader culture wars, and they often took the form of skirmishes over taste. When it comes to taste, which was defined as a moral and national issue, the satiric violence of the reviews I focus on reflects an emerging consensus that the poetry they attacked—sentimental, Della Cruscan, Cockney, Lake School, Satanic School—was part of a dangerous new epidemic, but one that might still respond to the harsh treatment of satire on behalf of the literary world whose authority it represented. The new poetries of the era, these reviews assumed, were a hydra-headed mutant species that abhorred satire as much as they were abhorred by it. It is too easy to underestimate the significance of that basic, seemingly common-sense assumption: that satire and the new poetry were antithetical, even hostile, species. Over time, it is remarkable how often Romantic or sentimental modes come to be defined negatively, as meaning something very close to "un-satiric." In most of the famous cases cited above, the abusive sarcasm of the reviewers half-intentionally imitates the alternative satiric modes—"manly," public, worldly, aggressive—that defined by their very absence the emerging Romantic canon. This is more than merely recognizing again the well-known opposition of neoclassical and Romantic, although that more universal critical observation was in its general outlines formulated during the same era and surely accompanied the more local effect I am highlighting. My purpose is more specific: to provide a local habitation and a name to one aspect of that hoary universal generalization, to give a concrete body—one important set of actual modal and generic conflicts—to that theoretical idea.

One word here about terminology. Though I will use the terms "genre" and "mode" more or less interchangeably in this study, I do not mean that a given work fits a predetermined literary form, or even that it exhibits a discrete set of inherited conventions. Instead, I mean that the work is situated in recognizable contexts, which may include literary as well as subliterary satiric conventions, among which may be found ritualistic name-calling, punning, parody, and mock-heroic comparisons; but also cartoon and caricature, carnivalesque absurdity and disgust, and scapegoating violence. Competent and persuaded readers of satire in context usually expect that it can serve pragmatic social functions, such as enforcing the status quo or social *données* by punishing women writers, social parvenus, closet Jacobins, and apostate poets, but they also may believe that it can be subversive or oppositional, a way of rallying collective radical anger around a shared target or defying gag laws on principle.

These expectations and the conventions of satire are the function of public performances in specific situations, and these often resist being separated into "literary" versus "cultural" performances. Like the most vivid and most widespread form of satire at the time, graphic satiric prints, early-nineteenth-century satires tend to be *medleys*, of topics or subgenres (this is to be expected from the mixed-feast or *satura* that is satire) but also of discourses high and low, of texts and images, and of seemingly incompatible modes. Even literary satires often work by making gestures towards this promiscuous feast of discursive possibilities. As Mikhail Bakhtin has shown, such mixtures partake of the carnivalesque as it descends from the genres of parody, satyr play, and Menippean satire to the modern novel. But as Peter Stally-brass and Allon White have argued, the carnival is the site of demonization and violence as well as subversive laughter, and any study of satire in an era of social and political conflict must be alert to both the popular rough music and the normative, authoritarian uses of satiric modes.[17]

This is another way of getting at the problem of the "topicality" of satire, its reliance on contexts as much as on texts. Topical satire depends on customary gestures, such as a nonverbal wink across a crowded room, witnessed by all but only fully understood by the intended recipient.[18] Satiric allusions are encoded to be experienced on multiple levels, to function through various forms of indirection—not all of them controllable by the author's intentions. On one level, Arabella Fermor is (ideally) made to laugh at herself; on another, her family cools its desire for public retribution in an ongoing feud. On yet another, savvy male readers in Pope's circle are encouraged through traditional satiric misogyny to ridicule Arabella in Belinda—as the representative of all womankind. But on still another level, some readers may revel in the enchanted machinery at the expense of Pope's satiric messages. In the course of accumulating layers of reception history, as contexts continue to change, an Aubrey Beardsley may arise to satirize the satirist in acidly ironic illustrations of the text.[19] Relying on context as much as text, satire is the genre most likely to be understood in purely intrinsic or essentialist terms, the genre most likely to require the audience to make the meaning of the text. There is little or nothing essential and self-sufficient *in* satire; it is constructed in performance before an audience or, in some cases, many different audiences.

Therefore I prefer definitions of both satire and Romanticism that are local, specific, and relational, connected to the performance and reception of works in their immediate contexts. My purpose is to identify the ways the terms "Romantic" and "satiric" were constructed through processes of struggle and mutual definition. I avoid those larger-than-history generic labels, "Juvenalian," "Horatian," or "Persian," in favor of more pragmatic modal positions taken by specific authors and works vis-à-vis other authors and works. Mary Robinson wrote under the pseudonym of "Horace Juvenal," and Byron may have called William Gifford "Juvenal" (while composing his own "Hints from Horace"); undoubtedly, a late-eighteenth-century idea of Juvenal's satire had important implications for Gifford's own satiric practice, but for the most part I leave those implications to others. For my purposes here, Gifford's version of satire is best located not in a transhistorical literary tradition but at the battlefront of the culture wars of the 1790s, where it was shaped by the strategic moves and countermoves of his own work, the work of his intended targets, and all those looking on who took a lesson from the struggle, all of which helped to shape emergent ideas of canonical poetry.

The works I examine in this book define themselves as satires in very specific terms, and they do so in relation to a particular opposite: sentimental, Della Cruscan, Lake School, Anti-Jacobin, coterie, or cant. Especially in chapters 1, 2, and 4, I make use of case studies in conflict and relational definition, focusing on representative interactions between satiric and Romantic works that contribute to the emerging construction of a recognizable Romanticism. Throughout, my case studies are chosen because the relations they embody are significant, and I see these relations as real events in history (including literary history), documented confrontations, struggles, parodies, or satiric commentaries, interactions along a complex front. That front is permeable and the interactions work both ways. As chapters 3, 6, and 7 demonstrate, emergent Romantic or sentimental modes find their way into early nineteenth-century satire, including popular and radical forms such as journalism and the pantomime. And more often than traditional criticism has been prepared to recognize, Romantic works are influenced by, infected with, and enfold within themselves examples of satiric writing. In my view Byron (the subject of chapters 5 and 6) is simply the most vivid representation of the ambivalent relation of Romantic and satiric modes in the period, a relation evident as early as Coleridge's writings in the 1790s, which begin with potentially self-parodic modes and then proceed to open themselves to parody, in the process making themselves ready for the canon. The satiric and the Romantic are shown by my evidence to interpenetrate one another, to be related in ways that finally go well beyond mere dialectical opposition.

My procedure is to focus on examples of satire being written to vital effect long after the conventionally recognized decline of the mode at the end of the eighteenth century, reading them alongside poetry later canonized as dominating its age. Thus I view satire in action, as part of a relational definition, a struggle for the not-yet-accomplished dominance of the literary field. I also emphasize works and authors that might escape notice as trivial (a "mere squib"), aesthetically inferior (sentimental, popular, vicious), or interstitial in terms of literary period (Crabbe, Elliott). This means, for example, that I deliberately foreground the popular gothic and sentimental elements in Coleridge's *Rime of the Ancient Mariner,* or that I pay more attention to Byron's relatively slight skit, "The Blues," than to the much-analyzed *Don Juan.* The result, however, is a wide historical sweep connecting important moments of the period—from poetic ruralism and supernatural gothicism in the Lake Country in the 1790s to radicalism and sentimentalism in post-Waterloo London, to the broadly influential gestures of Byron in exile, to the newly respectable movement for reform and the making of the canon in the 1820s and 1830s. In each case I zoom in on telling details, because the generic devil is in the details, in the subtle breakaway gestures that strike out, erode resistance, and survive to form new channels of understanding. The detailed picture of literary history thereby produced is more "fractal" than simply linear in its effects. That is to say, the dynamic relation between Crabbe and Wordsworth resembles the dynamic relation between the Della Cruscans and Keats, because both sets of relations are iterations on their limited scales of a larger process going on at a higher scale in literary culture, a process retrospectively recognizable as the emergence of the dominantly Romantic canon.

In describing this process, I sometimes find it useful to invoke a related metaphor for emergence and change in cultural history, for systems operating through competitive interaction, that of evolution. Despite some reservations, I find stimulating Gary Taylor's argument that literary history and its result, the canon, can be better understood in light of evolutionary models—as a process of local struggles for productive niches from which to dominate and survive.[20]

> The history of literature, then, is the history of innumerable struggles for cultural space and time, and the results are as unforeseeable as the outcome of any competition. The struggle is not periodic; it does not happen in recurring cycles. Moreover, the randomness created by competition and individual evaluation is multiplied by the fact that literature is not a closed system. The tragedies performed at Athenian festivals are not simply literary texts; like Broadway musicals, they compound verbal with visual, musical, and choreographic art in an unstable mixture that emphasizes first one constituent, then another. And all these arts interact in complex unique combinations with the larger human social environment in which they are evaluated and selected for recollection or oblivion. (*Cultural Selection,* 19)

Taylor is aware that he is treading a fine line between metaphor and specious homology in this thesis, and he admits that "works of art are not themselves living organisms" but then goes on to suggest that "their creators are, and culture—like life—is created by endlessly reiterated combinations of struggle, death, and survival" (*Cultural Selection,* 46). I find the metaphor of evolutionary selection productive for creative thinking about cultural competition—so long as it is treated as a metaphor. In these terms, literary works, forms, and generic modes, like individuals and their respective species, interact in competition for openings or niches in the cultural economy; the borders between them fluctuate and blur, then fix into newly demarcated forms whose very identities continue to depend on a certain family resemblance, and on what they are *not*. Such metaphorical thinking about genre or mode provides a useful context for more narrowly literary descriptions.

But it is important to think through such metaphors in the context of culture and its *made,* human complexities, and here I often find salutary the sociological theories of Pierre Bourdieu, who reminds us that competitive struggles in culture are not natural but are the result of institutional social structures. These struggles take place for many reasons, including unconscious motives and the press of material necessity, and ultimately they are less like natural selection, however complexly conceived, than they are like the socially constructed and yet determining rules of a "game" played for dominance in a given "field."[21] Competition in the literary field takes place for resources (for readers in the marketplace, for example, or the symbolic capital of prestige and reputation) and according to the rules of a game, the object of which is to "win," to survive, in part by defining what will henceforth count as winning. In the realm of culture, what counts as winning is often what counts by the standards of taste. As Bourdieu says, this struggle is not limited to "the ethereal realm of ideas," or even to "the confrontation between 'canonized' and 'non-canonized texts'"; instead, change in the literary field depends on "the balance of forces between social agents who have entirely real interests in the different possibilities available to them as stakes and who deploy every sort of strategy to make one set or another prevail."[22]

Cultural capital and what counts as winning the struggle for dominance in the field are matters of value and evaluation, inclusion and exclusion, part of the "stakes" to which Bourdieu refers. The canonical work—and the complex symbolic process of recognizing and valuing that work—helps reflexively to define the taste and the procedures of competition and judgment that lead to the canonization of that work and others. Wordsworth put it somewhat differently, that representative artists must create the taste by which they are to be appreciated. Being able to do so is one of the defining criteria of canonical status. According to the rules of the game, such definitions of taste and canon frequently take place over and against something, in opposition to what is less worthy of later recognition (by definition). In the case of emergent Romanticism, this something often turns out to be satire. As it entered the canon, Romanticism in effect turned the tables on contemporary satiric critics of the new mode. Tracing that double process of critique and canonization can help us to better understand the canonical status of Romanticism, and how that was achieved by defining it as countersatiric writing. That, to put it as simply as possible, is the rationale for what follows.

In chapter 1 I argue that Romantic rusticity emerges over and against the satire of George Crabbe—as a form of sentimental countersatire. Wordsworth's way of representing rusticity is deliberately, strategically countersatiric, evincing a sincerity defined against Crabbe's kind of perspective on the rural poor. This opposition is usefully complicated in relation to the counterpastoral tradition and the satiric "counter-counterpastoral" of

Stephen Duck and Mary Collier, in which the rustics turn the tables and represent themselves. Chapter 2 looks at Coleridge's best-known poem of the high Romantic canon, *The Rime of the Ancient Mariner,* in order to explore the subtle role of parody and self-parody in the revisionist project by which Coleridge helped to make Romanticism. By examining parodies of the ballad as well as Coleridge's history of preemptive self-parody, I suggest that the parodists are merely developing the potential within the Romantic text for turning satire into encomium. Chapter 3 cites the strong example of the radical satirist and popular journalist, T. J. Wooler, editor of *The Black Dwarf.* The titular persona, which I suggest may have been a parody and appropriation of Walter Scott's Romantic Black Dwarf, bestrides both carnivalesque satire and Romantic modes of address. Wooler's *Dwarf* thus embodies some fundamental anxieties of the public-sphere discourse it commanded.

In chapter 4 I look at the most famous *targets* of Romantic-era satire, the sentimental and erotic Della Cruscan school. In the context of their public pillorying, I read John Keats—especially in "The Jealousies"—as a Della Cruscan attempting reflexively to administer his own satiric remedy. I then point to the Romantic defense of Keats, Shelley's *Adonais,* as the quintessential late Della Cruscan poem, a countersatiric work that seeks the victims' revenge against the violent hand of satire. Then the focus of the study shifts to the one recognized master-satirist among the canonical Romantics, Lord Byron. Chapter 5 examines that enormously popular eighteenth-century straw woman, the "bluestocking," as she was reconstructed by Byron's late satire "The Blues" and a family of related satiric works, which I read as an anxious defense of male authority in the new marketplace of literature, over and against what was perceived as the dangerous potential of salon culture to patronize or threaten that authority.

That potential was based in the "colloquial wit" of conversation. Chapter 6 looks at the very different "visual wit" of the popular theatrical form, the pantomime. This English adaptation of the Italian *commedia dell'arte* was, according to Leigh Hunt, "the best dramatic satire of the age." The *commedia* (and its modern revival) was also a favorite of German Romantic theorists—and I argue that the English pantomime was the most prominent mainstream conduit and visible arena in early nineteenth-century England for "Romantic irony"—and can thus be directly connected to the greatest canonical satire of the era, Byron's *Don Juan.* Much of the satire in the poem is best understood as a conflicted and materialist, *pantomimic* kind of satire. Whereas the pantomime transforms a romance plot into a raucous harlequinade, criticism has systematically turned what was once burlesque and satiric—in *Don Juan* and other works of the period—into something more sincere, sentimental, Romantic.

Chapter 7 moves into the late 1820s with the work of Ebenezer Elliott, the self-styled "Corn Law Rhymer." Represented as an uneducated poet of earnest sentiment and honest indignation, Elliott was actually an extremely direct satirist, one often accused of violent "sarcasm." But he was widely respected in his day, a day of reform in which the context for political satire was changing. As the canon-building Thomas Carlyle recognizes, Elliott seems to point beyond Romanticism, but in order for his work to be valued and survive, it must measure up to standards already established by Romanticism. Since Elliott's work cannot be construed as countersatiric, in the end it cannot enter the (Romantic) canon.

Chapter 1 ～

Representing Rustics:
Satire, Countersatire,
and Emergent Romanticism

In 1808 William Wordsworth wrote to Samuel Rogers thanking him for his charity donation to the orphans of Grasmere. He also happened to mention a recent publication of mutual interest to the correspondents on the general topic of sympathy for the rural poor: "I am happy to find we coincide in opinion about Crabbe's *verses;* for *Poetry* in no sense can they be called."

> I mentioned in my last that there was nothing in the last publication so good as the description of the Parish workhouse, Apothecary, etc. This is true—and it is no less true that the passage which I commended is of no great merit. . . . After all, if the Picture were true to nature, what claim would it have to be called Poetry? At the best, it is the meanest kind of satire, except the merely personal.[1]

Wordsworth here invokes a whole set of evaluative oppositions through which he is to decide the "merits" of Crabbe's writing. On the one hand, he offers the touchstone of "Poetry"; on the other hand, an array of related pejoratives: mere "verses," a "Picture . . . true to nature" such that it amounts to almost "the meanest kind of satire"—second only to personal invective. The result is that Wordsworth implies an important definition of "Poetry"—as the opposite of at least this "kind of satire."

The purpose of this chapter is to examine this implied definition and its standards of evaluation, because I believe that the definition and evaluation represent more than merely personal taste on Wordsworth's part. These revealing remarks represent one of those small moments in which the dominant definition of "Poetry" gets formulated by those in a position to help make the taste by which they will be appreciated, one small exchange of the kind through which literary history gets written by the (eventual) winners. With his casual judgment Wordsworth reveals a series of assumptions about what counts—what deserves a place—in the canon of poetry. What interests me is that Wordsworth's construction of "Poetry," one that was quickly becoming normative for emergent Romanticism, takes the form of a direct opposition with "satire." In the event, literary history has so closely agreed with Wordsworth on the merits of these competing modes of writing—true poetry versus mere satire—that it is now very difficult to imagine a time when they were still contestable. But such imagining is worth the effort; it may lead to a clearer understanding of the role of "satire" as a negative standard for the construction of canonical Romanticism.

Crabbe's Rustics and Romantic Rusticity

Wordsworth's letter probably refers to the *Parish Register,* published in Crabbe's *Poems* of 1807, a volume that marked a kind of comeback by Crabbe after a hiatus from poetry; he had first made a name for himself with *The Village* (1783), the work Wordsworth damns with comparatively faint praise, and essentially a satiric refutation of Oliver Goldsmith's sentimental rural scenes in *The Deserted Village.*[2] For many years after 1807, Crabbe continued to publish with wide popular success. As late as 1818 John Murray offered and paid £3,000 for the copyright of his works.[3] Since the Victorian era, however, it has been the custom to assume that the Romantics in effect took away Crabbe's audience—that the stronger poets of the age, those more in touch with the progressive Zeitgeist, free of the tradition of "Augustanism," simply displaced the weaker Crabbe and his outdated "verses," however well crafted. He has generally been treated as a literary anachronism, a holdout, a living fossil preserved beyond his time into a new age in which he did not belong. Since he wrote about the minute particulars of the rural poor, and nevertheless did so in Popean couplets—as primarily a satirist rather than a celebrator of "low and rustic life"—his work has always made a useful backdrop for sincere ruralism or primitivism, as exemplified and then canonized in the *Lyrical Ballads* and its prefaces.

But all this is to read the triumphal narrative of the canon in place of the messier, complex history of the field of literature in the nineteenth century. In the contemporary documents of that more complex history, Crabbe's name is everywhere. It is clear his contemporaries viewed Crabbe as extremely important. Even Hazlitt, for example, who criticized him severely, was forced to admit that he was "one of the most popular and admired of our living authors."[4] A clear trajectory of decline in reputation is traceable, however: after the 1820s Crabbe is increasingly treated as secondary, something between a "minor" author and a major talent unfortunately out of sync with the artistic progress of his day. By the twentieth century, this evaluation has become the norm. A. O. Lovejoy mentions him as one of the anomalies defeating attempts at a unified-field theory of Romanticism; more recently, Jerome McGann cites him as a revisionary example, a dialectical reminder of the distinction between the "Romantic period" (including un-Romantic writing like Crabbe's) and "Romanticism" itself; Raymond Williams famously finds in his "realism" a "counter-pastoral" that helps us to demystify the shift to agrarian capitalism; one early critic neatly summarizes the conventional view of most literary historians: "Crabbe's realism, in harmony with the tradition of the eighteenth century in England, is opposed to the dawning Romanticism."[5] That simple term "opposed" is the sign under which Crabbe has appeared in most studies of his own historical era, when he has appeared at all. Very early on Byron opposed Crabbe (as related to Pope) to all his contemporaries practicing under the "wrong revolutionary poetical system."[6] Leslie Stephen, writing in 1874, automatically situates him at "the very opposite pole from Keats" (but then goes on to use the opposition to undermine Keats's own relative status); Coventry Patmore (1887) treats Crabbe and Shelley as the exemplary polar opposites, using the pair to illustrate the worst excesses of those overdetermined terms of art, "reason" and "imagination."[7] All this is in marked contrast to the kind of attention Crabbe received in his own lifetime: Scott praised him highly; Byron quotably pronounced him "Nature's sternest Painter, yet the best"; most significant for my purposes, however, is the estimate of Francis Jeffrey, who judged Crabbe the "most original writer" of his age but also the sometimes "disgusting" satirist of "low life."[8]

Jeffrey may have been the earliest critic to employ in print the defining opposition between Crabbe and Wordsworth—an "entire opposition," in his words—as a way to set Crabbe over and against a whole "set" of poets, the emerging "school" that would soon come to be called "Romantic." His April 1808 review of the *Parish Register* (only months before Wordsworth's letter to Rogers) puts it this way:

> There is one set of writers, indeed, from whose works those of Mr. Crabbe might receive all that elucidation which results from contrast, and from an entire opposition in all points of taste and opinion. We allude now to the Wordsworths, and the Southeys, and Coleridges, and all that misguided fraternity, that, with good intentions and extraordinary talents, are labouring to bring back our poetry to the fantastical oddity and puling childishness of Withers, Quarles, or Marvel. These gentlemen write a great deal about rustic life, as well as Mr. Crabbe; and they even agree with him in dwelling much

on its discomforts; but nothing can be more opposite than the views they take of the subject, or the manner in which they execute their representation of them. (*Edinburgh Review*, April 1808, 131–51)

The passage is better known for its remarks on the Romantics than its setting them against Crabbe. But I take seriously Jeffrey's suggestion that a comparison of these poets can be salutary (less so his critical judgments on the relative value of the poets). Such a comparison may contribute to a subtler understanding of the historical construction of this "fraternity" as the dominant literary movement of its day. In this I would attempt to examine the particular ways in which "Romantic judgements upon Crabbe eventually became normative."[9] Beginning with Jeffrey's assumed contrast between Crabbe and the Romantics, I intend to pursue the terms of the contrast, but then to end by asking how that contrast itself came to be.

Though Jeffrey was later to chastise Crabbe repeatedly for dwelling on "disgusting" subjects and call him by one of modern criticism's dirtiest names—"mannerist"—[10] the burden of this 1808 review is to build him up as the wholesome alternative and antidote to the excesses of the Lake School. From the other side, Wordsworth himself helped to reinforce the same opposition, in the letter to Rogers quoted above and as late as an 1843 note dictated to Isabella Fenwick, in which he suggests that "Lucy Gray"—one of his most (literally) sentimental lyrical ballads—would make an instructive case-study for those who wished to contrast his and Crabbe's treatments of similar rural subjects.[11] Though "founded on circumstances" based in fact, Wordsworth says, "the way in which the incident was treated and the spiritualizing of the character might furnish hints for contrasting the imaginative influences which I have endeavoured to throw over common life with Crabbe's matter of fact style of treating subjects of the same kind." Here Wordsworth reinscribes Jeffrey's earlier contrast with Crabbe's kind of "spiritualizing," which was in 1808 partly a matter of cultural politics: the clergyman's stern moralism is more acceptable to him than the still-threatening leveling tendency of the Lake School.

This preference is explicitly represented by Jeffrey in terms of public taste: what Pierre Bourdieu would later call the "peremptory verdicts which, in the name of taste, condemn to ridicule, indignity, shame, silence," persons and works.[12] "Distinction," Bourdieu argues, is a "serious game" played for dominance in the "field" of legitimate "taste," a struggle involving (unacknowledged, euphemized) acts of rhetorical competition and symbolic violence. Symbolic violence, I would add, is the customary weapon of satiric writing. Bourdieu's theoretical terms are helpful in explaining how certain intertextual relations go beyond mere linguistic inevitability or traditional genetic influence—how they are exponents of real struggles for dominance and legitimacy in the social field.[13] In that context, the point I wish to underscore at the outset of this chapter is that the conventional opposition between Crabbe and the Romantics (for whom Wordsworth, as he so often has, will stand as a useful representative) almost always depends upon a kind of differentiation of species—on identifying Crabbe *as a satirist* so the Romantics can be established as unsatiric. A closer look at this critical commonplace—satire as the "natural" opposite of Romanticism with Crabbe as a key anti-Romantic—clarifies the terms at stake, allowing us to trace the then-emerging border between Romantic and un-Romantic modes. The actual process of competitive struggle and relational construction at this border is remarkably complex, far from clear-cut. For one thing, satiric modes and figures inevitably survive within Romantic writing as the by-products of such an act of oppositional definition, of the struggle for difference and dominance in the field of poetry.

Wordsworth and Crabbe's Poetic Presence

First, I want briefly to consider the evidence for direct "influence" between Crabbe and Wordsworth—slim and mostly circumstantial—before moving to a more capacious (and ultimately more interesting) way of comparing the two poets. Obviously the two would have read one another's works, at least to some extent. It is believed that Wordsworth first encountered extracts of *The Village* in the *Annual Register* of 1783 and, as explained above, he knew the *Poems* of 1807.[14] Crabbe's son said that his father was "a cool admirer of the earlier and shorter poems of what is called the Lake School," and Crabbe himself, on the occasion of finding himself parodied in the *Rejected Addresses* of 1813 ("The Theatre"), referred to "Wordsworth whom I read & laughed at till I caught a touch of his disease & now really like many of the simplicities."[15] Crabbe laughing at Wordsworth; Wordsworth condemning Crabbe as a mean satirist; both eventually becoming to some degree infected with the other. What begins to come into focus in these remarks is a dynamic interaction, a process more like a competition for the same market than a linear succession of minor to major author, or Augustan to Romantic ages. Crabbe's own metaphor of infection is apt, and can serve as a useful reminder of the actual closeness of the two poets—the similarities of their themes, general verbal intertextuality, and a generic family resemblance.

Though Crabbe was already well known by the time of the publication of *Lyrical Ballads* (1798), his later poetry continued to draw upon a common ground of culture and literary fashion from the 1780s and 1790s (especially in magazine verse)—the wave of sentimental representations of rural life, including the destitute, the mad, criminals, women, and outcasts. His response in *The Village* to Goldsmith's idealized picture of subsistence-agriculture in a composite-portrait village established him in the general tradition of neopastoral and prospect poetry, which includes (besides Gold-smith) Gay, Thomson, Dyer, Duck, Collier, Gray, and Cowper—a tradition, taken as a whole, that was extremely important for Wordsworth. But Crabbe's place is on the opposition side of this tradition; he is the author of counterpastoral on the true harshness of rural life. As early as *The Village*, and certainly in the later tales, Crabbe frequently represents the meanness of the peasants themselves at the center of what he calls "the real picture of the poor." "Rank weeds" and high tides in place of bucolic fields, and a cynicism about the (rhetorical) search for "the simple life" in nature, are the background of Crabbe's counterpastoral; the foreground always teems with grubby rustics.

> Here joyless roam a wild amphibious race,
> With sullen woe displayed in every face;
> Who far from civil arts and social fly,
> And scowl at strangers with suspicious eye.[16]

Crabbe's satire is thus aimed at the poor themselves as well as at their sentimental patrons and historical (mis)representations. Take, for example, this passage on the follies of pastoral poetry, which becomes an ironic apostrophe to the semiliterate poor:

> Nor you, ye poor, of lettered scorn complain,
> To you the smoothest song is smooth in vain;
> O'ercome by labor, and bowed down by time,
> Feel you the barren flattery of rhyme?
> Can poets soothe you, when you pine for bread?
> By winding myrtles round your ruined shed?
> (ll. 55–60)

It is true that in this and other passages in *The Village* (as Raymond Williams rightly observed) the structural distance between rich and poor is highlighted, a distance elided or ignored by most country-house pastoral before Crabbe.[17] But this distance is also a matter of literacy and thus access to the canon *as* cultural power, and the poem reinforces the distance it describes. As John Guillory has recently put it, the unlettered poor could never complain of a "lettered scorn" of which they could not read in the first place; Crabbe's lines "describe a repression so successful that its victims have not even the means to detect its operation," and Guillory reads in this passage a "maudlin irony,"[18] but I would resist his hint that Crabbe may have happened upon this effect in pursuit of other rhetorical goals. In context, the apostrophe is actually a kind of deflected satire pitched to middling and privileged readers, and the poem seems quite aware—ironically aware—of this satiric effect. My point is that this kind of rhetorical irony serves to sharpen the edge of Crabbe's satire. It reminds the reader that Crabbe's own performance in these very lines is another kind of "lettered scorn." Frank Whitehead shows that, although Crabbe's readers are frequently made to "empathize" with the characters of his tales, their "satisfactions" derive mainly from the "cool, objective, carefully balanced evaluative judgments that the author communicates."[19] In this way, the reader's viewpoint is frequently realigned with the satirist's, over and against the rustics who are otherwise depicted relatively sympathetically.

Much of Wordsworth's writing directly or indirectly refutes or opposes such a relationship to rustic subjects, particularly the definitive Preface of 1805. The conflict of Goldsmith versus Crabbe, as it culminated in *The Village,* formed part of the context for Wordsworth's defense of his choice of subjects from among "low and rustic life," his celebration of natural simplicity (especially in the language of poetry itself), and his argument that "the manners of rural life," rather than being hopelessly corrupted by harsh nature or unjust society, "germinate from" and remain tied to "elementary feelings" of human nature. It has long been recognized that the Preface, with the *Lyrical Ballads* in general, participates in the most definitive of all canonical battles—the "Pope controversy." But Pope's legacy as a satirist survived in a direct competitor to Wordsworth, a poet closer to hand and one who also took as his material (and in part his targets) the very rural subjects that would soon come to be associated with Wordsworth's name and style of poetry—Crabbe himself.

When in late 1835 Wordsworth wrote the "Extempore Effusion Upon the Death of James Hogg," Crabbe was commemorated in these lines:

> Our haughty life is crowned with darkness,
> Like London with its own black wreath,
> On which with thee, O Crabbe! Forth-looking,
> I gazed from Hampstead's breezy heath.
>
> As if but yesterday departed,
> Thou too art gone before; but why,
> O'er ripe fruit. Seasonably gathered,
> Should frail survivors heave a sigh?[20]

This is in the voice of the "survivor," certainly, but he is anything but "frail." Note that there may even be a hint of satiric chastisement implied in "haughty" and "darkness," which may represent Wordsworth's final judgment on Crabbe's style. But as important as any didactic content communicated between these lines is the very fact of the lines themselves. For Wordsworth has of course in 1835 survived Crabbe in more than the physical, medical sense. He has gained a canonical ascendancy that will persist to our own day. Why mourn, indeed, the victim of what appear to be natural processes—or processes of natural selection? When Wordsworth later declared in 1839 that Crabbe fit into the lineage of what he called the "natural and sensual school"—Chaucer-Burns-Crabbe-himself—[21] he completed a process and spoke as the recognized legitimizer of taste, dominating the field, the one who is empowered to make distinctions and establish value, to tell the story of poetic inheritance with himself as the strongest, latest scion, the survivor. No longer a mere satirist, Crabbe has been more or less canonized here, but only as a foil—as a lesser, "minor" example of one strain of Wordsworth's own poetic strength. Eventually, in the course of literary history, he will simply be displaced, if not excluded from the field, then reduced to its margins, to the leftover pages of the anthologies.

Wordsworth's self-definitions vis-à-vis Cabbe and satire are clarified by his *Essays on Epitaphs,* written around 1810. Here the immediate context is the "Pope controversy." For Wordsworth Pope represents eighteenth-century rhetorical modes in general and satire in particular; and these contrast with elegiac modes of sensibility Wordsworth wishes to claim as his own (with some important qualifications). Robert Griffin has demonstrated—in part by reading the *Essays on Epitaphs*—how important Pope remained for Wordsworth's poetics.[22] Griffin anticipates my thesis to the extent that he suggests that the opposition between Pope and Romanticism "is in some way constitutive of Romantic identity," and that "What is denied as an alien Other [represented by Pope] is actually an inseparable part of the internal structure of the Romantic subject" (3, 5). This approaches the point I wish to make about Crabbe, but I want to shift the focus from "Romantic identity" or "the Romantic subject" per se, to literary-historical constructions of "Romanticism" as a movement, one characterized by certain recognizable modes and generic conventions and thematic preoccupations. In order to shift the focus to satire, I deliberately look past Pope to the less considered—but I think as important—pressure on Wordsworth's developing poetics: this is the context that might be called the "Crabbe controversy."

Paul de Man has argued that the *Essays on Epitaphs* rest on the opposition of Wordsworth's own epitaphic ideal over and against "the antithetical language of satire and invective," yet themselves indulge in antithetical and aggressive language in their attacks on Pope.[23] Wordsworth situates the *Essays* in the village churchyard, and therefore in the highly recognizable field of Gray's *Elegy* and—I would argue—Goldsmith's and Crabbe's opposing views of pastoral, as well. (*The Village* concludes in the churchyard, with a pauper's bleak burial its final scene.) Throughout, the chief topic of the *Es-*

says is competing ways of representing rustic life. Wordsworth argues for a kind of willful and imaginative idealization (or "spiritualizing" as he says in the Fenwick note on "Lucy Gray") versus Pope's kind of display of wit and satire at the expense of, or by using as a mere excuse, the departed villagers themselves.

> Without being so far lulled as to imagine I saw in a Village Church-yard the eye or central point of rural Arcadia, I have felt that with all the vague and general expressions of love, gratitude, and praise with which it is usually crowded, it is a far more faithful representation of homely life as existing among a Community in which circumstances have not been untoward, than any report which might be made by a rigorous observer deficient in that spirit of forebearance and those kindly prepossessions, without which human life can in no condition be profitably looked at or described. For we must remember that it is the nature of Vice to force itself upon notice.[24]

Later in the essay Wordsworth critiques Pope's epitaph on Mrs. Corbet at great length, the very lines that Johnson had claimed were among Pope's best. According to Wordsworth, the passage indulges in artificial wit and "an oblique and ill-timed stroke of satire" where there should have been only sincerity and sympathy. In the essay on epitaphs that follows, Wordsworth opens with a direct attack on Pope—the passage of aggressive rhetoric de Man discusses—as an author whose "mind has been employed chiefly in observation upon the vices and follies of men"—that is to say, an author employed as a satirist. This comes just before the famous passage on the power of words, which de Man deconstructs as enfolding within itself a bitter invective against language as a whole:

> Words are too awful an instrument for good and evil to be trifled with. . . . If words be not (recurring to a metaphor before used) an incarnation of the thought but only a clothing for it, then surely will they prove an ill gift; such a one as those poisoned vestments, read of in the stories of superstitious times, which had power to consume and to alienate from his right mind the victim who put them on. (84–85)

I would argue, contra de Man, that in context this is less a metaphysical or metalinguistic than a rhetorically instrumental passage, less a general utterance revealing language's inevitable self-canceling negation than a specific, strategic attack on particular violent modes of language inherited with the Pope tradition. As I understand Wordsworth's expressed anxiety here the corrosive power of ill-used language, its ability to create victims, stands out as the chief danger. In other words, I read the passage as a kind of deliberate and serious satire upon satire:

Language, if it do not uphold, and feed, and leave in quiet, like the power of gravitation or the air we breathe, is a counter-spirit, unremittingly and noiselessly at work to derange, to subvert, to lay waste, to vitiate, and to dissolve. (85)

Wordsworth's is an ethical argument concerning coercion versus imagination, destruction versus sympathetic reconstruction. It places the negations of language—exemplified in satiric modes—in opposition to modes of imaginative sympathy and suggests that it is only such sympathy that can express the "gravity" of universal nature. Satire is unnatural to the degree that it is judgmental, and even violent in its judgments. De Man correctly notes that Wordsworth himself deploys an aggressive, vitiating language against what he paints as a violent rhetorical tradition. But I suspect he does so quite deliberately, as a way of neutralizing traditional claims for the moral force of satire and thus clearing a space for something new—an *un*satiric, Romantic mode of representation.

Wordsworth uses the representation of rusticity as the proving ground for true poetry, which suggests that the essays on epitaphs and the larger project of Lake School Romanticism must take into account Crabbe and the question of satire. It seems highly likely that in the period of 1809 to 1810 Crabbe is an unnamed co-defendant in Wordsworth's suit against Pope. This satirist of rustic life had already been prominently contrasted by critics with Wordsworth, and his choice of subjects and, to some degree, interest in narrative were uncomfortably close to Wordsworth's own.[25] It is clear that Wordsworth was consciously invoking recent variations on the pastoral or georgic, including Goldsmith, Thomson, and Cowper (as well as Crabbe), in his arguments against satiric modes for representing "low life." And that context was itself highly charged with the competing energies of sympathy and satire. One well-known example will suffice: the cynical village priest at the conclusion of Crabbe's *Village,* who is a satire on the preacher of Goldsmith's *Deserted Village,* a man all compassion and sympathy, rather than judgment.

> Pleas'd with his guests, the good man learn'd to glow,
> And quite forgot their vices in their woe;
> Careless their merits or their faults to scan,
> His pity gave ere charity began.[26]

It is Crabbe's work, however (rather than say Cowper's more genial, comedic satire), that marks the real challenge to Wordsworth. After Crabbe's satire of Goldsmith, Wordsworth could no longer simply align himself with Goldsmith's sensibility. He was compelled to answer a potent and popular satire of such sensibility, a living, well-received author—and that imperative is perhaps reflected in the *Essays on Epitaphs*. From Wordsworth's point of view (and that of posterity), Crabbe could be the one described in the *Essays*, "an observer deficient in that spirit of forebearance and those kindly prepossessions," who, unlike Goldsmith's preacher (and more like Pope), paid too much attention to folly and vice, to "faults" rather than "woe"—and thus overlooked the natural goodness of village life, a depth of goodness only sensibility and its true, imaginative sympathy could reveal (or project).

> The afflictions which Peasants and rural Artizans have to struggle with are for the most part secret; the tears which they wipe away, and the sighs which they stifle,—this is all a labour of privacy. (*Essays*, 64–65)

This "labour" is best communicated to or shared with a "gentle reader" rather than judged before the public. It is knowledge best shared by an individual poet whose sensibility is grounded in empirical sense. Wordsworth claims that he could "illustrate" the "self-forgetfulness" of the "noble" poor "by many examples, which are now before [his] eyes," but that he will not digress from his argument (65). Having plenty of lurid tales to tell, he deliberately chooses to hold his pen and shift the focus to thoughts too deep for tears. Nonetheless, his appeal to real, first-hand experience or "matters of fact" is an interesting recourse in an argument in defense of imaginative, emotional sympathy. In 1808 he had found such facts inadequate, distasteful bases for Crabbe's tales.

> After all, if the Picture were true to nature, what claim would it have to be called Poetry? At the best, it is the meanest kind of satire, except the merely personal. The sum of all is, that nineteen out of twenty of Crabbe's Pictures are mere matters of fact; with which the Muses have just about as much to do as they have with a Collection of medical reports, or of Law cases. (op. cit. letter to Rogers)

This is actually one of those characteristically Wordsworthian statements that is more radical than it at first appears. The "meanest kind of satire"— the lowest or most base, except for merely personal invective—is rhetorically pointed realism. It is mean in part because it is unimaginative: it merely reports versified facts, then claims a moral authority for having done so.

This raises the larger question of empiricism versus imagination and touches on some of the more complicated psychological and epistemological debates of the age. But keeping my focus on the practice of genre, I want to suggest something of what was meant by "imagination" and "fact" in the context of these debates about poetry. For one thing, it became a commonplace in Wordsworth's circle that Crabbe lacked imagination and therefore lacked true poetry. Coleridge found in him "an absolute defect of the high imagination"[27] and Hazlitt saw in his work "one sad reality," thus characterizing him as "of all poets the least poetical."

> Literal fidelity serves him in the place of invention; he assumes importance by a number of petty details; he rivets attention by being tedious. He not only deals in incessant matters of fact, but in matters of fact of the most familiar, the least animating, and the most unpleasant kind.[28]

But along these same lines, Leigh Hunt's *Feast of the Poets* intriguingly compares Crabbe's poetry to a camera obscura—that technological device for objective representation, the passive recording of perceived reality.[29] Using a related metaphor, an anonymous reviewer in the 1819 *Edinburgh Review* said that whereas Crabbe was "the poet of actual life," Wordsworth "exhibits it [human life] in a phantasmagoria. He presents to you, not living creatures, but the vivid images of forms which he himself has fashioned, which he moves by his own agency, and tints with his own colours. From all these faults Crabbe is free."[30] As the (Romantic) canon takes shape in the nineteenth century, this reviewer's values are simply inverted: "faults" become virtues as phantasmagoria comes to sit above camera obscura. This is a useful way to revisit M. H. Abrams's famous opposition of the mirror and the lamp (or mimetic and expressivist modes of writing); the camera and the phantasmagoria, however, are metaphors for competing technologies of representation.

These technologies are not transparent in their relation to nature. The phantasmagoria or magic lantern projected illusions, not illumination. Magic-lantern shows always involved distortions of images: miniaturization or enlargement, apparent movement toward or away from the spectator, translucence, superimposition, and—at least by the Victorian period—various kinds of kinetic effects, including panoramic slides and levered and geared mechanical animations.[31] Even the early camera obscura is far from a merely passive or realistic mirror of nature, based as it is on the projected and distorted image of the object caught in its dark aperture. Both technological inventions offer rhetorical special effects and manipulate the perception of the viewer/reader. Behind these competing modes of representation stands the opposition of Romantic-period satire and Romantic sensibility—inflected by the contemporary participants (as well as by later critics) as a struggle for the heart of the moral purpose of poetry. Hazlitt escalates the conflict by writing in 1818 that Crabbe "collects all the petty vices of the human heart, and superintends, as in a Panopticon, a select circle of rural malefactors."[32] Here the potential of the recording camera is put to use as the controlling gaze of power. With Crabbe as high-tech

Benthamite prison warden, his (moralistic, utilitarian) poetry is "naturally" opposed to emerging Romantic values: liberty of the imagination for the free individual. Hazlitt vividly prefigures the terms of the coming critical devaluation of Crabbe and of satiric writing in general. Crabbe's moralism is suspect; he loads the deck by surveying only a "select group" of representative types, his "rural malefactors." Hazlitt's figure, when applied to Wordsworth, foreshadows a familiar characterization of Romanticism by modern criticism: as a willful effort to project its own self-generated illusions on the scene. But the point to keep in mind is that to characterize poetry as being like the phantasmagoria is to suggest that it projects special effects—of movement, life, organic transformations, and even "gothic" or supernatural visitations.

Modern readers miss the importance of the contrast because from the distance of two centuries a magic-lantern show of the imagination seems so different from Wordsworth's self-ideal of simplicity, sincerity, and authenticity. Yet in his praise of the unself-conscious encomiastic language of rural epitaphs (with which he wishes to identify his own poetry of sympathy) Wordsworth says equivocally that such tombstones do "not so far exceed reality as might be lightly supposed" (65). But they *do* exceed them. Like true poetry, the epitaphs project their own deliberate coloring of the imagination over perceived realities. Imagination, always for Wordsworth at least one half of the perceptual process, by definition is not literal reality but contrary to fact or in excess of it. Self-generated projections of the imagination in rustic epitaphs point toward the highest kind of poetry. The ethical language of the *Essays* calls for "kindly prepossessions" over "rigorous" observation, for projection of imaginative images over objective surveillance, and it does so by making use of the conventional language of sensibility: sympathy, forbearance, tears for another's suffering.

In this scheme, deep natural feeling serves as the limit of objectivity, the place where one's critical observations are halted and one's imaginative projections come to the rescue. In the following personal anecdote, Wordsworth dramatizes the preliminary stage in the process of such self-generated positive illusions, the tendency to objective judgment:

> When a Stranger has walked round a Country Church-yard and glanced his eye over so many brief Chronicles, as the tomb-stones usually contain, of faithful Wives, tender husbands, dutiful Children, and good Men of all classes; he will be tempted to exclaim, in the language of one of the Characters of a modern Tale in a similar situation, "Where are all the *bad* people buried?" He may smile to himself an answer to this question, and may regret that it has intruded upon him so soon. For my own part such has been my lot. (63)

The quiet tranquility of the country churchyard is at times disrupted, subverted, dissolved by the "counter-spirit" of such ironic skeptical realism, even for Wordsworth himself; even he has been visited by unwanted thoughts of the "vices and rancorous dispositions, by which the hearts of those who lie under so smooth a surface and so fair and outside must have been agitated" (64). The judgmental tendency to look beneath the surface, as it were, is what threatens the peace of the churchyard scene and must be deliberately offset by a sentimental perspective, a conscious cultivation of heightened sensibility that smoothes over satiric judgments.

Wordsworth's particular kind of sensibility here goes beyond the literature of sensibility. It is also more than merely a call for "sincerity"—though it surely contributes to how that term comes to be defined as quintessentially Romantic. In Wordsworth's *Essays* the problem is revealed as a choice of modes, and the right choice is defined by its difference from the satiric. It is a countersatiric mode produced in strategic resistance to the human tendency to "smile" at folly and vice, to react skeptically or with implied ridicule in the face of imaginative, sympathetic idealizations, to give in to the corrosively satiric "counter-spirit." As I read them, the *Essays on Epitaphs* share a larger purpose behind the *Lyrical Ballads* and *The Excursion* (in other words, Wordsworth's most important contributions to canonical notions of Romanticism)—to promote countersatiric modes of representing rusticity, which is to say elemental, natural human existence. In this he succeeded brilliantly, and important features of canonical Romanticism are the result. But it is important to remember that the pathos of such elemental human existence, too deep for tears, a pathos which those Romantic modes are created to represent, remains only one dialectical step away from the unwanted but sometimes unavoidable, intrusive, and ironic smile against which it is defined.

Wordsworth's Countersatire

This countersatiric purpose, so defined, is everywhere evident in Wordsworth's poetry of 1798 to 1819. It has been suggested that Wordsworth quite possibly revised *The Excursion* (including the introduction of the Vicar), just to name one example, as a direct response to the influence of Crabbe.[33] But the ambivalent counter-satiric urge in his writing goes far beyond the literal question of influence.

The contrast between the narrative portraits of Crabbe, the "Hogarth of verse," and an antinarrative like "Simon Lee," for example, is instructive, as Karl Kroeber has suggested.[34] Crabbe's tales follow a "progress" (usually a decline) as if in the busy, fact-crowded panels of Hogarth's narratives. Crabbe's verbal portraits are appealing more for these particulars—and how they pull us into the frame—than for the moral they lead us to in linear fashion. The eye may follow any number of digressive paths in one of Hogarth's panels, may stop any number of times on a miniature vignette within the tableau, and one gets the same sense of inhabiting a story in reading Crabbe. Caricature and exposure of lurid truths within the details are as important to the large satiric purpose of both works as the outcome of the story. Indeed, readers of Crabbe, like viewers of Hogarth, may find the narrative denouement strangely beside the point, either a foregone conclusion or a discontinuous coda. Wordsworth's ballads often go one step further and deliberately defeat the reader's expectations for a conclusion to a tale altogether. The best-known examples are the apostrophic intrusions of "The Idiot Boy" and "Simon Lee," both subjects that could easily have appeared in one of Crabbe's collections.

> My gentle Reader, I perceive
> How patiently you've waited,
> And now I fear that you expect
> Some tale will be related.
>
> O Reader! Had you in your mind
> Such stores as silent thought can bring,
> O gentle Reader! You would find
> A tale in every thing.
> What more I have to say is short,
> And you must kindly take it:
> It is no tale; but should you think,
> Perhaps a tale you'll make it.[35]

This, after declaring matter-of-factly how the old man's "weak ankles swell" and before closing anecdotally with the severed root and self-consciously elegiac tears of the speaker.

Partly because the final word of the poem is "mourning," although "Simon Lee" appeared in 1798, it is tempting to read it as a poetic exemplification of the argument of the *Essays on Epitaphs*. Once the *Essays* are read in the way I have suggested, they make possible a reading of this lyrical ballad as containing Wordsworth's speaker's suppressed smile—even in the face of such a tale of suffering. It helps to see the exaggerated confrontational pathos of "Simon Lee," the poem's highly charged sensibility, as a kind of defiance of the counter spirit that would dwell too long on human folly and vice instead of simple suffering. Like the Leech Gatherer or the Idiot Boy, Simon Lee is a sentimental character always teetering on the brink of representational violence—literally of caricature. Those swollen ankles are like the exaggerated features in numerous satiric prints of rural bumpkins or clowns but, turned to the uses of sympathy, made an awkward touchstone for the speaker's—and the gentle reader's—Romantic sensibility. The "tale" the reader expects is likely to be the kind of satiric moral tale for which Crabbe is famous. In this way the ironic potential of the poem—so strangely present even in the midst of its sentiment—is redirected reflexively back upon the reader's own "satiric" tendencies. The tendency to satire is being redefined as a failure of imagination.[36]

The satiric cartoonist's smile is of course even closer to the surface in "The Idiot Boy," as its many parodists were immediately aware. Its oddly burlesque invocation to the muses in the middle of its narrative (non)action again taunts the reader for seeking a "tale" in the silent and openly mystified experience of the natural holy fool. Johnny's nonce couplet on the cocks/owls mocks the reader, trained on Crabbe and his moralist colleagues, who would anatomize human "folly" in verse. "And that was all his travel's story." Such frame-breaking apostrophes in Wordsworth have been much discussed as reader-response cues for invoking a collaborative or dialogic performance between text and reader, as linguistic openings to the polyvocal potential of the texts. The Romantics themselves claimed that such moments provided an engagement with the reader as "fellow-labourer."[37] But I want to suggest that such rhetoric may work negatively, calling attention to the reader's complicity in latent satiric judgments. I would redirect attention to the surface effects of the rhetoric, which turn about on the reader and his or her expectations. But I also want to augment those "expectations," to define them more precisely than as simple narrative closure, to see that they include the desire for moral teaching—a desire most often gratified, according to convention, by satiric modes. Wordsworth's experiments in this vein often hold up a potentially ridiculous or disgusting (if rarely vicious) subject and then dare his reader to react as he or she has been conditioned to: with a satiric smile. In this way such poems satirize their readers' predispositions for satire; they are not merely idealizing or escapist pastorals: they are truly countersatires.

Look for a moment at one of Wordsworth's *Lyrical Ballads* that would seem to *intend* a satiric judgment on its subject: "Andrew Jones." It was added to volume II in 1800 but was omitted after 1815, and stands out in this present context in part because it refuses to repress or redirect its aggression towards a subject from low life. Its story, at least, could well have been found among Crabbe's tales of coarse village characters.

> I hate that Andrew Jones: he'll breed
> His children up to waste and pillage.
> I wish the press-gang or the drum
> With its tantara sound would come,
> And sweep him from the village![38]

Wordsworth explains this venom with a single narrative instance of cruelty and dishonesty, in which Jones stole the alms from a crippled itinerant beggar he encountered on the road. After a simple relation of the crime, the final stanza recaps the first with a "hence," explaining and justifying the condemnation of this Crabbean rustic. A companion to "Old Man Travelling" and other poems on vagrants and charity by Wordsworth, this is obviously a statement on the radical danger of greed in a community built on charity. The honest public hatred of the speaker points us past Jones's vice to the binding communal virtue he fails to exhibit. In place of the "cripple" from outside the community, Andrew becomes the true pariah to be driven out for the greater good of all.

This is a rare case of aggressive rhetorical attack in Wordsworth's lyrical-ballad oeuvre. More characteristic—and more open itself to parody and ridicule—is *Peter Bell*, which tells the story of a similarly antisocial character, with a similarly "low" generic name, who also steals from the helpless:

> And passing by a twisted elm
> Again poor Peter thus began
> "'Twas just by such another tree
> I robbed of sixpence half-penny
> A Boy that led a poor blind man.

As the editors of the Cornell edition point out, the Alfoxden Notebook provides evidence of an even closer connection between the two poems, showing that lines describing "Andrew Jones" once had the villain named "Peter."

> And he bethinks him then of one
> To whom a foul deed had been done
> A helpless man a travelling cripple
> For this poor crawling helpless wretch
> It chanced some traveller passing by
> A penny on the ground had thrown
> But the poor cripple was alone
> And could not stoop no help was nigh
> Inch-thick the dust lay on the ground
> for it had long been droughty weather
> So with his staff the cripple brought
> The halfpennies together—
> It chanced that Peter passed that way
> Just at the time & there he found
> The cripple in the mid-day heat
> Standing alone and at his feet
> He saw the penny on the ground

> He stooped and took the penny up
> And when the cripple nearer drew
> Quoth Peter under half a crown
> What a man finds is all his own
> And so my friend good day to you—[39]

With the name altered, most of this incident finds its way into "Andrew Jones," where it becomes the cause for the speaker's expressed hatred. Andrew's poetic cousin, the infamous Peter Bell, is described long after he has committed his similar crime (and others). In the end, he proves capable of being affected by guilt when he remembers stealing from the blind man. His story tells of his largely self-inflicted punishment, final redemption, and restoration to the community.

In light of the argument I have been making, it would appear that the many parodies of Wordsworth's poem brought out its own latent satiric tendencies, tendencies that it was part of Wordsworth's deliberate intention to displace or subsume into the narrative's redemptive ending. As with the Leech Gatherer, the seeds of absurdity are planted in the text as part of its dialectical potential—then are resisted or displaced. *Peter Bell* is a conversion story, told as a sometimes self-mocking ballad, that pointedly does not satirize Methodist enthusiasm—and this fact was its most noticeable feature to many of its critics in 1819. It is a tale that transforms a stock clown, a caricaturable rough who abuses dumb animals, into the object of sympathy, even reverence. In the end, the reader is back in the village churchyard being dared *not* to "smile."

Interestingly enough, the story of Peter Bell, like many of Crabbe's tales, was based on a newspaper anecdote about an ass found standing by the water who pointed the way to the drowned corpse of its master. Other features of the tale were taken from the poet's direct experience of rural life; he enumerates them in support of his claim to first-hand knowledge, as well as to establish some distance from the rudeness of his subjects: "The countenance, gait, and figure of Peter," Wordsworth said, were based on a "wild rover" he had encountered and from whom he heard "strange stories." In his rambles, he avers, he always takes the opportunity to become acquainted with "this class of people." The Methodist worship service heard amidst the beauties of nature, he says (to the urban critics), is an actual feature of the quiet summer countryside. "In both the psalmody and the voice of the preacher there is, not unfrequently, much solemnity likely to impress the feelings of the rudest characters under favorable circumstances."[40]

Here is raw material for Wordsworth's sympathetic and synthetic imagination. The framing prologue is at great pains to introduce what follows as "poetry" rather than mere "verses"—serving as a kind of apologetic preface. Still, the prologue attempts to establish the narrator's credibility on all fronts: as an imaginative poet who gazes at the moon and a local resident who addresses his fellow villagers, the vicar and a little girl (emblems of piety and simplicity), in his own garden. The narrator first sails and then abandons his fantastic "flying boat" of romance, comes down to earth, and tells his tale; in the 1819 dedication to Southey, Wordsworth openly insists he will move the reader and affect the imagination but without recourse to "supernatural machinery." Like "Goody Blake and Harry Gill" (a poem written around the same time as the first version of *Peter Bell*), this claims to be a kind of experiment in "superstition," but from an anthropological or social-psychological point of view.[41]

Peter is a ruffian who, though he has lived a simple life amidst natural scenery, remains rough, hard-hearted, "wild," "rude," and "savage." He has had twelve wives and is possibly a felon, a veritable walking catalogue of vice and folly, and he behaves like a stage buffoon—until the climactic moment he is frightened into an evangelical Christian repentance. The crisis comes in a moonlit, deserted quarry, where Peter sees something reflected in a dark pool and lets his imagination run away with him. Even less equivocally than Robert Burns's Tam O' Shanter, Wordsworth's unlikely hero is a victim of psychological and moral horrors—"spirits of the mind," the poem openly calls them—at least until Peter discovers a drowned corpse. The ultimate effect is remorse and his own moral transformation, apparently merely aided by the trappings of rural Methodism. The tale ends in a tableau of sensibility revealed, with the orphan children and widow of the drowned man mourning before their cottage door ad Peter sobbing in contrition. The final stanza quickly became notorious:

> And Peter Bell, who, till that night,
> Had been the wildest of his clan,
> Forsook his crimes, renounced his folly,
> And after ten months' melancholy,
> Became a good and honest man.
> (ll. 131–35)

It hardly needs to be said that this outcome is precisely that which satire has traditionally claimed as its own special aim to achieve: moral reform, the scourging of vice and folly. My point, however (and one reinforced by the glee of many parodists), is that the outcome is the opposite of satire. Everything about the subject, setting, and narrative structure would lead a reading audience to *expect* the satire Wordsworth so studiously avoids; instead he provides an apotheosis of the sympathetic imagination. What seems now so recognizably Romantic about *Peter Bell* has its basis in Wordsworth's desire to produce countersatire.

Crabbe's Satire: "Peter Grimes"

In the midst of his reading of *Peter Bell*, Alan Liu notes in passing that Wordsworth's Peter is "ancestral to such literary types as Crabbe's Peter Grimes," then in a footnote further remarks: "It seems clear that there is a tradition here."[42] Leslie Stephen had observed much the same in 1874:

> Peter Grimes was doubtless a close relation of Peter Bell. Bell having the advantage of Wordsworth's interpretation, leads us to many thoughts which lie altogether beyond Crabbe's reach; but, looking simply at the sheer tragic force of the two characters, Grimes is to Bell what Brandy is to small beer. He would never have shown the white feather like his successor.[43]

True, *Peter Bell* was begun (and in some versions finished) long before "Peter Grimes" came into the world (in 1810); this is not influence per se but something more like family resemblance.

As Liu hints, the two Peters can be triangulated with another famous "Grimes," a secondary character in Godwin's Jacobin novel, *Caleb Williams*. Like Crabbe's tale, Godwin's novel is about the horrors of rural life from the perspective of the powerless—the indentured or apprenticed—and as a result of the corrupt and unequal system of justice. The villains in both cases are supported by corrupt systems. Caleb himself is a socially subordinate "boy" who becomes a victim of class violence at the hands of Tyrrel, the tyrannical landlord, in part over what happens to a proud but doomed tenant farmer, Hawkins. Godwin's Grimes is a secondary character, but like Crabbe's Peter, he is "boorish," "uncouth," and "coarse"—a "half-civilised animal." Like both poetic Peters, Bell and Grimes, Godwin's character exhibits a failure of feeling. He is "a total stranger to tenderness; he could not feel for those refinements in others, of which he had no experience in himself."[44] One other trait stands out in this triangular comparison: the lack of sympathetic imagination in Godwin's Grimes is accompanied by a tendency to "sarcasm." Godwin's Grimes, Wordsworth's Peter Bell, and Crabbe's Peter Grimes—all three are rude and uncouth satiric objects who themselves participate in the negative, judgmental spirit of satire. Crabbe hints at an affective vulnerability, at least, in his ruffian, and Wordsworth makes it the whole purpose of his ballad to reveal and exploit the dramatic potential of such vulnerability. Wordsworth's Peter is a convert to true feeling.

Such comparisons are helpful because they do not merely repeat the well-established opposition between Crabbe and Wordsworth but usefully complicate the terms of that opposition, help to tell its history. The family resemblance between the two Peters is clear: it runs much deeper than their names or the stereotypes they represent. The differences between the two characters, therefore, are more subtle than the terms "realism" and "romance," under which they have come down to us in (and in the margins of) the canon, can possibly account for.

The inadequacy of received critical terminology is revealed by another of Crabbe's tales, even closer in its narrative particulars to *Peter Bell* than "Peter Grimes," "The Convert" (1812). In it John Dighton, a mobile, malleable, shifting personality, is seized with a fever, plunged into abject terror, then abruptly converted to Methodism—but only tenuously, because merely emotionally, converted.

> A convert meek, obedient, and afraid.
> His manners strict, though form'd on fear alone,
> Pleas'd the grave friends, nor less the solemn tone,
> The lengthen'd face of care, the low and inward groan:
> The stern food men exulted, when they saw
> Those timid looks of penitence and awe;
> Nor thought that one so passive, humble, meek,
> Had yet a creed and principles to seek.
>
> The faith that Reason finds, confirms, avows,
> The hopes, the views, the comforts she allows,—
> These were not his, who by his feelings found,
> And by them only, that his faith was sound;
> Feelings of terror these, for evil past,
> Feelings of hope, to be receiv'd at last;
> Now weak, now lively, changing with the day,
> These we his feelings, and he felt his way.
> (ll. 77–92)[45]

Compare Wordsworth's pointed lines from the strange prologue to *Peter Bell:*

> "A potent wand doth Sorrow wield;
> What spell so strong as guilty Fear!
> Repentance is a tender Sprite;
> If aught on earth have heavenly might,
> 'Tis lodged within her silent tear."
> (ll. 146–50)

These lines by Wordsworth are a helpful base from which to examine Shelley's satire "Peter Bell the Third," which (as I have argued elsewhere)[46] focuses the ideological differences between the two Romantic poets. For Shelley, Wordsworth's poem represents a defense of Methodism as a moral force—at least among naive rustics—and thus amounts to a failure of imagination. Though Shelley was probably responding to rumors about the

poem as well as other satires and criticisms of Wordsworth, his parody avant
la lettre hit the mark to this extent: when it comes to *Peter Bell*'s central device, Wordsworth does aim to convince his reader that even negative emotion—including "primitive" religious guilt—can move the hardened heart.
Before Wordsworth's Peter Bell appeared before the public, however, and before Shelley could parody him, George Crabbe had already created a volatile
"Convert" who may be just as easily unconverted, backsliding into the role
of worldly stationer, corrupted into doubt by reading "Satiric novels, poets
bold and free, / And what their writers term philosophy" (ll. 163–64). His
faith, being built upon the sand of "guilty fear," cannot support him, and he
dies in confusion. Wordsworth's Peter Bell moves from such fear to deep
sympathy with the suffering of others, "sobs even like a child" and is therefore finally saved.

Peter Grimes, on the other hand, is wholly beyond redemption. A fisherman, poacher, thief, drunkard, sacreligious parricide, he suddenly (but in
that suddenness, with psychological verisimilitude) develops the sadistic desire for an apprentice to control and abuse.

> *Peter* had heard there were in London then,—
> Still have they being?—Workhouse-clearing Men,
> Who, undisturb'd by Feelings just or kind,
> Would Parish-Boys to needy tradesmen bind:
> They in their want a trifling Sum would take,
> And toiling Slaves of piteous Orphans make.
>
> Such *Peter* sought, and when a Lad was found,
> The Sum was dealt him and the Slave was bound.
> Some few in Town observ'd in *Peter*'s Trap
> A Boy, with Jacket blue and woollen Cap;
> But none enquir'd how *Peter* us'd the Rope,
> Or what the Bruise, that made the Stripling stoop;
> None could the Ridges on his Back behold,
> None sought him shiv'ring in the Winter's Cold;
> None put the question,—'*Peter*, dost thou give
> The Boy his Food?—What, Man! The Lad must live:
> Consider, *Peter*, let the Child have Bread,
> He'll serve thee better if he's stok'd and fed.'
> None reason'd thus—and some, on hearing Cries,
> Said calmly, '*Grimes* is at his Exercise.'
> (ll. 59–78)

This horrifying, lucid moment early in the tale gives way to a long passage of gothic melodrama, as apprentices are murdered one by one. But in

the verse paragraph above (and in this way like some of Blake's *Songs*), the social conscience of the reader is challenged along with those of the silent and complicitous villagers. This is a story about getting away with murder, at least for a time. The most frightening villain of the poem is collective: the close-knit village and system of justice that perpetuates such evil and allows Peter to continue to repeat his abuse, even when everyone knows what is going on.[47] As in some abolitionist literature of the period, the poem seems to demand merely a more benignly humane treatment of sufferers but not the liberty of the "slaves." Yet even that limited demand goes unmade. In the end, excepting his inner torments, the worst that is done to Peter in this life is that he is deprived of his heretofore steady supply of apprentices and is forced to fish alone. Eventually, however, Peter becomes increasingly disturbed by repressed guilt, until in a kind of madness he sees the ghosts of his father and the dead boys on the water; finally, he thinks he sees the father fling water in his face and that water turns to fire and blood—an effect Crabbe's footnote explains as the result of aqueous phosphorescence. Peter sees a vision of Hell, then dies, and the tale simply ends.

In some ways a Hogarthian "progress," "Peter Grimes" is also a kind of gothic melodrama in verse, complete with supernatural (or psychological) scenery. But these strains are mixed in a *satura:* it satirizes (in the serious, moral sense of the term) its titular rustic, it satirizes the workhouse and the justice system, it satirizes the villagers (and all of us) who turn a blind eye. At times it verges on the kind of misanthropic satire on humanity associated with the darkest moments in Swift. But then there are the boys, Peter's victims. As Wordsworth said, much of Crabbe's material came from the newspapers or direct experience, "matters of fact," which Wordsworth deemed unworthy of poetry and compared to a mere "Collection of Medical reports, or of Law cases." This accurately describes the genesis of "Peter Grimes," truly a "Newgate pastoral." Crabbe's son said that the "original" of Grimes was a "Law case" regarding an old fisherman named Tom Brown of Aldborough, of whom Crabbe knew while practicing there as a surgeon: "He had a succession of apprentices from London, and a certain sum with each. As the boys all disappeared under circumstances of strong suspicion, the man was warned that if another followed in like manner, he should certainly be charged with murder."[48] Like Grimes, Brown suffered from imaginary "terrors."

Such "parish apprenticeships," in which entrepreneurial workhouse clearingmen would bind over children of paupers and foundlings to rural masters—usually with no questions asked and worth a premium of about five pounds—were common practice. The economic purpose was to relieve the poor-rate, to shift the burden of support to another parish; this most often meant London boys were sent into the country, where they were even more unconnected, protected only by magistrates appointed by the Crown from among the local gentry.

The system was notorious for abuse, even at the time. One farmer near Malmesbury was tried in 1764 for maiming and castrating two apprentices bound to him and for whom he had been paid premiums (it was also said that he tried to infect them with smallpox).[49] One famous case of apprenticide, reported in the *Newgate Calendar*, was that of "Mother" Brownrigg; the story became a device in one of the *Anti-Jacobin* satires of 1790s. The young Southey had written a sympathetic "Inscription" on the civil-war regicide Henry Marten, who had been imprisoned in Chepstow Castle for 30 years after the restoration. The satire retorts with an "Inscription" for the door of Mrs. Brownrigg's cell:

> For one long term, or e'er her trial came,
> Here BROWNRIGG linger'd. Often have these cells
> Echoed her blasphemies, as with shrill voice
> She scream'd for fresh Geneva. Not to her
> Did the blithe fields of Tothill, or thy street,
> St. Giles, its fair varieties expand;
> Till at the last in slow-drawn cart she went
> To execution. Dost thou ask her crime?
> SHE WHIPP'D TWO FEMALE 'PRENTICES TO DEATH,
> AND HID THEM IN THE COAL-HOLE. For her mind
> Shap'd strictest plans of discipline. Sage Schemes!
> Such as LYCURGUS taught, when at the shrine
> Of the Orthyran Goddess he bade flog
> The little Spartans ; such as erst chastised
> Our MILTON, when at College. For this act
> Did BROWNRIGG swing. Harsh laws! But time shall come,
> When France shall reign, and Laws be all repealed![50]

This serves to remind us that "apprenticide" was a socially emblematic crime, sure to provoke radical political sympathy and a structural analysis of the "Laws." Blackstone is instructive in this regard, as much as for what the law assumes as for what it says, and as much for its ambiguities as for its definitions: "Assaults committed by masters and mistresses on apprentices or servants (persons whom they are naturally bound to protect), so as to endanger life, or permanently injure health, constitute a misdemeanor punishable by imprisonment not exceeding three years . . ."[51] Only if a master should deny the apprentice food or "treat him with such continual harshness and severity, that his death is occasioned thereby, the law will imply malice, and the offence will be murder." The previous discussion of "murder" cites cases behind the law that could have supplied any number of Crabbe's tales:

> As when a park-keeper tied a boy, that was stealing wood, to a horse's tail, and dragged him along the park; when a master corrected his servant with an iron bar; and a schoolmaster stamped on his scholar's belly; so that each of the sufferers died; these were justly held to be murders, because the correction begin excessive, and such as could not proceed but from a bad heart, it was equivalent to a deliberate act of slaughter. (IV, 222)

Even read in terms of genre, this text makes a very interesting comparison with Crabbe's. Like one of his poetic tales, the legal commentary works by citing cases—in this instance vivid, even lurid narrative anecdotes—and in each of these legal tales of violence against the young and poor, the law must interpret the tale, must detect "a bad heart" in the perpetrator. Sensibility is made the normative standard for rendering judgment in such cases. All the more striking then, that Crabbe's "Peter Grimes" represents itself coolly, with a certain distance from its material, as a sort of forensic anecdote—a satire on the black heart of its protagonist, yes, but based on the facts of the case as they are narrated, and with an implied indictment of the community as a whole. Hazlitt's image of the panopticon begins to make a deeper sense in this context—as a vivid reminder of how modern and "progressive" Crabbe's version of satiric judgment was, as a kind of controlling rhetorical technology.

Wordsworth's effects, by contrast, are aimed at more obviously emotional responses from his reader, but beyond this, the comparison of Crabbe and Wordsworth refuses to yield absolute or clear-cut binary oppositions. Wordsworth's rhetorical judgments are more often turned back on the reader, or on an interlocutor figure who stands in for the reader, most famously in the dialogues that Stuart Curran has shown to play on conventions of the eclogue, the father in "Anecdote for Fathers" and the speaker in "We Are Seven."[52] In *Peter Bell* Wordsworth refuses to complete the satiric judgment of either Methodism or his protagonist, despite the evidence, and in effect rehabilitates his criminal at the end, with the aid of imagination, "guilty fear," and powerful emotion. But rather than merely avoiding judgment, this ending directs the judgment to other targets: among other things, it becomes a kind of affront to readers and a challenge to their sensibilities. Political and ideological differences between Crabbe and Wordsworth result in different final outcomes for the two sadistic ruffians. Like Crabbe's, Wordsworth's tale also has a "purpose," as he insists in the Preface. His argument that this is what sets him far apart from "mean" verses like Crabbe's, however, is difficult to accept at face value. In 1825, John Wilson described Crabbe's effect on his reader again in terms of a sentimental contrast with Wordsworth:

> Unlike to that of Burns and Wordsworth, may it not be said that the genius
> of this author alienates the spirit of his reader? . . . We have found no friend
> in the poet, to whom we were willing to surrender our hearts, but too often a
> sneering cynic, who shows us insultingly that he knows and understands the
> beauty we prize, and then plucks it to pieces before our very face.[53]

What separates the two poets is less "realism" and "imagination," or purpose and its lack, than fundamentally different metaphysics and politics.
But in formal terms these differences are seen as a difference between the
"sneer" and the "heart." This is reminiscent of Wordsworth's resistance to
the ironic "smile" in the face of human folly and vice, a smile and a cynical
sneer displaced in his ideal poetry by imaginative sympathy with the represented subjects. In place of a shared smile the reader and author are related
as "friends," the text made a kind of provocation to shared feeling, a work
before which we are asked to "surrender our heart." The judgment is rendered against (or for) us.

Thus readers can pick up Crabbe to remind them that Wordsworth's is a
poetry of resistance, a "counter" to the "counter-spirit" of satire, to Crabbe
and the satiric tradition he represents. By extension and a logical turnabout,
some of the many parodies of Wordsworth's rustic mode help remind us of
this resistance within the Romantic. In parody after parody, the poet is represented as painfully earnest in the face of knowing, leering rustics who are
as much the satirists as the butts of satire. Take for example an 1822 speci-
men, titled simply "Lyrical Ballad."

> 'TWAS a March morning, about nine o'clock,
>   The Lark sung clear from an iron-grey cloud,
> I past an old man on an Upping-stock,
>   And, as I passed him, he sneez'd aloud.
> In pious courtesy I blessed him,
> Whilst he, with penetrating eye and keen,
> Held forth a bottle, tied down round the rim
> With an old rag of thread-bare velveteen.
> And in my lonely thought I did surmise,
> That the same velveteen had clothed his thighs.[54]

The speaker muses deeply on the man's breeches and the bottle for another
stanza or so, observes of the rustic that after all he is human, "as much alive
as I," and produces in himself appropriate sympathetic emotion: "a gust of
fellow feeling thrill'd my soul." At this point the old man interrupts his
thoughts to tell the speaker that the bottle contains leeches, writhing water
snakes that the speaker cannot help but reimagine:

In water pure they swam;—quoth I, "'tis good,
Man hath not taught them yet to thirst for blood:"—
With that a harden'd smile gleam'd in his eye,
And, leering on me, this was his reply;—
"They don't lack teaching. Put your hand and try!"—
I turn'd me from that leering grey-beard crone
And, marvelling deeply, sate me all alone
Upon a stone.

And though that flinty stone was ridged and bare,
　No moss nor lichen made a cushion on it,
Though it most sharply gall'd my kerseymere.
Doing a rude stamp-office duty there,
　I'll take my oath upon it,
The rugged surface of that flinty stone
Hurt not my bone,
Nor to my outward self caus'd such deep smart,
As that old man's harsh leer smote on my inmost heart.

　　That man was Peter Bell—alas! alas!
　　Yea, though he kissed his own ass,
　　Yet unredeem'd! But I will try once again
　　Try to reclaim him in some future strain.
　　—Amen.

This parody is funny, but it is also a parable of competing poetic modes (and the inevitability of their continuing admixture). Indeed, it provides a perfect picture of the very dynamic I have been describing: Wordsworth's counter-satiric turn and the return of satire. Here the "harsh leer" is set in opposition to the purity of nature and the "inmost heart," and the solipsistic poet of sensibility literally turns away from the "penetrating eye" of the leering, sarcastic old man, retreating into meditative feeling ("deep smart") and projecting onto the rustic his phantasmagoric idealization of human (and leech) nature—a Romantic reclamation project. It is only poetic justice that the satiric old man should turn out to be a grotesque avatar of that deliberately countersatiric creation, Peter Bell.

Rustics Representing Themselves:
Duck, Collier, Elliott

Wordsworth's and Crabbe's rustics are represented differently but in a direct competition for the same marketplace of polite, middling-type, and learned readers of literature. There were alternatives to both, of course, when it came to representing rusticity, chief among them the poets who were themselves rustics—or at least of rustic stock—for which there was a vogue in the nineteenth century. It will be useful in closing to examine the role of those self-representations in setting some of the terms for Wordsworth's and Crabbe's "competition."

Raymond Williams has most clearly articulated Crabbe's deliberate alignment of his own work with the debunking poetry of Stephen Duck, "the Thresher Poet."[55] Duck described the "melancholy scene" of agricultural labor and its economic and social relations from the un-idyllic laborer's point of view—as dull, "endless Toils, which always grow anew"—and always in obedience to the Master and his economic imperatives. In *The Village* Crabbe claims to "paint the cot, / As truth will paint it, and as bards will not" (I, 53–54).

> Yes, thus the Muses sing of happy swains,
> Because the Muses never knew their pains:
> They boast their peasants' pipes, but peasants now
> Resign their pipes and plod behind the plough;
> And few amid the rural tribe have time
> To number syllables and play with rhyme;
> Save honest DUCK, what son of verse could share
> The poet's rapture and the peasant's care?
>
> (I, 21–28)

In reacting (most immediately) to Goldsmith's neopastoral, Crabbe's 1783 counterpastoralism identifies with this tradition of what John Goodridge has called "proletarian counter-pastoral"[56] by authors such as Duck and Mary Collier in the 1730s. But this specific tradition falls within the larger mock-pastoral line, including Gay's mock-Spenserian poetry of the early eighteenth century or even Swift's later urban mock-pastoral (indeed, Swift is credited with the idea for Gay's *Beggar's Opera*—the "Newgate pastoral"). As Goodridge argues, the illusions and idealizations of the pastoral have always contained within them the (urban, realistic, modern) "reality" that helps define them (3). The pastoral idyll always implies its opposite, the counterpastoral, even since Theocritus and Virgil: *et in Arcadia ego.* Stuart Curran usefully traces the serpentine developments of Romantic-period pastoral, antipastoral, and the "countergenre" of late neopastoral.[57] Crabbe's poetry, Curran notes, is the inevitable result of this generic counterinsurgence (93). He also points to the sublimely Juvenalian *Prophecy of Famine* by Charles Churchill (1763), with its "knowing deconstruction of pastoral paradigms" (93), and then, in response to such antipastoral as Churchill's and Crabbe's, the rise of the neo-idylls of Collins, Southey, and even Wordsworth and Coleridge in the *Lyrical Ballads,* which after 1802 was subtitled *with Pastoral and Other Poems.* Wordsworth's Preface, as Curran says, is "an extended defense of the new pastoral . . ." (98–99). It is only an additional step from these observations to my thesis that Wordsworth's pro-pastoral stance is at bottom frequently antisatire.

Tracing the interrelations of such subgeneric identities has this advantage: it highlights the identifying marks through which authors and works establish intertextual family resemblances, thus establishing lineages that continue to affect later competitions and struggles for dominance. Delineating some of the particular versions of counterpastoral, and then showing how those bleed over into versions of countersatire, reveals connections that have become obscured by chronological lists and anthologies. In the present case, they help us get at the relative importance of Crabbe over Pope when it comes to the emergence of Romantic modes of representing rustics. The "field" in this case—and thus the differentiations of taste on which canon formation and the construction of a dominant "movement" depends—involves the vagaries of satiric and sincere modes as these interweave themselves with conventions for representing rural life. Finer distinctions yield subtler understanding of the struggles for dominance in the poetic field.

To begin with, both George Crabbe and Stephen Duck produce antipastoral poetry, and both include in their projects satiric modes of attack. But as his own epithet reveals, Crabbe patronizes "honest Duck" [58] even as he praises him, thus clearing a space for his own superior version of debunking. Crabbe's middle-class perspective lacks Duck's angry "we," the thresher's participatory sense that the inexorable forces of nature are no more compelling than the "dehumanising machine, controlled by 'The Master,' and driving the farm workers relentlessly through a never-ending cycle of backbreaking work," as Goodridge puts it (12). For Duck, the "golden harvest" reveals itself to be about "gold" itself—a question of someone else's profits. But this is seen simply as the way of the world. There is little nostalgia reaching beyond a single generation, little real temptation to appeal to a golden age. Surveying his English landscape, Duck sees before him only "Thistles," "And Corn blown adverse with the ruffling Wind;" and behind him,

> Our Master waits; and if he spies
> One charitable Ear, he grudging cries,
> "Ye scatter half you Wages o'er the Land."
> Then scrapes the Stubble with his greedy Hand.[59]

This is writing at the crossroad of georgic and Juvenalian satire, a picture of the poor Crabbe, for all his stern "realism," never quite provides.

Such satiric effects in Duck are accompanied by another perennial Juvenalian convention: satiric misogyny. Thirty-six lines are given over to the ridicule of women workers, "a Throng / Of prattling Females, arm'd with rake and Prong," who sit down on the job and chatter at every opportunity ("Ah! Were their Hands so active as their Tongues, / How nimbly then would move the rakes and Prongs!"). At a sudden rain-shower, Duck pauses for a long mock-epic simile comparing the women to a flock of sparrows scattered by a storm. These lines inspired their own countersatire by Mary Collier in her poem *The Woman's Labor* (1739), which astutely mocks Duck's poem while answering his misogyny. Collier deploys complex satiric devices, matching Duck point for point. Moira Ferguson has aptly called the poem a "one-sided flyting"—one of the oldest kind of verbal performances, the duel or contest of insults, identifiable as "satiric"—by an author who may be "the first known rural laboring woman in England to publish creative work."[60] The gist of Collier's countersatire is the "double shift" that women must work, and the double standard to which they are held.

> No Learning ever was bestowed on me;
> My life was always spent in Drudgery;
> And not alone; alas! With Grief I find,
> It is the Portion of poor Woman-kind. (6)
>
> When Ev'ning's come, you Homeward take your Way,
> We, till our Work is done, are forc'd to stay;
> And after all our Toil and labor past,
> Six-pence or Eight-pence pays us off at last; (15)

Like the women gleaners in her verse, Collier comes along behind Duck and with parodic ingenuity picks up the satiric potential of counterpastoral, then turns it against the male poet. As Goodridge notes, Collier shows "mock sympathy" in this Popean zeugma alluding to Duck's bleak landscape: "Those mighty Troubles which perplex your Mind, / (*Thistles* before, and *Females* come behind)" (14). Collier continued to labor as a washerwoman after Duck had been established under the patronage of Queen Caroline; and his place at the margins of the canon is nonetheless more visible than hers. Her example, more than his alone, reminds us that satiric dialogue and countersatiric retort can never be disentangled from the pastoral/counterpastoral struggles of the eighteenth century.

Though the close, yet oppositional dialogue between their works has been obscured over time, Wordsworth himself came to see Crabbe as one (lesser) member of his poetic lineage. The point of this chapter has been to suggest that asking about the reciprocal relation of satiric and coun-

tersatiric modes is a useful way to reconsider such constructed succes-
sions, to reillumine long-forgotten subtleties of similarity and difference
and to reengage in the competitive struggles that led to the construction
of the evaluative categories by which the result of those struggles has
come down to posterity as a fait accompli. Otherwise, looking back from
the long perspective of (post-Romantic) literary history, important distinctions are collapsed and important family resemblances—on the
grounds of which competing "movements" or modes get declared dominant or subordinate—are lost to us. In the usual view, Crabbe and Duck
and Collier all fade into a background meant to set off Wordsworthian
"pastoral" in all its triumphal inevitability, as using rustics to represent
the decidedly unsatiric, Romantic spirit of the age.

Chapter 2 ⁓

"Supernatural, or at Least Romantic": The *Ancient Mariner* and Parody

An ancient literary practice often aligned with satire, parody "comes of age as a major comic expression during the Romantic period," as Marilyn Gaull has observed, the same era that celebrated and became known for the literary virtues of sincerity, authenticity, and originality.[1] The era of Romantic poetry was also the era of biting parodies in the *Anti-Jacobin* and the radical weeklies, and in reviews such as *Blackwood's;* of the politically influential parodies of the Bible or nursery rhymes by William Hone, as well as collections of poems such as Horace and James Smith's *Rejected Addresses* (1812) and James Hogg's *Poetic Mirror* (1816); and of novelistic parodies such as Jane Austen's *Northanger Abbey* or the "Menippean" satires of Thomas Love Peacock. Most students of the period are aware that Wordsworth, Coleridge, and Southey were widely lampooned, as in the parody of Wordsworth's rural subjects discussed in chapter 1, and some are familiar with the flurry of parodies surrounding Wordsworth's *Peter Bell,* notably including Percy Bysshe Shelley's *Peter Bell the Third.*

But these are only the better-known examples. Significant recent anthologies of Romantic-period parodies make the sheer bulk and topical range of such imitative works available for readers and critics for the first time, providing ample evidence for the prominence of the form.[2] Taken as a whole, the weight of evidence in these collections should also put to rest the widespread assumption that parody is *inevitably* "comic" or gentler than satire—that is, essentially in good fun (though there are always such comic parodies in evidence). At least during the politically volatile Romantic period, as Linda Hutcheon has asserted, parody "is almost always aligned with satire; that is to say, parody is the literary shape taken by social satire."[3] Even in these extreme examples, the very act of imitation implies a closeness and familiarity rather than a mere dismissal of the target. This is why much parody has historically been seen as a form of flattery, a tribute to the original. As Hutcheon says elsewhere, parody is "imitation with a critical ironic distance, whose irony can cut both ways," producing in some cases "scornful ridicule" and in others what looks like "reverential homage."[4] Nonetheless, in the hands of the editors of the *Anti-Jacobin,* for example, or any number of radical pamphleteers, parody often served as a powerful mode of topical satire—a particularly galling and intimate way of ridiculing by stealing and distorting one's very voice. There is something primitive and childlike in this mode of parodic satire, its mockery so often taking the form of mere verbal mimicry and caricature rather than the subtly ironic intellectual criticism its practitioners sometimes claim.

It is often observed that, considered etymologically, "parody" can mean either "beside" or "against" another poem, and that parodies can serve either to pay tribute to or to ridicule the targeted work. Samuel Taylor Coleridge approached the same matter from a slightly different direction in the following epigram for anonymous inclusion in Robert Southey's *Omniana:*

> Parodies on new poems are read as satires; on old ones, (the soliloquy of Hamlet for instance) as compliments. A man of genius may securely laugh at a mode of attack, by which his reviler in half a century or less, becomes his encomiast.[5]

This way of putting it helpfully focuses on historical context as necessary to any interpretation of the tone and purpose of parody; but it also emphasizes by implication the canonical status of the targeted work. The difference between parodic "satire" and parodic "compliment" is time, according to Coleridge: the distance traveled from a "new" to an "old" poem. But the chosen example of an old poem is telling; in 1812, when Coleridge wrote the passage, Shakespeare had just begun to stand at the head of an English vernacular canon. The kind of old poem that both survives the test of time and is at the end still considered worthy of parody is likely to be a work of recognized "genius," which is to say, a canonical work.

Coleridge's gnomic remark suggests that whether a parody counts as satire or compliment depends in part upon the process of canonization, a process in turn dependent upon the kind of critical judgments offered by parody. Such parodic judgments identify the works worthy of being remembered and taken seriously enough to be parodied in the first place, and help to define the qualities of those works that make them worthy of (even negative) attention. There is a double circularity at work in this scheme: parody helps to shape the context that partly determines the effect of other parodies; and in a kind of poetic Doctrine of the Elect, only the man of genius can rest secure in eventual victory, in the promise that his satiric "attackers" will eventually, in the due course of cultural change, be transformed into his encomiasts. The canonical have the last laugh. But whether a work is worthy of such canonization becomes known only when the work is no longer "new" but still considered significant, literally imitable. In most cases, true security is only certain after the death of the author. Beneath these paradoxes, Coleridge's parable speaks to the dialectical relationship of satire and poetic expression in literary history. Parody and satiric commentary help not only to cull and determine the works that remain in the field; sometimes they help through their overall contributions to its critical reception to shape a movement-defining, major work—even after the fact of its publication—as in the case of Coleridge's *Rime of the Ancient Mariner*.

This chapter will look through the lens of parody at one of Coleridge's most characteristically "romantic" works, his famous ballad of the supernatural, *The Rime of the Ancient Mariner*. Along with the other so-called Mystery Poems—*Christabel* and "Kubla Khan"—this is among his most significant generic contributions to the developing idea of Romanticism, the kind of work that comes through synecdoche to stand for the whole movement as it was conceived. According to his own statement of intentions, these poems represent his "supernatural, or at least romantic" mode, which served as a pendant to Wordsworth's "natural," rustic simplicity in the *Lyrical Ballads* project.[6] In what follows I place the *Rime* in the context of Coleridge's changing conception of the work and his own satiric practice, including his propensity for self-parody and the parody of his fellow poets. In the late 1790s Coleridge joined a literary trend, producing supernatural works so deliberately extreme they were always on the verge of self-parody. Over the course of the following three decades he attempted to distance himself from the more fashionably romantic works of the same generic family, and from those qualities in his own works, representing them as part of a more metaphysical kind, constructing a philosophically coherent corpus fit for a place in the canon. Parody, broadly conceived, plays a role at every stage of this process. Coleridge's self-revisions take place in dialectical relation with parodic and satiric modes of writing, his own and those of others, with the result that these modes are deeply embedded within some of the foundational texts of Romanticism.

The *Ancient Mariner* and the Romantic Canon

My choice of poem in this chapter is no accident. *The Rime of the Ancient Mariner* is rooted in Coleridge's most "romantic" early works (as the term was understood at the time), but it is also an exemplary Romantic poem (in the canonical sense), and can thus, in more than one way, be considered one of the "first" among Romantic works. Wordsworth's and Coleridge's own accounts of the composition and publication history of the ballad make up one of the founding myths of English Romanticism, beginning with their attempts to collaborate on it and publish it in the *Monthly Magazine* as a way to pay the expenses of a walking tour. Coleridge quickly took over the composition but was then caught up in the larger plan for a volume of poems on rustic and supernatural subjects. In the event, the *Rime* was the first poem readers encountered in the first edition of *Lyrical Ballads* in 1798. It was also one of the works in that collection that contemporary readers would have immediately recognized as fashionably romantic in the German style, a kind of gothic horror ballad then popular in the magazines. As an anonymous reviewer looking back from twenty years later noted, *The Rime of the Ancient Mariner*

> appeared at a time when, to use a bold but just expression, with reference to our literary taste, *"Hell made holiday,"* and *"Raw heads and bloody-bones"* were the only fashionable entertainment for man or woman. Then Germany was poured forth into England, in all her flood of sculls and numsculls: then the romancing novelist ran raving about with midnight torches, to shew death's heads on horseback, and to frighten full-grown children with mysteries and band-boxes, hidden behind curtains in bedrooms . . . [7]

I believe that this reviewer is essentially correct about the origins of the *Rime:* it began as a romantic horror ballad in the popular sense, and only later was made over into the quintessentially Romantic poem.[8] When it first appeared, it was in a self-consciously archaic form, and in these terms Wordsworth's brief Advertisement to *Lyrical Ballads* offered a kind of preemptive apology for it, saying that it was "professedly written in imitation of the *style,* as well as of the spirit of the elder poets." Privately Wordsworth said that he believed it had "upon the whole been an injury to the volume," that "the old words and the strangeness of it have deterred readers from going on;" he wrote an apologetic note for its appearance, near the back of the collection, in the 1800 edition. Between 1798 and 1817, Coleridge continued to revise the poem, producing a number of different versions, but by far the most significant version is the one he prepared for publication in his own *Sibylline leaves* of 1817.[9]

During the intervening years the poem and its author had become famous. Coleridge's brother-in-law, Robert Southey, wrote one of the earliest reviews of the *Lyrical Ballads,* a scathing attack satirizing the *Ancient Mariner* as a "Dutch attempt at German sublimity"; another friend, Charles Lamb, strongly disagreed at the time, saying that it was on the contrary a successful, "right English attempt" to "dethrone German sublimity," and confessing elsewhere that he "was never so affected with any human Tale. After first reading it, I was totally possessed with it for many days."[10] Lamb's respectful point of view was widely shared. Even critics who were sometimes unsympathetic to the Lake School's poetry professed admiration for the ballad, most notably John Gibson Lockhart, who said that this "most wonderful" of the poems in *Sibylline leaves* was the most Coleridgean: "From it alone, we are inclined to think an idea of the whole poetical genius of Mr. Coleridge might be gathered, such as could scarcely receive any important addition either of extent or distinctness, from a perusal of the whole of his other works."[11] The anonymous *Monthly Review* writer cited above, while attacking the German influence and lurid poetry of the ballad, quotes other passages with approval, specifically avoiding what he calls "the horrors of the poem." In *The Spirit of the Age* William Hazlitt summed up the positive view of the ballad and located its place in Coleridge's oeuvre:

> Of all Mr. Coleridge's productions, the *Ancient Mariner* is the only one that we could with confidence put into any person's hands, on whom we wished to impress a favourable idea of his extraordinary powers. Let whatever other objections be made to it, it is unquestionably a work of genius—of wild, irregular, overwhelming imagination, and has that rich, varied movement in the verse, which gives a distant idea of the lofty of changeful tones of Mr. Coleridge's voice.[12]

Hazlitt describes the poem in terms that would later be seen as essentially Romantic ("a work of genius—of wild, irregular, overwhelming imagination") and associates it with the author's name and even his very voice, the authority under which it is to enter the canon.[13] Notice as well how his terms of sometimes equivocal praise—"wild, irregular . . . rich, varied movement"—anticipate, acknowledge, and answer the very kind of criticism (those "other objections") Southey and others made of the poem. Hazlitt's description participates in making the poem into what Coleridge called it (recorded in *Table Talk*):"a work of . . . pure imagination."[14] Among the so-called younger generation of Romantics the poem became a touchstone of themes and techniques, narrative and lyrical. Byron admired it. Shelley borrowed from it. The young Mary Godwin heard the author recite it in her father's home; later it served as a key influence on her own work of gothic horror, *Frankenstein*. In the nineteenth and twentieth centuries it has retained a place of preeminence in the canon and has entered the public consciousness and the culture at large, producing its own extensive academic Midrash of critical commentary and a long chain of multiple editions, versions, imitations, and parodies.

That process of commentary and canonization was begun by Coleridge himself in collaboration with his audiences and critics, even before he revised it for publication in 1817. In that decisive, authoritative version he added as a kind of integrated paratext the famous marginal gloss, as if in the hand of some later (but still "antique") hermeneut. By doing so, as well as through his own critical remarks in the *Biographia Literaria* and elsewhere, he in effect collaborated with readers, critics, and parodists in determining the form in which it would be handed on to the canon and literary history. The gloss, itself a parody of "academic" or monkish interpretation, has proven to be a continuous source of hermeneutic questions about the poem and about hermeneutics in general.[15] It is by now a critical commonplace that the gloss offers a kind of enfolded dialectical or ironic perspective on the main text of the ballad, though critical disagreement persists as to how to read the precise tone of the marginal text. Huntington Brown treats as separable the narrator and gloss-writer; Lawrence Lipking reads it in a tradition of glossed texts; Tilottama Rajan reads the poem with its gloss as a reflexively dialogic, self-deconstructing text; David Simpson finds a species of Romantic irony at work in the way the gloss parodies "the habit of overinscription" by critics; Kathleen Wheeler reads the gloss as "a parody of the process of perception" itself; and Jerome McGann connects the structure of the work, with its narrative and marginal annotation, to biblical Higher Criticism and the history of nineteenth-century philology.[16]

For my purposes here, it is enough to acknowledge that there are places in the text where the gloss opens up an ironic countervoice on the main action of the ballad, in effect anticipating the inevitable parodies. This may be discerned as early as the use of the word "Gallants" adjacent to the first stanza; but it is a clearer possibility in stanzas 9–10:

> The bride hath paced into the hall,
> Red as a rose is she;
> Nodding their heads before her goes
> The merry minstrelsy.

> The Wedding-Guest he beat his breast,
> Yet he can not chuse but hear;
> And thus spake on that ancient man,
> The bright-eyed Mariner.

The gloss merely says in deadpan fashion: "the wedding-guest heareth the bridal music; but the mariner continueth his tale."[17] The simple discrepancy in tone between the agony of the Guest and the gloss-writer's imperturbability is potentially parodic, whatever Coleridge's specific intentions. Elsewhere, specific moral-theological judgments are offered, or quirky, seemingly personal, and sometimes overobvious reactions are recorded. When the poem describes in lurid detail the gothic appearance of Life-in-Death and her mate (III.10–11), the glossist simply observes, "Like vessel, like crew!" In other instances, the key discrepancy is between the pace of the ballad meter and of the glossist's terse remarks, as when the moon rises and two hundred sailors one by one silently curse the Mariner and drop dead, told by the ballad in four full stanzas (the first of which is extra long at nine lines); synchronized with the slow motion of the "star-dogg'd Moon" (III.16), their souls fly away. The gloss, by contrast, moves quickly through three phrases: "At the rising of the Moon . . . One after another . . . His shipmates drop down dead." the parody here is a matter of style: a play between "scholarly" understatement and sentimental overstatement. It is difficult to separate intended from unintended ironic effects in the interpenetrating texts of gloss and ballad, but the possibility of parody—in the full range of its senses, from iterative tribute to allusive appropriation to satiric mimicry—is anticipated and subsumed in the structure of Coleridge's dialogic text of 1817. This merely brings to an initial climax (but does not end) a process of effusion and parody that was intimately bound up with the composition, revision, and reception of this most "romantic" of Romantic works.

Two Parodies: 1819, 1989

What is it about the *Ancient Mariner* that parodists continue to find imitable and risible? I would suggest that parodies of this work are useful precisely because they target the *Ancient Mariner* based on its family resemblance to the gothic ballad tradition, which persisted despite Coleridge's attempts to turn the poem into something of a higher kind. Especially after 1817, parodies offer a satiric perspective on the whole process of revising the poem and thus on the making of Romanticism itself out of "romantic" elements in popular and fashionable literature. Looking at the poem through parodists' eyes is a useful dialectical exercise and one that provides a counterweight to the institutionalized academic readings of the poem as a central text in the High Romantic canon. The parodists of the "romantic" elements in the *Ancient Mariner* include, first and foremost, Coleridge himself.

From the many possible examples of parodies by others I have deliberately selected two representative works widely separated by era and cultural context, a poetic imitation from 1819 and a comic-book adaptation from 1989. These serve first to dramatize the extension of the cultural capital of the poem into the late twentieth century—and well outside the academy—

but also to demonstrate the specific ways in which both parodies make much of what Coleridge had already provided in the way of dialogic and parodic openings, openings he himself responded to with revisionary moves even as he was creating them. Already in 1819 *The Rime of the Ancient Mariner*, though a "new" poem still in terms of Coleridge's dichotomy, had achieved the kind of fame that turned the "satire" of any parody into something of a "compliment." The reception and legacy of the work was shaped by the interaction of such canonizing compliment and satiric commentary.

I. 1819

Less than two years after the publication of *Sibylline leaves* and only months before Lockhart's praise of the *Ancient Mariner* appeared in *Blackwood's,* an anonymous parody was printed whose title suggests a satire on Wordsworth along with Coleridge, "The Rime of the Auncient Waggonere." Its author was David Macbeth Moir, who would a short time later also publish a parody of *Christabel* purporting to complete the fragment. The effect of the parody, technically a burlesque in its treatment of a base subject in Coleridge's sublime tones, is based on verbal mimicry and on various substitutions for elements in the original, but also on exploiting the discrepancies between gloss and main text.

> IT is an auncient Waggonere,
>   And he stoppeth one of nine:—
> "Now wherefore dost thou grip me soe
> With that horny fist of thine?
>
> "The bridegroom's doors are opened wide,
>   And thither I must walke;
> Soe, by youre leave, I muste be gone,
>   I have noe time for talke!"
>
> Hee holds him with his horny fist—
>   "There was a wain," quothe hee,
> "Hold offe, thou raggamouffine tykke,"
>   Eftsoones his fist dropped hee.[18]

The gloss to the second stanza merely reads: "The waggonere in mood for chate, and admits of no excuse." So far this is very much like the effect in the 1817 original of discrepant tones and ironic understatement, but with coarser northern slang in place of Coleridge's vaguely medieval or Renaissance language. At times this effect takes the form of slapstick bathos, though again, the original had provided the example and pointed the way:

> "The wain is fulle, the horses pulle,
>   Merrilye did we trotte
> Alonge the bridge, alonge the road,
>   A jolly crewe, I wotte:"—
> And here the tailore smotte his breaste,
>   He smelte the cabbage potte! (164)

The gloss merely repeats the event, like a mindless refrain, but with something like the pedantic long-windedness of the original: "The appetite of the Tailore whetted by the smell of cabbage." (There is surely a pun on Coleridge's name in "Tailore.") In this passage Coleridge's ethereal wedding music is brought down to the level of the cabbage (and the baser sense of smell), the social class of the wedding party is made clear, and the parody mocks the intrusion of quotidian details (and the body) into the melodramatic action and supernatural or psychological effects of the original ballad.

As the parody continues, the main joke, emphasized by this play of gloss against text, turns out to be the blatant physical violence of the Waggonere, which satirizes the Mariner's violent act against the albatross but also generally punctures the metaphysical pretensions of the original. Coleridge's first version and what survives in 1817 of the gothic horror ballad decorum—whose conventions can compass ghost ships, waking corpses, and slimy things—are satirically debunked by the direct knockabout of the parody, as the Waggonere proves himself the low ruffian who might be expected by *Blackwood's* readers to appear in a ballad.

> "At lengthe we spied a goode grey goose,
>   Thorough the snow it came;
> And with the butte ende of my whippe,
>   I hailed it in Goddhis name.
>
> "It staggered as it had been drunke,
>   So dexterous was it hitte;
> Of broken boughs we made a fire,
>   Thomme Loncheone roasted itte."—(164)

Signaling that it is subtle enough to mimic Coleridge's archaic diction ("thorough," for example, and the excessive e's), the parody remains otherwise deliberately crude, thus taking aim at the whole Lake School's favorite poetic virtue of "simplicity." The power of the Waggonere to hold the Tailore as an audience begins to look increasingly like thuggish intimidation.

In "Part Second," as the Waggonere rides away, conventional balladic questions, including for a moment an allusion to the Albatross ("a foreigne bird"), come to a mundane anticlimax. As the gloss says: "Various hypotheses on the subject, frome which the passengers draw wronge conclusions."

> "Some saide itte was ane apple tree,
>   Laden with goodlye fruite,
> Some swore itte was ane foreigne birde,
>   Some said it was ane brute;
> Alas! It was ane bumbailliffe,
>   Riding in pursuite! (165)

Not surprisingly, the Waggonere "complimenteth the bumbailiffe with ane Mendoza" (a special boxing blow): "Why star'st thoue soe?—With one goode blow, / I felled the bumbailiffe." So it is with less metaphysical than physical dread (what the gloss names "Corporal Feare") that *this* interlocutor says,

> "I feare thee, auncient waggonere,
>   I fear thy hornye fist,
> For itte is stained with gooses gore,
>   And bailiffe's blood, I wist. (166)

The parody ends by tacking on an explicitly labeled, clumsy "MORALE" (168), thus going right to the heart of what was and remained perhaps the key interpretive question of Coleridge's poem, beginning with the legendary comments of Anna Barbauld (she remarked that the poem lacked a moral) and continuing for the next two hundred years. Making fun of the summarizing stanzas of the *Rime,* the moral of the parody is bluntly explicit. It simply cautions "foolish men" to avoid "bade companye," implying again the danger of treating too seriously ill-mannered, low-life rustics like the Waggonere and demonstrating why it is better to avoid than indulge "simple" strangers on the road. Instead of a narrative of increasing mystery and wonder, the Waggonere tells an all-too mundane story of quotidian rough behavior. In the same way the whole parody demystifies with a vengeance (by caricaturing and domesticating) the exotic, "wild" atmosphere and machinery of the 1817 original, reducing the sublime to the ridiculous—with a brickbat.

What is clear in the design of the parody is, first, that Moir reads even the 1817 text as pretentiously romantic in its mystified supernaturalism, and second, that he is aware of and willing to capitalize on the ironic openings provided by Coleridge's dialogic gloss. This revision was precisely the device through which Coleridge also enhanced the susceptibility of the ballad to "Romantic" interpretations—as a metaphysically transcendent and aesthetically symbolic text. The parody returns to the half-buried romantic qualities of the ballad, which persist despite Coleridge's attempts to revise them away; in fact it calls attention to how the layered revisions of the poem work to dress up the simple narrative events, thus encoding the shifting senses of "r/Romantic" as they apply to—indeed, as they are in part defined by—Coleridge's poetry.

II. 1989

Similar demystifications of the poem continue in the partly "underground" and extra-academic tradition of parodies and popular adaptations of the *Rime,* from Coleridge's own time, through the Victorian era, to the present.[19] One striking twentieth-century example is Hunt Emerson's 1989 comic-book version, which includes Coleridge's text in word bubbles and panel captions, according to comic-book conventions, but also supplements it with additional speeches, and parodies the text through its illustrations.[20] Emerson's no-holds-barred lampoon style originates in the underground comics of the early 1970s and makes use of a conventional repertoire of psychedelic distortions, hallucinatory and surrealistic fantasies, and gleeful bodily humor, including puns and slapstick jokes of questionable taste. Within those conventions—I would argue because it *is* within them—it offers a remarkable parodic tribute to *and* satiric commentary on Coleridge's ballad and on its long reputation and vast store of accumulated cultural capital.

Emerson's percipience is evident from the frontispiece to the comic book, a brilliantly grotesque full-page representation of a textual passage in the 1798 version of the poem, later deleted by Coleridge as too luridly "German," in which the living-dead sailors raise their arms to burn as lurid torches (see figure 2.1):

> A little distance from the prow
>   Those dark-red shadows were;
> But soon I saw that my own flesh
>   Was red as in a glare.
>
> I turn'd my head in fear and dread,
>   And by the holy rood,
> The bodies had advanc'd, and now
>   Before the mast they stood.
>
> They lifted up their stiff right arms,
>   They held them strait and tight;
> And each right-arm burnt like a torch,
>   A torch that's borne upright.
> Their stony eye-balls glitter'd on
>   In the red and smoky light.
>
>   (VI, sts. 18–20)[21]

Emerson cannily chooses to restore this deleted passage to his overall "text" by way of this silent image, thus foregrounding the kinship of the original poem to his own version. The comic-book panel could almost be an illustration of the nineteenth-century review quoted above, with its "*Raw heads and bloody-bones*" entertainments. Uncaptioned and wordless (except for the T-shirt on one of the figures), the image reminds us of the "silenced" text Coleridge deleted and in effect declares it as a measure of what is to follow, establishing the spirit and tone of the rest of Emerson's parody. It shows a line of five zombie sailors on the deck, with eyeless skulls, rotting flesh, protruding bones, and grotesque entrails, but the effect of horror is undercut by numerous broadly comic details—an airhorn, opium pipe, chicken bone, aged cheese, and a dead bird extending out of the skulls, held aloft by extra hands, repeating the image of the burning fists. One holds what appears to be a frog, one a flaming cigarette lighter, the universal signal calling for an encore at a rock concert, and wears a T-shirt reading "Bob Dylan World Tour 1795." In the center of the composition, the albatross itself pecks angrily at a sailor's silly animal slippers. The slapstick anachronisms are licensed by the irreverence of the comic-book form and by the mode of parody itself. The flouting of historical boundaries is only one way the parody targets the stuffy academic ownership of this text. As if in anticipatory defiance of conventional distaste, one of the sailors thumbs his nose at us in the frontispiece tableau.

In his playful treatment of the grotesque and macabre, as if in a dream or drug-induced hallucination, Emerson is exploiting the distant family resemblance between this countercultural art form and Coleridge's own opium-induced reveries. The mixture of horror and humor is also profoundly true to the contradictory effects of Coleridge's ballad from the start, but especially after the gloss was added for the 1817 version, effects of which Moir's 1819 parody is well aware. The exaggerated sensibility and "supernatural" and sublime pyrotechnics of late eighteenth-century gothic balladry, novels, and theater already at their inception opened themselves up to the possibility of caricature and parody by their very nature. By design, the artists who began at the time systematically to use these effects for their own purposes created works self-consciously in excess, sentimental, passionate, lurid, and wild in their imaginative intensity—in a word, "romantic." Defining themselves as "against" or "beside" conventional morality and decorum, such expressions come into being as part of a "parodic" relationship to the status quo, which is easily enough turned back upon them, reversed in actual parody. These "outsider" qualities, still present in fossil form within the long history of the *Rime*'s reception, are brought out by the historically distant and yet generically consonant, exaggerated, and distorted psychedelic exuberance of Emerson's comic-book style.

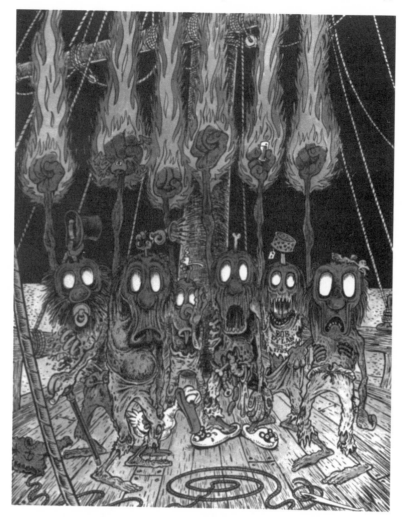

Figure 2.1   Hunt Emerson, *The Rime of The Ancient Mariner* (frontispiece)

Emerson places Coleridge's gloss as an "argument" at the beginning of each part of the poem, but he also "glosses" the text himself in various ways, first in the images, which often comment on the text, but also in additional speeches put in the mouths of the characters, and finally in completely new interpolated sequences, bits of comic business that comment on the "real" plot like theatrical asides or parabases to the audience, as if improvised by actors performing a well-known script. One of the funniest of these is his depiction of the early plot crisis, the actual shooting of the Albatross. Emerson has the Mariner use his crossbow but with a suction-cup-tipped arrow. He repeatedly fires at the bird and misses in a series of snapshot images, panel by panel. When he finally hits it, the Albatross hams it up, reeling and staggering around the deck, one brief panel at a time, in a burlesque-melodramatic dying scene, the arrow protruding ridiculously from its head (see figure 2.2). The staring sailors at first form a stone-faced audience to this performance, growing more frustrated as they listen to the brief moral-mongering speeches (in the word balloons: "martyred to man's dominion! . . . DEAD!"), until the Mariner grimly returns with a large gun and blasts the bird in the final panel. The comic timing of this use of the rhythmic transitions between the closely articulated panels here is impeccable, but what is so successfully parodic about this interlude is its targeting of the incipient tropes of sensibility inherited by Coleridge with his chosen form. From the initial reception through much of twentieth-century criticism, it has been clear to readers that the "bird of ill-omen" has to bear an inordinate weight of emotional significance in the narrative. The "dying" of Emerson's Albatross is a pop cliché straight out of Tex Avery's animated cartoons, for example, but is ultimately derived from the same kind of sentimental melodrama that was popular in the 1790s. The comic-book bird serves simultaneously as a sentimental hero and as its own long-winded exegete, and in one sense the gun-toting Mariner acts on behalf of countless readers who have been frustrated with the sententiousness of much of the critical tradition and the seemingly disproportionate significance attached to the ornithological protagonist. A wicked satiric relief comes from watching the feathers fly from this most famous Coleridgean symbol.

Similarly, at the strange climax ("Part Fourth"), Emerson parodies the famous blessing of living things by the Mariner, with the Albatross very much alive again ("Aw—give us a break, boss—there aren't many good parts in literature for albatrosses," it pleads), hanging around his neck, indulging in a crude visual pun on "spring of love" (the Mariner's heart protrudes from his chest on a spring), as a punning reply to sneezing water snakes ("bless you"). At the conclusion, Emerson further demonstrates his awareness of the history of interpretation. After an extraordinary sequence of 21 separate panels across two pages in which the Mariner recites as if on stage the famous lines summarizing the purported moral of the poem ("O Sweeter than the marriage-feast . . . He prayeth well who loveth well . . ."), Emerson provides another silent graphic interlude. The Wedding Guest—obviously sadder and wiser, indeed looking properly "stunned"—wanders along the road, as the backdrop changes like a panoramic stage set to suggest the miles and perhaps ages he is traversing, until he is tapped from behind by the revivified Albatross, still wearing the suction-cup arrow but now carrying a beggar's tin cup. The Wedding Guest drops two coins into the cup, then watches as the bird

Figure 2.2   Hunt Emerson, *The Rime of The Ancient Mariner*

walks away, presumably joining his nemesis the Mariner on the road as an itinerant opportunity (or nuisance) for hapless charitable interlocutors. The final two stanzas of the poem, in which the Mariner turns and goes on his way, are illustrated in a ⅓-page borderless panel containing Emerson's caricature of Coleridge himself, quill in hand, completing the poem in a state of laudanum intoxication (figure 2.3). The poet's wicked grin suggests a conspiracy of satire with the comic-book artist, and Emerson seems to have caricatured himself as well, making a cameo appearance earlier in the text as the drunken Hermit. It is as if the lurid gothic effects, arcane symbolism, and narrative ambiguities were all part of a plan of self-parodic poetic effects that were merely imitated, illustrated, and exaggerated by Emerson.

The reception of a canonical work is ultimately an uncontrollable process. A work like the *Rime* (or to name another example, and one inspired by the *Rime,* Mary Shelley's *Frankenstein*) can possess for a time a sort of super-canonical status, claimed by popular or even mass culture as well as

Figure 2.3   Hunt Emerson, *The Rime of The Ancient Mariner*

elite intellectual culture, that allows its reception to exceed by far its official interpretations by academic critics, the contemporary clerisy. Knowledge of such a work—often through a diverse array of versions and adaptations in various media—functions as a marker of cultural capital for a wide range of readers.[22] Hunt Emerson's parody is aimed at this kind of wide audience, and is enjoyable on a number of levels. Though he includes the gloss and uses the basic text from 1817, he also makes good use of variants from earlier versions, and, as I have been suggesting, highlights the general gothic tone descended from the 1798 version. Emerson's comic book is a parody of the composite artifact that might be called the vulgate *Rime of the Ancient Mariner.* One of the reasons his parody works so well is that there is a happy consonance between the lurid effects of underground comic-book art and the lurid effects of gothic horror balladry, the "gross and violent stimulants" that Wordsworth denounced in the culture of his time and that found their way into Coleridge's ballad at its inception. Emerson brings out in high relief precisely those qualities of the *Rime* that Coleridge partly effaced in re-vision but that still mark its family resemblance to Bürger's ballads or the plays of Kotzebue,[23] the very qualities that most opened it up to parody in the first place, as Coleridge was well aware.

The Roots of the *Ancient Mariner:*
Mystery and Parody

Since the publication of John Livingston Lowes's exhaustive study, *The Road to Xanadu,* the question of the sources of the *Ancient Mariner* has become a singularly uninteresting topic, taken on its own.[24] In this case, however, I am interested in a particular kind of source, exemplified in Bürger's "Lenore," which almost everyone agrees was an inspiration for Coleridge's ballad. I am interested less in the private imagination of Coleridge during composition, or in specific intertextual echoes (though they exist, particularly with the trans-lations by Walter Scott), than in the generic family to which the two ballads belong and what this family tie tells us about how the "romantic" qualities of Coleridge's poem would have been perceived by his contemporary audience.

"Lenore" was translated by Thomas Taylor and published in the *Monthly Magazine* of March 1796 (as "Lenora"), whence it "awakened a native strain of 'spook' balladry," in England, as it has been pointed out, "at a time when an interest in gothic horror had reached a peak in both the novel and the drama."[25] The ballad had been imitated in the first place in 1773 from a Scottish original. Walter Scott translated it and reportedly said it inspired him to turn to poetry; it helped to inspire his *Minstrelsy of the Scottish Bor-der* (1803) and reinforced the widespread influence of Percy's *Reliques* and the ballad as a form. Among a more limited circle of influential writers, "Lenore" was a decisive text. An excited Charles Lamb called it to Co-leridge's attention in a letter of 6 July 1796.[26] In the same issue of the *Monthly Magazine* in which his translation appeared, Taylor published a note arguing that Bürger's poetry was "singularly fitted to become national popular song" because of his "impetuous diction," and praised his style in terms now recognizably Romantic:

> Bürger is every where distinguished for manly sentiment and force of style. His extraordinary powers of language are founded on a rejection of the con-ventional phraseology of regular poetry, in favour of popular forms of ex-pression, caught by the listening artist from the voice of agitated nature. (117–18)

Note that the gothic subjects of Bürger's works are never mentioned here. Instead Taylor stresses the vehicle of his vernacular style in terms that align him with the literature of sensibility—"manly sentiment" expressed in "the voice of agitated nature."

Lenore foresees her lover's death in "frightful dreams," and he eventually does return as a revenant to take her away with him. Thinking him dead, she then falls into "furious despair" when he fails to return home from the crusades:

> "Go out, go out, my lamp of life;
>   In endless darkness die:
> Without him I must loathe the earth,
>   Without him scorne the skye."
>
> And so despaire did rave and rage
>   Athwarte her boiling veins;
> Against the Providence of God
>   She hurlde her impious strains.
>
> She bet her breaste, and wrung her hands,
>   And rollde her tearlesse eye,
> From rise of morne, till the pale stars
>   Again did freeke the skye.
>
> (sts. 21–23)

The melodramatic passions of horror ballads, like those expressed in this passage, would have been for many contemporary critics subsumed in the larger vogue for sentimental effusions, and both would have been seen as the result of a new dominance in literature of the "popular" taste.

Coleridge seems to have seen it this way and to have been deeply ambivalent about the degree to which his own work was implicated in such taste. A February 1797 review of M. G. Lewis's *The Monk* attributed to Coleridge opens by declaring that "The horrible and preternatural have usually seized on the popular taste, at the rise and decline of literature."

> Most powerful stimulants, they can never be required except by the torpor of an unawakened, or the languor of an exhausted, appetite. The same phaenomenon, therefore, which we hail as a favourable omen in the *belles lettres* of Germany, impresses a degree of gloom in the compositions of our countrymen. We trust, however, that satiety will banish what good sense should have prevented; and that, wearied with fiends, incomprehensible characters, with shrieks, murders, and subterraneous dungeons, the public will learn, by the multitude of the manufacturers, with how little expense of thought or imagination this species of composition is manufactured. But, cheaply as we estimate romances in general, we acknowledge, in the work before us, the offspring of no common genius.[27]

Though he decries the proliferation of such "powerful stimulants" (foreshadowing Wordsworth's attack in the Preface to *Lyrical Ballads*) and suggests they represent a decline in taste in England, he values this movement more highly in the German context, perhaps even hinting that it is the novelistic form—"romances in general"—that he particularly regrets; poetry may be another matter. And Coleridge goes on to praise *The Monk,* including its embedded gothic tale of the bleeding nun and the character of the Wandering Jew, extremely romantic devices. Coleridge's own professed weariness with gothic conventions cannot be taken at face value as his final or unambivalent judgment on the value of sentimental and romantic writing, but he did profess such weariness. One month after this review appeared, he wrote to William Lisle Bowles:

> indeed I am almost weary of the Terrible, having been a hireling in the Critical Review for the last six or eight months—I have been lately reviewing the Monk, the Italian, Hubert de Sevrac & &c & &c—in all of which dungeons, and old castles, & solitary Houses by the Sea Side, & Caverns, & Woods, & extraordinary characters, & all the tribe of Horror & Mystery, have crowded on me—even to surfeiting.—[28]

If Coleridge was indeed becoming surfeited with "Horror & Mystery" in early 1797, it is likely because he had been devouring it over the past year—in order to prepare the reviews, as he implies in this letter, but also in pursuit of his own taste. A self-protective irony seems during these months to accompany a submersion in popular romantic literature, so decisive to the production of his so-called Mystery Poems. Here is a chronology of significant events: Bürger's "Lenore" appears (translated by Taylor) in March 1796 and Lamb and Coleridge correspond about it; less than one year later Coleridge writes the review and letter quoted above. Shortly thereafter (within months) he composes *The Rime of the Ancient Mariner* and begins to conceive of the *Lyrical Ballads* collection with Wordsworth. During this same time span Coleridge published a collection of sentimental effusions (as sonnets were seen at the time) by himself, Lamb, and Lloyd, and then shortly thereafter parodied this very form himself in the *Monthly Magazine,* the same venue in which such sentimental poetry was often printed and in which "Lenore" had appeared the previous spring. In the letter to Joseph Cottle (ca. November 1797) in which he first reveals that he has written *The Rime of the Ancient Mariner*—"a ballad of about 300 lines"—he also says that he sent to the *Monthly Magazine*

> three mock Sonnets in ridicule of my own, & Charles Lloyd's, & Lamb's, &c&c—in ridicule of that affectation of unaffectedness, of jumping &

misplaced accent on common-place epithets, flat lines forced into poetry by Italics (signifying how well & mouthis[h]ly the Author could read them, puny pathos &c&c—the instances are almost all taken from mine & Lloyd's poems—I signed them Nehemiah Higginbottom. I think they may do good to our young Bards.—[29]

These three "Sonnets, attempted in the Manner of Contemporary Writers" are apt parodies of the exaggerated simplicity and sentimental effusion that had recently been so much in vogue in Coleridge's own circle. It has been pointed out that the first poem works best as a self-parody.[30]

> PENSIVE at eve on the *hard* world I mused,
> And *my poor* heart was sad; so at the MOON
> I gazed, and sighed, and sighed; for ah how soon
> Eve saddens into night! mine eyes perused
> With tearful vacancy the *dampy* grass
> That wept and glitter'd in the *paly* ray:
> And I *did pause me* on my lonely way
> And *mused me* on the *wretched ones* that pass
> Oe'r the bleak heath of sorrow. But alas!
> Most of *myself* I thought! when it befel,
> That the *soothe* spirit of the *breezy* wood
> Breath'd in mine ear: "All this is very well,
> But much of ONE thing, is for NO thing good."
> Oh *my poor heart's* INEXPLICABLE SWELL!

This is loaded with parodic effects, beginning with the "mouthish" italics that Coleridge explicitly called attention to. The limp surprise of "myself" in line 10 and the sententiousness with which cliché is dispensed as if from the oracle in the quoted passage in lines 12–13 contribute to a sharp satire on the gloomy narcissism, "breezy" pantheism, melodramatic sentiment, and exaggerated treatment of trivial things common in this poetry of romantic sensibility.

The second sonnet is a parody on the vogue for "simplicity" and the third, it has been argued, amounts to an oblique parody of Wordsworthian ruralism as well as Coleridge's own poetry, echoing the manuscript poem by Wordsworth that was appropriated by Coleridge to become "Lewti."[31]

ON A RUINED HOUSE IN A ROMANTIC COUNTRY

> And this reft house is that, the which he built,
> Lamented Jack! And here his malt he pil'd,
> Cautious in vain! These rats, that squeak so wild,
> Squeak not unconscious of their father's guilt.
> Did he not see her gleaming thro' the glade!

Belike 'twas she, the maiden all forlorn.
What tho' she milk no cow with crumpled horn,
Yet, *aye* she haunts the dale where erst she stray'd:
And *aye,* beside her stalks her amorous knight!
Still on his thighs their wonted brogues are worn,
And thro' those brogues, still tatter'd and betorn,
His hindward charms gleam an unearthly white.
Ah! Thus thro' broken clouds at night's high Noon
Peeps in fair fragments forth the full-orb'd harvest-moon!
(Stones and Strachan, II, 52)

The romantic setting gives way to rustic lunacy, as the quixotic knight obscenely "moons" the unsuspecting reader of the sonnet, satirizing the taste that had produced the sonnets by Coleridge's circle in the first place. Coleridge later told the story of a "celebrated physician"'s being warned before meeting him not to mention this poem, since it was assumed that he was "sore as a boil about that sonnet."[32]

In the *Biographia Literaria* Coleridge cited this anecdote and the existence of these sonnets—including texts of the sonnets themselves—as if in self-defense. It appears in the midst of a discussion of canonical virtues in chapter 1, of what makes Milton's or Shakespeare's texts *"essential poetry,"* and of the effect on his own developing style of Bowles's sonnets of feeling (along with Cowper, he had been the first to combine "natural thoughts with natural diction"). He admits that he had earlier "adopted a laborious and florid diction," but implies that he has now moved beyond such youthful romantic excess:

> Every reform, however necessary, will by weak minds be carried to an excess, that itself will need reforming. The reader will excuse me for noticing, that I myself was the first to expose *risu honesto* [with honest laughter] the three sins of poetry, one or the other of which is the most likely to beset a young writer. So long ago as the publication of the second number of the monthly magazine, under the name of NEHEMIAH HIGGINBOTTOM I contributed three sonnets, the first of which had for its object to excite a good-natured laugh at the spirit of *doleful egotism,* and at the recurrence of favorite phrases, with the double defect of being at once trite, and licentious. (I, 26–27)

He then reprints the sonnets so the reader can see the evidence of his own skill at parody. "I myself was the first," Coleridge here claims, thus situating himself as the premiere parodist of the youthful romanticism so many had found so risible. This amounts to revisionist literary history in the guise of autobiography, a preemptive or talismanic self-parody protecting him against other parodies, then and now. In yet another such gesture, he appends a second anecdote to the note containing the parodic sonnets, telling of an amateur versifier who claimed to have written a "severe epigram" on the *Ancient Mariner*. The joke is on the foolish would-be parodist, however, when Coleridge reveals to his readers that "to my no less surprise than amusement, it proved to be one which I had myself some time before written and inserted in the Morning Post."

> To the Author of the Ancient Mariner.
>
> Your poem must eternal be,
> Dear sir! it cannot fail,
> For 'tis incomprehensible
> And without head or tail. (I, 28)

The act of telling the story is itself satiric, and reclaiming his authorship of the epigram returns the advantage to Coleridge, but this is nothing compared to the original act itself. This small playful act uses the press for the purposes of public relations, a secret parody of the practice of puffery then common, in which authors or their literary agents would write the early reviews of their own works. Even in this small way satirizing himself in public only enhances Coleridge's reputation as someone worth satirizing. Most significantly, the humorous focus of the epigram is on the canonical status of the poem in question, which is linked (however humorously) to its opacity and incomprehensible qualities.

The *Biographia* is a self-promotional work. It often takes the form of a self-parodic purge in the pursuit of a more mature style and reputation. By reprinting the sonnets and his own satiric epigram, then staking the claim to have been the first to parody his own youthful indiscretions, Coleridge would place himself in 1817 on a plane far above such flaws of sentimentality. Such "doleful egotism" and excess in diction were charges that continued to be leveled against Coleridge's poetry, as was incomprehensibility. The revisionism of these passage works by exaggerating the differences between then and now, 1796–98 and 1817, in order to elevate the latter as a new era giving rise to a new species of poetry in Coleridge's oeuvre.

To a significant degree, Coleridge's romantic Mystery Poems, the *Ancient Mariner, Christabel,* and "Kubla Khan," were open to the same sort of charges he leveled at the sonnets, and they attracted their own criticism and parody after the publication of the *Biographia Literaria* and *Sibylline leaves.* As I have already mentioned, D. M. Moir's "Christabel, Part Third," satirized in 1819 Coleridge's irrationality, his "stance as a priest of the esoteric and as a poet of atmospheric effects."[33] The general consensus by about 1817 was that the romantic excesses of the Lake School as a group consisted in "sickly sentimentality," the tendency "to invest trifling subjects with an air and expression of great importance and interest," and to use vernacular language in exaggerated ways, "expressions which are merely vulgar or ridiculous"—all these terms come from an 1817 review of *The Rime of the Ancient Mariner* as it appeared in *Sibylline leaves.*[34] From his self-parodic position, Coleridge is well aware of all this. I would argue that even in 1797 he was writing romantic poetry with an ironic edge, with a self-conscious hint of the self-parodic tendencies of such writings. The Higginbottom sonnets attest to this, but it is also discernible from within Coleridge's romantic poetry, as the reviewer quoted above seems half-consciously to recognize. Speaking of the *The Rime of the Ancient Mariner,* he says that it "has always appeared to us in the light of a very good caricature of the genius of its author."

> It displays, in fact, all the strength and all the weakness, all the extravagances and eccentricities, all the bold features, and peculiar grimace, if we may so express ourselves, of his intellectual physiognomy, and in forming an opinion respecting the talents which he possesses, this composition may serve the very same purpose which an overcharged drawing of a countenance could answer. . . .

The Nehemiah Higginbottom sonnets merely reveal the degree to which Coleridge was prepared to parody before being parodied, even while producing his highly caricaturable romantic poetry of 1797–1800. But this tendency to self-parody as a self-protective—but also canon-forming—gesture was perhaps most systematically pursued in the strategic self-representations of 1816–17, which culminated in the revisions and revisionist self-editing of *Sibylline leaves* and the *Biographia Literaria.*

At the beginning of chapter 4 of the *Biographia,* Coleridge states his purpose to address the question of the causes of nascent Romanticism. He has been intent, he says, to prove that neither Southey's writings nor his own "furnished the original occasion to this fiction of a *new school* of poetry, and of clamors against its supposed founders and proselytes"(I, 69). He then goes on to attempt to prove a similar negative effect to the *Lyrical Ballads.* He would not deny that the Lake School had an effect on the culture, but wishes to persuade readers that its unique excesses had no major deleterious effect. The language of "a new school of poetry . . . founders and proselytes," is invoked to be refuted, but only in its weakest and most vulnerable, risible form. The implicit claim is that his more recent work is far superior to this early activity and superior to what he sees as the flaws of the *Lyrical Ballads*—and this is why he dwells so much on what is wrong with Wordsworth's poetry. The personal and artistic quarrels between the two poets may be behind this, but the passage also serves Coleridge as a tactical differentiation in the strategic wars of taste. His language establishes a distance between "Simon Lee" or "The Thorn," say, and what he considers notable and worthy in Wordsworth's and his own poetry. He argues that the famous Preface of 1800 called unnecessary attention to the defects of Wordsworth's poems on "low" subjects, what he calls the "humbler passages" or "minor poems," which "in and for themselves would have been either forgotten or forgiven as imperfections, or at least comparative failures"(I, 70–71). The hostility of the often-satiric critics is thereby deflected away from the "major" works of the Lake School by sacrificing the earlier poetry of extreme "simplicity," in the vogue for which Coleridge had once so eagerly participated. In one remarkable (essentially satiric) passage, Coleridge argues that such minor Romantic writing is simply not worth the strong opposition of an all-out cultural combat:

> The seductive faults, the dulcia vitia of Cowley, Marini, or Darwin might reasonably be thought capable of corrupting the public judgement for half a century, and require a twenty-years war, campaign after campaign, in order to dethrone the usurper and re-establish the legitimate taste. But that a downright simpleness, under the affectation of simplicity, prosaic words in feeble metre, silly thoughts in childish phrases, and a preference of mean, degrading, or at best trivial associations and characters, should succeed in forming a school of imitators, a company of almost *religious* admirers, and this too among young men of ardent minds, liberal education, and not
>
> with academic laurels unbestowed;
>
> and that this bare and bald *counterfeit* of poetry, which is characterized as *below* criticism, should for nearly twenty years have well-nigh *engrossed* criticism, as the main, if not the only, *butt* of review, magazine, pamphlets, poem, and paragraph;—this is indeed matter of wonder! Of yet greater is it, that the contest should still continue as undecided as that between Bacchus and the frogs in Aristophanes; when the former descended to the realms of the departed to bring back the spirit of old and genuine poesy. (I, 74–76)

As the chapter continues, Coleridge pays tribute to Wordsworth's "original poetic genius," and it is clear that the point of the passage is not to belittle Wordsworth but to discount the role of the poems of extreme "simplicity" in the founding of the school later to be identified with Romanticism, to satirize the simplest Romantic poetry in advance of other satires. But in the process, Coleridge manages to depict a heated war of taste with himself and his fellow poets at the heart of it. The language of his metaphor, while attempting to satirize the ardor of the combatants, manages to elevate the issues involved and suggest the actual importance of the more important works of this same group of poets—including himself. Wordsworth's minor poems cannot be the basis of the new school, Coleridge says, and are unworthy of parodic satire or compliment. Wordsworth himself belongs in the canon, and several times in proximity to this passage he has named "Tintern Abbey" as a more worthy example of Wordsworth's genius.

My point is that the revisions of *The Rime of the Ancient Mariner* serve much the same purpose: they substitute what is really a new poem—with a number of revisions including the added gloss and its layered effects, and in a new context as an independent poem published as the work of S. T. Coleridge—for the German-influenced horror ballad published in the 1798 collection that included "Simon Lee." In each case satiric and parodic modes come to the aid of revisionist tastemaking, helping Coleridge (and he hopes his readers) to make canon-defining distinctions. It is as if Coleridge first moved into and found himself occupying the same cultural niche as Bürger, Southey, the "minor" Wordsworth—the Nehemiah Higginbottoms of the fashionably sentimental literature of the period—and then set about destroying the competition, exaggerating distinctions in order to define a new species of poetic achievement to dominate that romantic niche: eventually, this species of poetry would come to be called "Romantic." Purged through self-parody and the parody of others of weaker strains, elevated through theory and a ubiquitous layered hermeneutic contextualization, this is romantic writing more philosophical, transcendent, self-aware, serious—in a word, more worthy of the canon than mere popular "'spook' balladry" could ever hope to be. It remains resilient and thus dominant in part through a self-generated openness to parody from within and without, which, as Coleridge himself pointed out, over the course of time and canonization, is one way to turn satire into encomium.

Political Coda

This chapter has so far bracketed off the obvious and yet important fact that much of this revisionist literary history-as-autobiography, as well as the revisions of actual poems by Coleridge, were pursued in the service of ideological as much as aesthetic goals. Call it the "apostasy" plot, or the internalization of the revolutionary quest, the narrative in which youthful Jacobinism, Pantisocracy, and Unitarianism—as part of a general cultural "set" that included a penchant for affiliating oneself with German ballads, for example, or writing sentimental effusions—are put away for a more orthodox and Tory nationalism, rooted in organic nature and leading to individual transcendence.[35] Though the shift was less dramatic than in the case of Southey, Coleridge's contemporaries explained his career in terms of this plot as well. Indeed they were prompted to do so by the poet himself in numerous public qualifications and recantations, including, for example, poems such as "France: An Ode." One of my basic assumptions in this chapter has been that the development of a Romantic canon of taste and this political plot are intertwined stories.

Take the early "Monody on the Death of Chatterton" (1790–94; republished 1796).[36] Therein Coleridge accuses England of causing the suicide of the young genius, in part by public ridicule and satire, having subjected him to "Neglect, and grinning Scorn, and Want combined!" (l. 100). Mourning the kindred spirit, the poet finds himself tempted by despair, effusing on his own suffering in a highly sentimental effusion: "For oh! big gall-drops, shook from FOLLY's wing, / Have blacken'd the fair promise of my spring" (ll. 136–37). But then he turns away for consolation and escape to a utopian vision of a new society on the banks of the Susquehanna:

> Wisely forgetful! O'er the ocean swell
> Sublime of Hope I seek the cottag'd dell
> Where VIRTUE calm with careless steps may stray;
> And, dancing to the moon-light roundelay,
> The wizard PASSIONS weave an holy spell!
>
> (ll. 143–47)

Coleridge ends by vowing to raise a monument to Chatterton—as a victim of English society—in the new Pantisocratic community. The quoted lines find their way into a sonnet "To Pantisocracy," and find an ultimate echo in the paradisal/demonic circle of dancers weaving their own "roundelay" around the prophetic "wizard" poet at the end of "Kubla Khan." The politically radical and aesthetically sentimental vision of utopia is transmuted eventually to a paradise of "pure imagination"—a "dome in air," enclosed and protected, though built from song rather than on the banks of the Susquehanna. The displacement of the early radicalism by the internalized prophetic vision is mirrored in Coleridge's general self-transformation, and it includes an aesthetic shift—from sentimental effusion to Mystery Poem—as well as a political one.[37]

In the *Sibylline leaves* volume that contained the revised and glossed *Ancient Mariner*, Coleridge also reprinted and recontextualized a number of poems "Occasioned by Political Events." Among these was his early political satire on the Pitt ministry, "Fire, Famine, and Slaughter," to which he added a long and somewhat disingenuous "Apologetic Preface" that attempted to diminish the incendiary intentions of the original production, along with all the journalistic satires he had written in the war years. The Preface tells the story of a dinner party at which Sir Walter Scott recited the squib.

This *he* could so with the better grace, being known to have ever been not only a firm and active Anti-Jacobin and Anti-Gallican, but likewise a zealous admirer of Mr. Pitt, both as a good man and a great Statesman. As a Poet exclusively, he had been amused with the Eclogue; as a Poet, he recited it; and in a spirit, which made it evident, that he would have read and repeated it with the same pleasure, had his own name been attached to the imaginary object or agent.[38]

One intended purpose of this strange anecdote is surely to clear the "name" that had most often become "attached to" the satire. It literally puts Coleridge's Jacobin words in the mouth of his Tory friend; if Scott can enjoy the poem without blaming the author, Coleridge suggests, anyone should be able to. Moreover, his enjoyment proves that the poem is available to readers on purely aesthetic grounds, since Scott reads it "as a Poet" and with "pleasure," rendering moot its original political purpose. Had he read the poem for the first time, Coleridge reportedly told the party (before revealing his authorship), he would conclude that

> the writer must have been some man of warm feelings and active fancy; that he had painted to himself the circumstances that accompany war in so many vivid and yet fantastic forms, as proved that neither the images nor the feelings were the result of observation, or in any way derived from realities. I should judge, that they were the product of his own seething imagination, and therefore impregnated with that pleasurable exultation which is experienced in all energetic exertion of intellectual power. (95)

There is scarcely a poem in Coleridge's entire corpus less likely to be taken as a work of "pure imagination," and the "Apologetic Preface" strains even to transform it into a harmless pleasure. But the attempt itself is significant, as is the opportunistic use of Walter Scott. Besides his political qualifications, he was a fellow antiquarian interested in German ballads—he had imitated Bürger's "Lenore"—and in the popular or folk imagery of superstition and witchcraft. This particular species of poetic pleasure, it is clear, depends on a taste, however tinged with irony, for romantic balladry. The anecdote thus displaces radical gothicism with a playful, *aesthetic* romanticism.

Coleridge's satire itself, which Carl Woodring calls "the fiercest pop-up" of the group of political poems,[39] was first published in the *Morning Post* of 8 January 1798, but was reprinted in the *Annual Anthology* for 1800. Set amidst the destruction of La Vendée, its titular allegories gossip like *Macbeth*'s weird sisters about who sent them to the battlefield; in the concluding lines Fire effectively damns Pitt: "I alone am faithful! I / Cling to him everlastingly." It is worth remembering that this antiwar satire was written and published at around the same time as the first version of *The Rime of the Ancient Mariner,* and one can see in it the same atmosphere of gothic hellfire common to that era when "Germany was poured forth into England," when "'*Hell made holiday,*' and '*Raw heads and bloody-bones*'" were fashionable.

> *Fam.* Sisters! sisters! Who sent you here?
> *Slau.* [*to Fire*] I will whisper it in her ear.
> *Fire.* No! no! no!
> Spirits hear what spirits tell:
> 'Twill make a holiday in Hell.

Woodring has said that this poem and others like it by Coleridge "were the carnival fireworks that crackled and hissed among the dragon-fires of more solemn prophecy," and while I agree that "carnival" is precisely the right term for this sort of popular satire, I would shift the emphasis to what this squib has in common with poems like the *Rime,* to the family resemblance that unites "romantic" with "Romantic" works before the process of canon-formation has sorted them out. The characters Fire, Famine, and Slaughter are the poor relations of Life-in-Death and her mate, their battlefield fires another version of the burning fists Hunt Emerson so well illustrates. Coleridge, still immersed in "Horror and Mystery" in 1797–98, applies a newsprint gothic style to the anti-Pitt cause, turning the satiric potential of Germanic melodrama outward to public figures in the government.

Grouped in *Sibylline leaves* with sublime political odes and *Fears in Solitude* (along with *Recantation* and *Parliamentary Oscillators*), and carefully buffered by the formidable "Apologetic Preface," this representative of an important satiric part of Coleridge's early practice is nearly reduced, as Coleridge might wish, to a youthful *jeu d'esprit,* and in context is turned into an autobiographical self-parody. Coleridge and Robert Southey had collaborated on another incendiary topical satire full of hellfire, *The Devil's Thoughts,* for the *Morning Post* of 6 September 1799, and Southey had recently suffered at the hands of parodists for his authorship of *Wat Tyler.* That republican play from 1794 by the young Oxonian became difficult for the older Tory Laureate to repudiate once radical publishers pirated a later edition of it in 1817, complete with a mocking introduction that might be viewed as the radicals' "unapologetic preface." The very act of piracy and republication itself became a metaparody, which worked by turning Southey's own words against him. He attempted to suppress the piracy and to prosecute the radicals, which only made matters worse. In like fashion, Leigh Hunt reprinted "Fire, Famine and Slaughter" in the *Examiner* in 1816, which may have prompted Coleridge's own reprint in 1817. One effect of Coleridge's riddling and multilayered self-parodies was surely to defuse and deflect such appropriative attacks, though they did not always succeed in doing so. It is said that the young Percy Bysshe Shelley and Mary Wollstonecraft Shelley memorized and liked to recite "Fire, Famine, and Slaughter" along with "France: An Ode" as late as 1815. The juxtaposition itself works as a verbal parody, both compliment to a poet they admired and satire on that poet's later politics.[40]

Chapter 3 ～

Satiric Performance in
The Black Dwarf

I n 1815 the Napoleonic wars ended and a new round of the culture wars began. One year after Coleridge published *Sibylline leaves* including the revised *Rime of the Ancient Mariner* and the same year the *Biographia Literaria* appeared (1817), a very different series of publications, of more material and immediate national concern, occupied the public. A series of pamphlet parodies and the radical journal *Hone's Reformist's Register* led in the spring to the arrest of William Hone for blasphemous and seditious libel. Far below the relatively respectable level even of Coleridge's newspaper satires of the 1790s, a cheap radical press had been thriving in London once again since the end of the war, despite a concentrated program of government repression. In 1817 an important new radical weekly debuted, edited, published, and mostly written by Thomas J. Wooler, *The Black Dwarf.* Wooler's rhetorical style is characterized by a potent mixture of impassioned sentiment and biting satire, and the purpose of this chapter is to illuminate this mixture and to measure the similarities and differences of Wooler's journalism from the Romantic literature then emerging. In Wooler's radical satire, for the most part produced and received outside the margins of "literature" proper—never mind the canon—there is more evidence of volatile self-display than subtle self-parody, more carnivalesque, polyvocal ventriloquism than careful demarcation of voice. In what follows I look at Wooler's opportunistic uses of potent mixtures of satiric and sentimental modes, showing how sentimental modes soon to be gathered into the term "Romantic" were present even at the heart of his radical satire and—conversely and somewhat more surprisingly—how radical satire influenced certain strains of emergent Romanticism. In Wooler's satiric performances, the two modes are often played against one another for their incendiary effect.

Wooler's satire is the product of the violent atmosphere of London politics in the years just after Waterloo. It is an often-recounted story: in London in January 1817, after a year of increasing popular unrest, an angry crowd attacked the regent's coach on its way to the opening of Parliament and a stone or other projectile (some thought a bullet) broke one of the coach windows. This well-known incident has become a symbolic narrative crisis in almost every history of the period, in part because of its emblematic qualities—the shattering of the fragile barrier separating the ruler from the faceless rabble—and in part because the year that followed became so important in the history of radical reform that it inevitably casts a shadow back over the January scene.[1] In the following spring and summer—in the wake of the attack on the regent but also of the longer-term effects of demobilization after Waterloo, the general economic crisis (especially the Corn Law of 1815 and commodity taxes of 1817), and the Spa Fields meetings of late 1816 to early 1817—a newly resurgent English radicalism was put under enormous pressure from above and below. When habeas corpus was suspended at the first of March, a number of legal actions were brought immediately. The most prominent radical journalist, William Cobbett, fled to America. With Cobbett out of the picture, as E. P. Thompson has pointed out, Thomas J. Wooler's new weekly, *The Black Dwarf*—which appeared for the first time the day after the attack on the regent—now took over as the dominant radical organ, giving its large readership (by 1819 probably as many as twelve thousand)[2] a potent "mixture of heavy-handed satire and libertarian rhetoric."[3]

This contradictory mixture of the satiric and the sincere will be a recurrent motif in this chapter. Whereas E. P. Thompson called Wooler's satire "heavy-handed," Jon Klancher has more precisely detected in *The Black Dwarf* "moments of heightened discursive anguish," in which "the language of satire merges with the excessive language of melodrama itself."[4] I want to join this discussion by suggesting that the mixed satiric and melodramatic modes of *The Black Dwarf* appear profoundly and strategically interdependent when placed in the context of the history of satire. When viewed as satire—a *satura* or mixed feast of unstable modes— Wooler's journalism reveals precisely how (and to what effect) melodrama or overperformed sincerity was becoming a useful tool of radical discourse during the period. Popular print culture, from prints and broadsides to newspapers, has traditionally made use of medleys and combinations of satiric and burlesque forms. In the case of Wooler's work and radical satire like it in the early nineteenth century, generic mixtures often serve as working rhetorical contradictions, contradictions that grow out of the position of the marginalized satirist addressing the "people" and the "nation." This paradoxical situation was deliberately exploited by some radical journalists for greater satiric effect, but nonetheless it was an inescapable consequence of the "unofficial," potent, threatening position from which many of them were forced to produce and publish, to perform. In *The Black Dwarf,* I argue, the conflict of modes and the conflicted situation of the editor (and almost exclusive author), inscribe in the text of the journal the heterogeneity of its expected reception.

Wooler's *Black Dwarf* serves as my prime exhibit because it is the opposite of seamless, because it so openly engages in a troubling display of the *volatility* of the modes it incorporates—sentimental and satirical, those associated with "high" as well as "low" discourses—and thus dramatizes the instability of such oppositions and of representation itself. The nature of this volatility will be brought into sharper focus later on in this chapter by way of a brief comparison with some closely related satiric productions by Keats and Shelley, examples of shared context overlapping with emergent Romantic poetry. As I will show through these comparisons of similar satires written from subtly different positions in the cultural economy, Wooler *must* write—and edit, compose pages, and publish his productions—from the position of the pariah-satirist. One of his favored techniques is a kind of discursive "terror": the creation and exploitation of instability (and the dread of social chaos) for subversive public effect. But what frightens one (sub)audience may seem gleefully funny to another, positioned to read it in another way, and it is this difference that his full satiric energy uncovers. Wooler's work is highly self-conscious about such heterogeneity; it deliberately capitalizes on its own relation to a moment of cultural instability by *representing* that instability back to itself—and in this sense the radical discourse of *The Black Dwarf* is a powerful satiric performance.

Wooler's Romantic-Satiric Dwarf

Who *was* the Black Dwarf? In *The Black Dwarf* no. 37 (8 October 1817), Wooler printed a fictional letter from a reader ("Peter Pry"), headed "What are you?" The letter ponders whether the Dwarf is a man, monster, or a devil with cloven hooves (617–19). Wooler's invented editorial persona is a cartoon figure right out of the popular prints, and indeed, caricaturists at that historical moment quickly moved to represent the Dwarf's image. In effect, Wooler preempted his own potential satirists by adopting such a persona in the first place. "Black" or exotically African (sometimes simply vaguely "oriental" or otherwise "non-Western"), he was also "black" in the sense of occult or diabolical, and of threateningly "low" or villainous, of the underworld. Finally, like his companion persona in the journal, the "Black Neb" (crow), the Dwarf was an elusive sign of a "dark" political radicalism or Jacobinism that appeared from the dominant perspective as synonymous with blackguardism, even the demonic. In a frontispiece engraved for the first collected volume of the journal (1818; see figure 3.1), a large Satyr holds the hand of the dancing Dwarf, whose grossly misshapen head wears an exotic turban with pen feathers—"radical crow quills" (12 January 1820) with which to write his satire. The foregrounded Satyr gestures with his free hand to a jumbled, smoking heap of the signs of "authority" about to be immolated: a crown (topped with fool's cap), scepter, judges' wigs, and state papers. The Dwarf remains a relatively free-floating icon; it is the Satyr (read: "satire") who makes the defining gesture at center stage, while the Dwarf remains a shadow-partner, celebrating impishly in the background. This persona is picked up by other illustrators, for example, in the famous satire on Robert Southey, *A Poet mounted, on the Court-Pegasus* (1817), in which Wooler's Dwarf leans out, leering, with horns and claws and devilish features, from behind the laureate's butt of sack, waving a pirated copy of *Wat Tyler.*

   It is possible that Wooler took the name and figure of the Black Dwarf from Sir Walter Scott's well-known novel of the same name, published as the first installment of *Tales of My Landlord* in early December 1816. So far as I know, no one has pursued the implications of this highly suggestive intertextual link, not to a single literary source (as will soon become clear, Wooler's sources were certainly legion) but to a particular literary, even Romantic, milieu Wooler may have been attempting to invoke. Scott's Dwarf is first of all an unmistakable *country* type, a misanthropic fairy or brownie of the Border, living wild on the moor, the picturesque relative of the local devil himself (who was sometimes known as "the Black Man"). Scott takes him almost whole cloth from antiquarian folklore, oral tradition, and ballads, as his notes to the novel indicate. He even cites a particular ethnographic informant for his version of the character and seems to have visited a real-life model—one David Ritchie—in 1796 or 1797.[5]

   The Dwarf of northern legend, I wish to argue, is a typical scapegoat-figure for the rural community, an outcast who lives just outside the pale but binds together the social group by serving as the focus of its superstition and xenophobia. Both feared and respected for his presumed supernatural powers (over cattle as well as people), he is shunned and yet prized—at a distance—and is presumed able to cure as well as to taint. The ambiguity of effect is part of his power. Here is Scott's first full physical description of his version of this legendary Dwarf, whom he says is known as "Canny Elshie," "the Wise Wight of Mucklestane Moor," or "the Brown Man of the Moor":

> The being . . . raised his eyes with a ghastly stare, and getting up from his stooping posture, stood before them in all his native deformity. His head was of immense size, covered with a fell of shaggy black hair, partly grizzled with

Frontispiece to the First Volume of the Black Dwarf.

Figure 3.1   *The Black Dwarf,* frontispiece to bound edition

age; his eye-brows, shaggy and prominent, overhung a pair of small, dark, piercing eyes, set far back in their sockets, that rolled with a portentous wildness, indicative of partial insanity. The rest of his features were of the coarse, rough-hewn stamp with which a painter would equip a giant in romance, to which was added, the wild, irregular, and peculiar expression so often seen in the countenances of those whose persons are deformed. (29)

This picturesque freak of nature is paradoxically (but conventionally) possessed of the most profound, essential powers of nature. Gothic, sublime, and darkly comic all at once, this Dwarf is the kind of sentimental invention Scott's readers would immediately recognize as "romantic."[6] Like Wordsworth's Idiot Boy or Leech Gatherer, his deformity sets him apart, provokes a sentimental response, and stands as a sign of his proximity to the power of nature. Although the fascination with deformity is ancient and widespread—and obviously profoundly overdetermined—one anthropological perspective explains traditional figures like the Black Dwarf socially, as functional scapegoats. From this perspective, such a figure is constructed by the community as its necessary other and underground self—the accursed focus of others' curses, a "natural wonder" onto which the collective fear of nature is projected, and a safe victim on which to displace collective aggression. By mediating between the natural and the cultural, the scapegoat or *pharmakos* deflects the feared threat from within the unstable cultural order.

The political plot of Scott's novel concerns the Jacobite uprising of 1708, a story of internecine political violence analogous to that of England in 1817. Scott's Black Dwarf is at the center of the conflict and is even appealed to at one point as a stabilizing force, a move paradoxically consistent with the logic by which Hobbie Elliot's wise grandmother associates his successive appearances on the moor with waves of political turmoil (chapter 13). This Black Dwarf, like natural prodigies everywhere, is seen as a sign of instability in the social realm; by a homeopathic or talismanic logic, therefore, he is the first one to be consulted for a remedy to such turmoil. "In short, the evils most dreaded and deprecated by the inhabitants of that pastoral country, are ascribed to the agency of the Black Dwarf," the novel concludes. His symbolic "sacrifice" (being ostracized and reviled), therefore, serves as a spell to ward off further troubles.

In this light it is highly significant that (as Robert C. Elliott has suggested) the satirist's role in society, especially in so called "primitive" society, is analogous to the role of the scapegoat.[7] Always the outsider within the group, the practitioner of rough magic and victim of "rough music," crying in the "wilderness" (even if from the town square), the satirist is superstitiously feared and respected. Tainted with the poison he wields against others, he must exist at the margin of society in order to serve his necessary function, but he always remains himself suspect, unpredictable—a volatile presence within the structures of normative authority, a projection of the "dark other" of authority, and a reminder of the volatile force on which such authority depends. Hence the etymological confusion in English of "satire" with "satyr."

Given these strata of popular tradition, Wooler's choice of persona seems an inspired act, and may have been a deliberately parodic gesture of reappropriation: he could well have "stolen" the Black Dwarf from the famous Tory novelist who so successfully reproduced Romantic local culture for his mass audience. If so, then taking over the Dwarf from Scott would have been Wooler's first satiric gesture in this new journal, a fascinating though unproven possibility. In any case, audiences in 1817 would have quickly been made aware of both Dwarves, and the comparison could only have intensified the oppositional effect of Wooler's dangerous form of popular satire, drawing upon an ancient version of the scapegoat in the context of contemporary political troubles. From the very beginning, with his 1817 "Prospectus," Wooler plays on the volatility of his figure by exploiting the Dwarf's ambiguous relation to customary superstitions.

> It may be required of us to declare whether the Black Dwarf emanates from the celestial regions, or from the shades of evil—whether he be an European sage, or an Indian savage. . . . We are not at liberty to unfold all the secrets of his prison-house, to ears of flesh and blood. . . . He intends to expose every species of vice and folly, with which this virtuous age, and enlightened metropolis abounds. . . . Secure from his invisibility, and dangerous from his power of division, (for like the polypus, he can divide and redivide himself, and each division remain a perfect animal . . .

Notice how this passage begins with uncertainty over the binary opposition of high and low ("celestial regions" / "shades of evil"), maps that uncertainty onto the division of "civilized" "European sage" from "primitive" "Indian savage," and then ends by claiming for the Dwarf the "dangerous" magical powers that go with blurring or transgressing such essential divisions: "invisibility" and a monstrous ability to "divide and redivide himself." Silence, exile, cunning, and collectivity: Wooler exploits what is truly fearful about his outwardly absurd, cartoonish character. Like Percy Shelley's Demogorgon and Milton's "darkness visible," this Dwarf works rhetorically through sublime negativity (though in a comic register). In this case, as with the figure on the masthead of another radical journal, the *Gorgon*, Wooler plays on the fear that such slipperiness is dangerous because it can quickly and unpredictably multiply itself: one Black Dwarf can metamorphose suddenly into a "mob" like the one that stoned the regent's coach.

Wooler satirized the stone-throwing incident in a famous bit of mock-reportage, speculating that the mob had thrown not stones but "Treasonable Potatoes" (writing that would ironically be cited against him at his own trials later in the year). The conceit of the potato carries Wooler into an imagined reactionary trial for treason while alluding to the true cause of unrest: the economic crisis and consequent suffering of the poor. As historians have shown, the consumption of potatoes by the English poor was symbolically charged in the context of the Corn Law controversy and the debate over the price of bread.[8] R. N. Salaman suggests that the substitution of the potato for high-priced bread may have actually forestalled a violent revolution in nineteenth-century England by allowing English laborers "to survive on the lowest possible wage";[9] E. P. Thompson adds that the "The Irish Immigrants with their potato diet (Ebenezer Elliott called them 'Erin's root-fed hordes') were seen as eloquent testimony, and many Englishmen agreed with Cobbett that the poor were victims of a conspiracy to reduce them to the Irish level" (315). When *The Black Dwarf* imagines a burlesque trial of the personified potatoes for treason, it openly links hard economic circumstance to the actions of the mob. The facts of poverty, like the supposed vegetable grenades, are therefore "thrown as it were in the very teeth of royalty," but in a satiric print environment—the journal itself—that emulates all the threatening instabilities of the mob. On the one hand, the joke is that such an incident could be seen by paranoid ministers as an organized conspiracy of "violent reformists" (as Wooler says); on the other hand, the extreme rhetoric of Wooler's own fictional reportage—and its evocation of a symbolic world in which nothing is at it appears to be—works to reinforce such ministerial paranoia. The Black Dwarf, like Scott's "Canny Elshie," only *appears* to be naive. The real threat lies in his impenetrability.

Any historian of the period would note that Wooler's Dwarf bears another family relation to a different stock character, one more at home in the London crowd, also descended from ancient lore but transplanted, modernized, and urbanized: the grotesque plebeian radical. Especially since the turbulent 1790s, London radicals learned to deliberately play on their own demonization in order to leverage a more effective political threat. Iain McCalman vividly depicts this milieu in his *Radical Underworld,* his primary example being the famous Mulatto Spencean orator, Thomas Wedderburn.[10] This son of a Kingston sugar-plantation owner and his African slave may have been a direct influence on Wooler's Dwarf, given the combination of his militant rhetoric and threatening blackness. Another, even more relevant analogue McCalman calls "the doyen of . . . blasphemous buffoonery," literally a dwarf and (like Wooler) a printer, Samuel Waddington, a.k.a. "Little Waddy" or—surely not coincidentally—"The Black Dwarf."

> If Wedderburn's performances bring melodrama to mind, Waddington's evoke the world of pantomime. His role was that of the "imp of mischief" or "genius of nonsense" portrayed in contemporary pantomimes such as John Rich's "Harlequin and the Red Dwarf"; or more pertinently, he personified Wooler's radical literary imp, "The Black Dwarf" (another of Waddington's nicknames).[11]

I discuss Wooler's own use of the pantomime in chapter 4 below. My point at present is simply that Wooler's Dwarf would have evoked for his readers simultaneously *both* strands of plebeian culture: the ancient rural tradition of "superstitious" beliefs and scapegoat figures, and the modern London underworld of grotesquely self-parodic and subversive radical orators, writers, artisans, and printers. The totemic persona of *The Black Dwarf* exists at the confluence of these two traditions and reveals their interdependence, while fusing the two in the potent farrago of its printed satiric performance.

The heteroglossic style of Wooler's journalism has been seen as an instance of the Bakhtinian carnivalesque, in its "riotous panoply of voices, speeches, quotations, answers, questions, mockeries, parodies, and harangues."[12] I would agree but would add (with Bakhtin) that it is parody, satyr play, and (eventually) satire itself that have the deepest roots in the collective rituals of carnival, its mix of "high" and "low" languages, transgressions, violations, and metamorphoses.[13] In other words, there is something intrinsically *satiric* about Wooler's brand of heteroglossia.

When considering the ramifications of "the carnivalesque" in 1817, it is worth keeping mind that actual black Africans and dwarves (and, indeed, "Black dwarves" or pygmies) were among the numerous "prodigies" that made up the staple sideshow exhibits at London carnivals well into the nineteenth century. For example, around the time of Wooler's first issues, Bartholomew Fair included among its display of (un)natural wonders "The Beautiful Spotted Negro Boy," dressed with bow and arrow as a "primitive" icon.[14] Dwarves and pygmies were always leading characters in the carnival, part of the racist and colonialist—generally scapegoating—energy that is the darker side of many plebeian customary practices. One example close to Wooler's time was one Mr. Simon Paap, "the celebrated Dutch Dwarf," who was only 28 inches high, and was presented with ceremony to the prince regent and the entire royal family before beginning his popular run at the 1815 Bartholomew Fair. Animals, colonized "primitives," and live "fairies" or mythological beings were often grouped together in such exhibits of symbolic otherness. One exotic menagerie of 1748 tellingly included a camel, a hyena, a panther, a "Young Oronutu Savage," and "the wonderful and surprising satyr, call'd by Latin authors, Pan." But even closer to Wooler's icon is the earlier advertisement from Queen Anne's reign, in which the Smithfield Fair boasts the display of a pygmy, a "little Black Man, being but 3 foot high"—an actual racist and imperialist icon, a black dwarf performing at the teeming center of the carnival.

The outsider status of these victims of popular culture was an open topic already in the early nineteenth century, especially in so far as the carnival displays participated in the slave trade. One document of the sentimental reaction is found in *Blackwood's* for March 1830 (502), a sentimental poem in the very voice of "The Exhibited Dwarf." It begins in Africa: "I lay without my father's door, / A wretched dwarfish boy," then tells the narrative of the foreign "stranger" who buys the boy, instructs him, and takes him to "his native shore" to perform at fairs.

> The secret was explain'd;
> I was a vile, degraded slave,

In mind and body chain'd!
  Condemn'd to face, day after day,
The rabble's ruffian gaze;
  To shrink before their merriment,
Or blush before their praise!

In anguish I must still perform
  The oft-repeated task;
And courteously reply to all
  Frivolity may ask!
And bear inhuman scrutiny,
  And hear the hateful jest!
And sing the song,—then crawl away
  To tears instead of rest!

I know I am diminutive,
  Aye, loathsome, if you will;
But say, ye hard hearts! am I not
  A human being still?
With feelings sensitive as *yours,*
  Perhaps I have been born;
I would not wound a fellow Man
  In mockery, or scorn!

This is a useful reminder that the carnival, that loaded "site" (both "real" and "virtual"), which Bakhtin calls "the public square where the folk gather,"[15] was a volatile field incorporating violence and sentiment, images of scapegoating and mob action as well as festivity and celebration. For his different rhetorical ends, but including inversions of the power relations between slave and master, Wooler uses his Dwarf to tap into this dark potential of the carnival.

Materially speaking, the English carnival is the one site contemporary with Wooler's publication at which the urban-artisanal and plebeian-rural cultures actually came together in "the public square," a space at once economic marketplace and cultural theater, where commodities were traded and melodramas performed. Given the potential violence associated with the fairs and the threatening otherness often on display there, their historical particulars seem to provide a way to rematerialize and particularize the notion of carnival, bringing the Bakhtinian abstraction down to earth in Smithfield. This, I would argue, is the context within which to understand the hybrid satiric/sentimental language of *The Black Dwarf.*

It may be useful to begin with the best known feature of the carnivalesque—the highly theatrical symbolic inversions of the "world turned upside down," topsy-turvy, boxing-day reversals and fool's reigns, a temporary and carefully contained license that nonetheless formed a site of potential transgression. The favorite English symbol of the carnival was the pig—the "low" creature with uncanny intelligence, raised for subsistence-consumption near the human household, possessing both sacrificial and comic-grotesque connotations, long before Edmund Burke's reference to the people as a "swinish multitude" became an ironic catchphrase.

For example, an advertisement for the 1748 Smithfield Fair touted a giant hog, to be viewed for only three pence, "The greatest Prodigy in Nature . . . near Twelve Feet long," whose keeper is "the amazing little Dwarf, Being the smallest Man in the World." A human dwarf tending a giant pig: for carnival-goers and readers among the self-consciously "swinish multitude," such inversions took on a heightened political explicitness in the early nineteenth century. *The Black Dwarf* for 7 July 1819 opens with a letter from the Dwarf to his even more exotic correspondent, "the Yellow Bonze, at Japan": "What, pigs rebel?"

> I verily believe, my yellow friend, that the "*lower* orders" of this country have begun to think they have as much sense as their *superiors!* They are holding meetings, and communing with each other in large bodies; and really from a comparison of the speeches, and proceedings of those insolent "*lower orders,*" I can see a very great difference of talent in favour of the "*swinish multitude!*" What if the *pigs* should eat and beat the gentlemen! As for so many ages the gentlemen have been eating and beating the *pigs!* This would be a *revolution* with a vengeance! (437)

Against the backdrop of carnival, the Black Dwarf appears as a human cousin of the plebeian "pigs"—hence the unsettling humorous effect of his serving as the polite "correspondent" who reports objectively on such inversions.

Wooler's Dwarf frequently addresses "high" power from his own grotesquely "low" position, and in the process both emphasizes the distance between them and simultaneously suggests how quickly that distance might be closed. This device is used ironically in an address from the Dwarf ("so insignificant a pigmy") to William Cobbett, for example ("such a stupendous political giant"), who is thus brought down to size (5 March 1817, pp. 89–92). Even the prince regent is not safe from the Dwarf's David-like presumption: "*You,* however, *are not quite a king,* and may listen to the voice of reason, even uttered by a Dwarf, if uttered loud enough to penetrate the forest of bayonets with which your ministers seclude you from public view. You do not treat *the nation* with much ceremony, and I am willing to follow an example of *sincerity* so important, given by an authority . . ." (10 September 1817, p. 513). Sincerity and the position from below become for Wooler counterpositions of power. But this satiric letter to the prince looks tame in comparison to its long postscript, which comes straight from the midst of the recent carnival to mock the fears of fairs (a near rhyme) in high places, the use of spies and coercive legislation.

> P.S. Your Royal Highness may not be aware of the *general alarm* felt by the *cowards* who pretend to watch for the public safety. *If you were,* you, who are certainly a *brave man,* would hesitate to adopt the *suspicions* of your ministers, which are merely the result of their *fears,* and a modest consciousness of what *they deserve. Bartholomew Fair,* Sir, has *terrors* for your advisers; and they would have probably prevented its being held, under the bill for regulating *seditious* assemblies, had an *earlier intimation* of *their danger* been forwarded to them, by the wag who announced the *intended insurrection* on Saturday last. Every thing, Sir, was stated to be ready to give a *mortal* wound to the constitution "*as by law established,*" by a combined force of *gingerbread Punches, wooden dolls, and pasteboard soldiers.* Two or three *Jack-in-the-boxes* were named as ring-leaders; and a *monkey,* escaped from Polito's collection, was suspected of having organized *the plot.* Your sage advisers, Sir, aware that in point of *intellect* the *conspirators of the Fair,* were nearly on a par with themselves, thought it as well to *take care,* lest the Bank, the Bridge, the Tower, and the River might be again endangered. (519–20)

As the Dwarf reports in mock concern, "the Punches, dolls, and pasteboard rebels never moved from their stalls! But, what of that? They *would,* no doubt, had they not been intimidated by the preparations made to defeat their seditious machinations!" In future, oaths of loyalty will be required not just of persons but of "all and every imitation of men, women, and children, that are admitted into the fair" (520)

"Seditious machinations" at the fair? ("What, pigs rebel?") Indeed, such fears were reasonable, given the history of the English carnival, a fact which puts the true sting in Wooler's burlesque. His contemporary readers would know that it was no joke to associate insurrection and riot with the carnival. While it is true that "there is no a priori revolutionary vector" to carnival, as Stallybrass and White have rightly argued, still, "it was only in the late eighteenth and early nineteenth centuries—and then only in certain areas—that one can reasonably talk of popular politics *dissociated* from the carnivalesque at all."[16] It is probably most useful, as they argue, simply to recognize that:

> for long periods carnival may be a stable and cyclical ritual with no noticeable politically transformative effects but that, given the presence of sharpened political antagonism, it may often act as *catalyst* and *site of actual and symbolic struggle.* (14)

Wooler's historical moment is characterized by just such a catalytic antagonism, but this was only one moment in the long history of territorial struggles over the carnival, one instance among many of its association with general political instability. As late as 1822 (two years before Wooler stopped publishing the *Dwarf*), there were riots when the government, in other attempts, tried to suppress the London fair.

Ostensibly mocking the confusion of reality with representation by the government ("every imitation"), Wooler's 1817 passage actually ends by reinforcing the potential danger of "mere" representations—and by emphasizing the radical instability of the relation between representation and reality. In this way it makes its own pages into a site of symbolic struggle. For his middling and artisanal readers, the references to the commerce and craft of the fair would be familiar, homey. But to the authorities, the satiric fair would be a frightening, uncanny place of hidden conspiracies, where nothing is at it seems and even the gingerbread simulacra may revolt. The joke would not seem funny to those in power. Instead, it would serve to confirm their insecurities and suspicions—and sort out the fears of readers among the middling types, as well. This is satire with a dagger in its cloak of humor, explicitly reinforcing the feeling that identity, truth, and value are rendered uncertain in the chaotic carnival atmosphere.

In a more conventionally Romantic strain, Wordsworth responded to this same deep fear, in well-known lines of *The Prelude* VII describing the "anarchy and din, / Barbarian and infernal" of Bartholomew Fair:

> with buffoons against buffoons
> Grimacing, writhing, screaming . . .
> The silver-collared Negro with his timbrel,
> Equestrians, tumblers, women, girls, and boys,
> Blue-breeched, pink-vested, with high-towering plumes.
> All moveables of wonder, from all parts,
> Are here—Albinos, painted Indians, Dwarfs,
> The Horse of knowledge, and the learned Pig.[17]

Again the Negro and the Dwarf are parts of the spectacle of the fair. As the catalogue continues, the neutral description gives way to fascinated revulsion and the language grows increasingly moralizing:

> The Stone-eater, the man that swallows fire,
> Giants, Ventriloquists, the Invisible Girl,
> The Bust that speaks and moves its goggling eyes,
> The Wax-works, Clockworks, all the marvellous craft
> Of modern Merlins, Wild Beasts, Puppet-shows,
> All out-o'-the-way, far-fetched, perverted things,

All freaks of nature, all Promethean thoughts
Of man, his dullness, madness, and their feats
All jumbled up together, to compose
A Parliament of Monsters, Tents and Booths
Meanwhile, as if the whole were one vast mill,
Are vomiting, receiving, on all sides,
Men, Women, three-years Children, Babes in arms.

(ll. 709–21)

The sentimental sketch of natural humanity in that final line contrasts sharply with the uncanny robot-Bust and wax-works—what man has *made* of man. This passage leads to a characteristic philosophical passage commenting on the description of the "blank confusion" of the London fair, and then on to the opening of the next book, with its contrasting image: a peaceable, wholesome "rustic fair" at Grasmere. At *this* fair there are no booths in which to offer sideshow freaks and diversions, only healthy livestock in a sublime natural setting and—the central attraction—a "sweet lass of the valley" modestly selling her honest and unalienated wares, the "Fruits of her father's orchard." Wordsworth makes of the fair a town-and-country parable that (like his parabolic poem, "Michael") turns on questions of the relative values—and of value itself—of opposed communities of value.

In the years just after Waterloo, parliamentary debates and pamphlet wars alike were occupied with the question of value—in the material, economic sense. The postwar crisis led to heated discussions on the prices of domestic and foreign grain and bread (the Corn Laws), taxation and the national debt, and the slippery value of currency. Ricardo and Malthus were the dominant "witnesses" or authorities, but these controversies were everywhere in the air. The discontent leading up to the suspension of habeas corpus, which included the burning of ricks in the country as well as protests in the city, was largely the result of this economic crisis and the discourse surrounding it. Faced with the problems of fluctuation in commodities and an unstable currency, Ricardo posited his famous "labor theory of value"—an attempt to stabilize in theory the concept of inherent value.

Wooler shows an awareness of the general context for these economic debates and, specifically, the instability of markets—even in this rather conventional satiric parody on the "Political Price Current":

Talent.—A very old commodity, not now deemed worth looking after; the reason will be found under the following head.

Impudence.—Amazingly in request, and fetches very high prices.

Elsewhere, he makes it clear that stable value can only be defined in class terms, as arising from the laboring People.

> The PEOPLE, of course means all that mass of the labouring, and industrious, and ingenious mechanics, merchants, agriculturalists, and traders, whose toils are the wealth, and whose sinews are the strength of a nation. We cannot mistake the term. It means all that is valuable, all that is important in the scale of being. And yet THE PEOPLE, have their BETTERS in England!!! (23 April 1817, pp. 199–202)

This is Wooler's own labor theory of value, and it is articulated in the context of class conflict. This letter from the Black Dwarf to the "Yellow Bonze" of Japan explains (and hence, for English readers defamiliarizes) the familiar phrase, "the people's betters"—which means, Wooler says, "all who live like locusts on the labours of the people ... every paltry scoundrel, however destitute of morality, or virtues, that possesses a legal qualification to kill a hare" (199).

The actual fair is "carnivalesque" in that it is an economic marketplace—a "public square where the folk gather" to display and sell commodities as well as be entertained. (This was especially true until the late eighteenth century, when the ceremonial and cultural aspects of the fair began to take on a life of their own, accompanied by increasing numbers of nostalgic treatments of the carnival tradition.) This is the general background to Wooler's apparent obsession with the trivial potato, which was a staple food among the poor. At first this seems a satiric *reductio ad absurdum,* but the trial of treasonable potatoes offers a stern materialist critique of poverty. The plebeian potato, possibly hurled at the regent by a hungry mob and tried for treason by a reactionary ministry, becomes in *The Black Dwarf* a recurrent symbol of government obtuseness in the face of popular suffering, a taunt pointing to both the callousness and the fears of those in power. It shows up again at the end of the carnival sketch above, when the Dwarf suggests in closing that the same magistrate who tried the potatoes for treason is on the case of the seditious gingerbread men and insurrectionary Punch puppets.

And the potato appears again as the suspicious sign of incriminating "associations" of the Dwarf himself, in this letter published just weeks before Wooler's actual arrest:

> Even I, a mere stranger, attracted by the renown of this country to sojourn for awhile beneath the protection of its laws, am now suddenly deprived of their benefit, and for ought I know, may tomorrow be incarcerated by an order from the office of a secretary of state. Nay, my danger is imminent, for I have

been credibly informed that a magistrate deems my very name suspicious; and the landlady of the garret where I lodge, often shakes her head with a suspicious leer when I order potatoes for dinner, a root of which I happen to be more than commonly fond; but which has lately been here deemed a treasonable sort of food, because some ragamuffins who *were fattened* upon it, pelted a man whom they call here the Prince Regent with it, as he went to the house of legislature. (26 March 1817, p. 137)

When Wooler imagines the people ("all that is valuable") flinging potatoes in the face of the regent, or pictures his Dwarf spied upon for eating potatoes, he is reminding his readers that public unrest is based in economic distress, pitting the undereconomy against its upper-level controls. The potatoes, like the gingerbread Punches and sweetmeats hawked at carnival, come to stand for the people's everyday trade, as opposed to the national economy—a gray- or black-market activity analogous to the place of *The Black Dwarf* in the generalized economy of public-sphere discourse. Such "unofficial" activity was sometimes tolerated as an escape valve; it was seen as fulfilling basic needs of the community not met by the dominant system. It remained, however, criminalized and subject to periodic sweeps and arrests like the purgative trials against radical speech and publications throughout 1817, which culminated in the three trials of William Hone in December.

Wooler's discourse stakes out an amorphous carnivalesque site from which to hawk its "unofficial" wares within the dominant discursive economy, and it is no surprise when he is finally arrested and tried for seditious libel. Wooler conducted his journalistic business in a kind of black market. He had learned from Cobbett the trick of undercutting the official press and avoiding the stamp duty by selling two-, four-, and (once the Six Acts of 1819 forced the price up), six-pence copies. In terms of their commodity value, actual copies of *The Black Dwarf* were products of an unofficial economy of discourse, part of a "counter-public sphere" which, I suggest, is best located in the "public square" of carnivalesque culture.[18] Wooler's most far-reaching satiric effect (to follow through the black-market analogy) lies less in his own avoidance of the Stamp Tax than in the way his example reveals the instabilities and vulnerabilities of the dominant discourse, just as the carnival itself is most threatening (to Wordsworth and others) when it exposes the chaos of modern economic and social relations, when it reveals the full extent of the destruction of the idealized economy and community symbolized by the rustic Grasmere lass selling her patrilineal produce. The existence of a black market, like the carnival culture to which it is linked, is a constant reminder of the vulnerabilities of the official economy and official culture.

The fair is a site where a great deal of shady, semi-unofficial economic activity takes place, a site therefore where the class basis of "values" is dramatized, which carnivalesque satirists can deliberately exploit for subversive effect. This view of the fair provides a counterweight to the many happy pictures of carnival as a *locus amoenus* of organic England, where different classes happily intermingle for the day. Take, for example, this commemorative verse on Bartholomew Fair from the mid-eighteenth century:

> Each wooden house then groans to bear
> The populace that croud the Fair. . . .
> The chambermaid and Countess sit
> Alike admirers of the wit:
> The Earl and footman *tête-à-tête*
> Sit down contented in one Seat.
> The Musick plays, the Curtain draws
> The Peer and 'prentice clap applause.
> The house is filled with roaring laughter
> From lowest pit, to highest rafter.[19]

There *were* royal visitors to the stalls at the fair, and entrepreneurs sometimes had to tidy up their facilities quickly in order to entice visiting patricians and to encourage a mixture of the higher orders in the crowd.[20] But these seem exceptions that prove the rule; their very deliberateness suggests that such visits amount to slumming. By 1817 the "roaring laughter" of the harmonious theatrical audience pictured above—had it continued—might well have covered nervousness about the dangers of such mixing.

It is also significant that the representative carnival crowd in this scene is a *theatrical audience,* for the carnival as a whole was obviously a metatheatrical experience, a feature recognized as early as Ben Jonson's *Bartholomew Fair,* with its knockabout puppet farce within the farce. Slapstick Punch puppet plays, pantomimes, interludes, melodramas, scenes from Shakespeare: all were to be witnessed in the makeshift theaters and stalls along the crowded lanes of the urban carnival, the booths of which formed a stage set for the larger, ongoing play of plays, the carnival itself. Bakhtin's generic categorizations connect the novel in particular to ancient satire, satyr-play, and parody, and all of these to the collective rituals and mummery of the carnival, precisely because of their shared theatricality. The carnival is performed by the "spectators," not merely witnessed by them, and satirical masks, he argues, indiscriminately "grant the right . . . to parody others, the right to act life as a comedy and to treat others as actors. . . ."[21]

Wooler's debut as an editor came with a journal on the theater, *The Stage* (1814–16), and one feature of *The Black Dwarf* took the form of criticism or review of the "theater" of politics. "State Theatricals" might report, for example, on government pageantry: "The first piece performed was a military melo drame, called the *Procession,* which did *not take* with the audience"; or, an entry might announce a "New Casting of the School for Scandal" (satirizing the emerging Queen Caroline affair), then simply list a parodic-allegoric dramatis personae, with contemporary figures in the roles of Teazle, Surface, and others (10 September 1817). This sort of mummery often appeared in the same issue with a serious theatrical review of, say, Booth and Kean in a Drury Lane *Othello.* The heterogeneous format of journalism makes possible Wooler's particular brand of intertextual and intergeneric satire. And it is the momentary lack of any sure demarcation between an actual review (serious discourse) and a political essay (satire masquerading as serious discourse) that creates the truly unsettling effect of the issue as a whole.

Even when the parodic intent is unmistakable, as in the following comparison of public figures to farcical pantomime characters, some readers may have experienced a momentary sense of disorientation when confronted with the headline, "CHANGE OF MINISTERS!":

> We are not yet able to present our readers with a correct list of the successors of the present ministers; but some of the appointments we have been enabled to ascertain, we believe, pretty accurately. *Grimaldi* has been named as the new Chancellor of the Exchequer; the P———e R———t having been struck with his dexterity in picking *pockets,* and *stealing in general,* at a visit *incog.* to Covent Garden during the performance of the last pantomime. Yet although Grimaldi is very clever in his way, some people think he will not be able to rival the past pick-pockets of the treasury bench. . . . for there are but few pockets in the nation that have anything left in them. (26 March 1817, p. 138)

Grimaldi, the most famous pantomime actor of all and the toast of the regent's London, is named as a political appointment of the prince, a comment on the true state of the royal dandy's interests and values—quite apart from the joke about pickpocketing based on the theatrical clown that Grimaldi portrayed. Even Wooler's way of putting the analogy blurs the line between stage and backstage life.

Wooler's self-conscious use of theatrical tropes is also evident in the following passage from a letter by the Black Dwarf on the parliamentary build-up to divorce proceedings against Queen Caroline:

> These *legislators* are really amusing animals. The world would run melancholy without having them to laugh at. They keep a national puppet-shew, and are constantly playing their antics in *front of their booth,* as well as in the interior. The public are not always admitted to the inner recesses, where I have been

informed Old Bags sometimes assumes the character of clown; but every now and then the gaping multitude are entertained by one of the performers stepping out to announce that the performances are about to begin, and exhibiting a few of his humours, as an inducement to latent curiosity. When the curtain shall fall on the last pranks of the puppets, I cannot pretend to foresee; but I can predict that they will not be so well paid for them much longer. (28 June 1820, p. 877)

The ominous note at the end is typical of Wooler's abrupt shifts from comic to prophetic mode, and the ominousness is heightened by the proximity to the adjacent absurdity.

Wooler's ability to play on the fears of those in power is best illustrated in this theatrical notice of an actual play: "*Frightened to Death.*—a farce produced at Drury lane, and attributed to Mr. C. Oulton" (19 February 1817, pp. 93–94). The title is at least appropriate; "these are *frightful* times," he says, since "The ministers *say* they are frightened to death at Hunt and the *Spenceans*—and Hunt and the *Spenceans* at them . . . the rich are frightened to death lest the poor should seize upon their wealth—and the poor are frightened to death lest starvation should lay hold on them." These days, Wooler says, such a farce is sure to be a hit, since English public life is itself both ridiculous and terrifying: "everyone might all be *frightened to death very comfortably together* at Drury, in the person of their representative, Mr. Harley, the hero of the piece; who, though absolutely frightened to death, eats, drinks, walks, and talks, as naturally as any of them." The frightened spectators are "represented" by the actor, but again, the initial mockery of those who would take representation for reality (or satire for straight reportage) gives way to the deeper recognition that such mimetic representation *is* truly terrifying, since it reflects back to the public, and forth again as if in a hall of mirrors, the rampant terror of the times. The advertising bill announcing this issue of *The Black Dwarf* simply mentions the "Notice of the New Farce of Frightened to *Death*. With a great many important Additions to the Dramatis Personae," thus blithely erasing the footlights and crossing the line between actor and spectator. As he did in his parodic announcement of the succession to a pantomime ministry, Wooler here calls into question accepted borderlines between representation and reality, play and politics, farce and history. Historians of satire might expect rather that such demarcations would be safely reasserted, as for example in Pope or Dryden, through what has been seen as the normalizing tendency of satiric modes. But such binaries are potentially unstable in most cases, which is one of the reasons the satirist may be called on to reassert them. Works like *The Dunciad* or *Mac Flecknoe* play upon a background recognition that writing (good or bad) and power are frequently interrelated.

In the issue for 12 January 1820, Wooler echoes the title of the farce in suggesting that the recent coercive legislation was "rather intended to *frighten me* to death, than to kill me by force of arms: but when my nerves are found to be too strong to be scared by the little bugbears placed before my eyes, I may be assailed by more powerful means. Nor should I be amazed if an especial act of parliament were to be directed against my pen . . ." (9–10). Two weeks later (26 January 1820), Wooler prints an "announcement" from the King's Theater, St. Stephens, "THEATRICALS EX-TRAORDINARY," stating that the "*Old English Drama* will no longer be performed in this theater, it having been ascertained to *shock* the *delicate nerves* of the people of fashion, who honor this place with their patronage. For the present, the Italian opera will be performed; but, as soon as possible, the *genuine pantomime* will be restored; and every thing transacted in *dumb shew.*"

Wooler then proceeds to some shocking Swiftian imagery of his own. From now on, he reports, costumes will be "entirely *military*," and "*Real cannon*" will be fired "for *effect.*" In the final scene, these "will be turned upon the *gallery spectators,* and discharged with *grape shot.* In the *combats,* the people are to be *really killed,* and *wounded* in the Manchester method: and in all cases, nature will be copied as closely as possible" (81). Also, Wooler adds, due to the "inattention of the underlings," which distracts from performances, "the public are respectfully informed, that in future they will be all made of *wood,* of the best mechanism, to sit upright, and nod, or shake the head, as may be required"(82). This is the carnivalesque mix in which mimetic art ("nature will be copied") becomes more a threat than a promise. These model spectators possess the same disturbing, uncanny quality as the gingerbread rebels at Bartholomew Fair, or Wordsworth's automaton "Bust that speaks and moves its goggling eyes"—because they actually blur rather than didactically reinforce the line between representation and reality. The point is clear: that the performance of real "actors" in the national "pageantry" (at Peterloo, for example), divided as they were along rigidly hostile but far from clear class lines, is more terrifying than anything in the "shocking" old drama. But in its violent imagery Wooler's satire deliberately exploits that terror, making itself into a mirror of its target, and going beyond didacticism to suggest a world of topsy-turvy possibilities. This violent rhetoric only partly conceals an ambivalence toward the passive spectators themselves, whom Wooler imagines being gunned down and replaced with dummies. Such a reading is in accord with the sentiments expressed in this earlier confession by Wooler himself:

> We sometimes go to the theater, and sit there with the utmost astonishment, at the indifference we see around us. The stage has many charms . . . What an

invaluable school would the stage be, if it were quite unfettered. What a powerful engine to correct the abuses; and lash the follies of the times. (26 February 1817, p. 78)

Wooler's wish is for the English theater to play the roles traditionally assigned to satire, the correction of abuses and the lashing of folly, and this passage—with much of Wooler's violent rhetoric—reveals a frustration with the limits of his own satiric effects. Such passages tellingly foreshadow his despairing remark in October 1824: "The nation is asleep, as dull as tortoises in winter, and nothing can stir them from their trance." Months later he announced the end of *The Black Dwarf* "to the Friends of Reform . . . if there are any left?"

Wooler's Radical Satiric Performance

To go back to the summer of 1820, however: the Queen Caroline affair at that time held the promise and threat of another major crisis for the Reform movement. Many actually hoped or feared a popular uprising was imminent. On 28 June, Wooler has his Dwarf deny rumors to the effect that Queen Caroline was to be publicly beheaded during her husband's coronation—"for the gratification of that part of the crowd which could not be accommodated at the west-end of town!" There is to be no royal execution, after all, he says; it was the administration who published such lies in the first place: "Their object was to *frighten* the Queen away, since she had frightened them so much, by arriving in the metropolis" (870). The humor in this passage incompletely covers over its rhetorical violence; it is no accident that Wooler thinks of the execution of the queen, here, just as Edmund Burke had for very different ends played upon the execution of another queen. Especially given its (weekly) repetitions, Wooler's rhetoric about the royal scandal, along with his ambivalent rhetoric about the crowd, has the effect of invoking and perpetuating an atmosphere of mutual "terror," in the French Revolutionary sense of the word, in anticipation of our modern sense: as an ad hoc political strategy of violence or the threat of violence, heightened uncertainty and instability, combined with mass publicity. In such a climate, Wooler's pages suggest, radical satire must put on a terrifying performance if it is to be efficacious against the official terror.

When James Anderson referred in 1790 to the "performance" of his new periodical, along with the contributing "performances" of his individual correspondents, he indicated that they played timely and occasional roles before the public, in the "theater" of "the world at large."[22] The pages of *The Black Dwarf* are performative, but they are always, even in their serious moments, part of a larger satiric performance, generically unstable and provocative of unstable receptions among heterogenous audiences. They usually display their provocations in character, *en masque*. Reflections of the nation's fears are acted out in a frame at once journalistic (reporting on reality) and fantastic (satirically distorting). And this occurs even at the level of the "bibliographic code" of the texts, "using typography to press words themselves toward an almost extralinguistic force," partly, as Jon Klancher suggests, in "an attempt to reproduce in print the emphatic gesture and timbre of voice."[23]

Wooler's advertising bills offer a flamboyant example. They post "headlines" and highlights from the current issue and often make satiric commentary of their own. An advertising flyer for issue no. 6 begins: "This Number contains an Article to prove the Nation has lost its Liberty and ought to go in MOUR [H.C.] NING," the letters surrounded by a coffin. Here the iconic sign, produced from a crude dingbat, literally invades the printed word, suggesting an unspoken, subtextual, cause at the heart of the national mood. In Wooler's flyer for issue no. 9, the icon of the black coffin appears again, this time embedded in the syntax of the famous exhortation of Milton's Satan: "Awake, [H. C.] Arise, / Or be for ever Fallen" (see figure 3.2). The black-inked coffin contains white letters for "Habeas Corpus" in the graphic, brutal simplicity found in the signs (in more than one sense) of advertising and the semiotics of reform-movement banners. This combined graphic and linguistic semiology, foregrounding the editor's (and printer's) artisanal concern with the appearance of the page, has an extremely complicated and long history. At Wooler's 1817 trial, the attorney general was forced to argue the technical point that Wooler was responsible for printing the alleged libels because he was able to act as his own compositor, without a manuscript, "from his mind . . . for he prints as another man would write."[24] In the end, Wooler was acquitted on the basis of the counterargument that he could not legally be considered the "writer" of works for which he was the physical compositor.

But such graphic self-consciousness is especially significant in the context of satire, which has family ties to the language of advertising.[25] This legacy extends through the twentieth century, in both high and low satiric forms, from playbills, prints, and pamphlets, to modernist appropriations (for example, Ezra Pound's and Wyndham Lewis's *BLAST!*), to various small-press or photocopy experiments in the postwar years, right up to the *samizdat* and communication experiments of latter decades, including the digitized, animated icons and ad hoc ASCII-text graphics of the World Wide Web and the Internet as a whole. In each case a self-consciously heightened opacity of the medium itself results from the technological and social limits on the act of publication, pushing printed expression into a deliberate print performance.[26]

Wooler was capable, for example, of issuing a black-border front page on 3 December 1817, less than one month after the death of Princess Char-

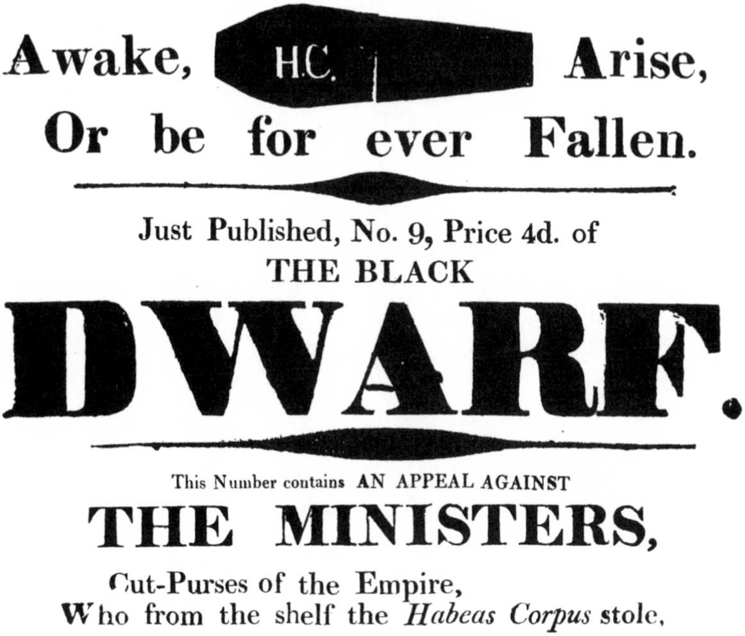

Awake, H.C. **Arise,**
Or be for ever Fallen.

Just Published, No. 9, Price 4d. of
THE BLACK
DWARF.

This Number contains AN APPEAL AGAINST
THE MINISTERS,
Cut-Purses of the Empire,
Who from the shelf the *Habeas Corpus* stole,

Figure 3.2 *The Black Dwarf,* flyer and advertisement

lotte. His headline, "Death of the Trial by Jury in Cases of Alleged Libel," mourns the abstract principles "executed" along with those hung in November as the result of the work of the *agent provocateur* Oliver. His observance of the mute printer's custom thus becomes flagrantly parodic. Or, as another example of his use of print conventions to break the frame of the printed page, take the set of typographic word-pictures reprinted (from a newspaper) in *The Black Dwarf* for 26 May 1819 (pp. 333–34), purporting to be subjects "for the improvement" of Carleton House by the regent. Readers can imagine the graphical arrangement of persons in a group portrait of the prince and his mistresses (including the "Hottentot Venus"), for example, based on the typographical arrangement of names in the space of the page. Placement and hierarchy are potentially symbolic, and Wooler adds commentary, as in this case: "N.B. *This picture should be veiled.*" Another "group" blocks off on the left the words, "An emblematical Painting of *False-hood.* 'False as Hell.'" "Trial of Wooler in the Court of King's Bench," lists judicial officials in the middle, and the blocks on the right: "Pluto's Regions. Trial of Hone in the Court of King's Bench." Another has the name of Lord Sidmouth and "Execution at Derby" literally flanked or hemmed in by the names of the spies, Oliver and Castles.

Wooler extended this technique of the verbal picture in *The Black Dwarf* for 26 January 1820 (pp. 93–104), "The Reformers' House that Jack Built, for 1820"—a parody of the most famous parody of the time, Hone and Cruikshank's "Political House that Jack Built." The children's rhyme had become by 1819 a recurrent source for political satire, from Rowlandson and the 1809 Old Price riots to a version by Leigh Hunt in the *Examiner,* to a well-known loyalist parody of Hone.[27] But Wooler's satire, coming quickly on the heels of Hone and Cruikshank's, is pitched as a direct reply, a new edition, "with *new readings.*" The *Black Dwarf* parody, however, includes no graphics to correspond to the memorable Cruikshank images. Instead, Wooler says, "we must draw from the imagination of the reader for the ENGRAVINGS, which we have endeavoured to describe" (93). Arranging type freely on the page, sometimes vertically, sometimes in simple line-drawn boxes, Wooler the working printer adds a set of labels and comments ["IMAGINE THIS SPACE, / [word boxed in:] HEAVEN"] to direct his readers' imagination and provide a graphic "layout" for his pages.[28]

His footnote to the parody connects it directly to "The House that Jack Built" but expresses the hope that this "edition" will be "acceptable to the friends of Reform" (93). The parody works to radicalize its model. For example, in Wooler, a Temple of Liberty is supported by "Magna Charta," "Trial by Jury," and "Liberty of the Press" and *supports* "Kings, Lords and Commons." These last three had made up the supporting columns of Cruikshank's less radical image. Hone had defiantly celebrated the printing press as "THE THING, / that, in spite of new Acts,"

> And attempts to restrain it,
> by Soldiers or Tax,
> Will poison the Vermin,
> That plunder the Wealth,
> That lay in the House,
> That Jack built.

As a persecuted editor and printer, Wooler should share this defiance, but his parody is throughout more demotic and more explicitly economic than Hone's. The *Black Dwarf* page stages its own radical economic critique of the "National Debt" (the words in a box):

> THE THING, that is nothing but *rags,*
> Manufactured and issued by paper-made hags,
> Who, to grow rich themselves, it is grown pretty clear,
> Have helped to encrease it, year after year.

When Sidmouth argued for the Habeas Corpus Suspension Bill in February, he cited the example of Hone's parodies, and the actions against Hone, Wooler, and Cobbett were among the first to follow the passing of the bill.[29] Hone was arrested on 3 May for his infamous parodies of the liturgy and the *Book of Common Prayer: The Late John Wilkes' Catechism,* the *Sinecurist's Creed,* and the *Political Litany.* When he was sent to prison only days later, Wooler was already there. Wooler was tried for two libels on 5 June, was at first found guilty (although the verdict was overthrown on a technicality), and then found innocent. By December he was present at Hone's trials; the Hone-Cruikshank *Political House* was published one year later, in December 1819. Wooler, who was to be imprisoned for 18 months after Peterloo (beginning autumn 1819), was acquitted in 1817. In *his* trials of 1817–18, Hone too was acquitted—to the delight of audiences in and out of the courtroom—at least in part on the grounds that parody was an ancient form of discourse not inherently dangerous to society.

But Wooler's own account of his first trials includes transcriptions of his prosecutor's case to the contrary, the general assumptions of which Wooler probably shared. Satiric works like *The Black Dwarf,* while humorous, are, the prosecutor argued, no less "libellous and dangerous."

> I dispute what has been laid down upon high authority, that ridicule is the best mode of reproof, for it may be made a most important, powerful and destructive engine:—attempting to turn those things that are valuable into ridicule, and to make them objects of scoff and contempt, is no slight offence. (*A Verbatim Report . . .*)

Wooler himself, upon hearing that his journal printed strong language about the ministry, said:

> I do not pretend to deny that this language is strong, and I will take leave to add, that I intended it to be strong, because I am firmly persuaded that nothing but the boldest language and the most determined energy (and if I had the good fortune to be a leader I should think so still) can rouse the nation to such a degree of exertion as to procure the dismissal of Ministers so odious and injurious, and so odious, because injurious.

This appears admirably sincere, if indignant, but it is also somewhat disingenuous. It was not for its passionate sincerity but for its destabilizing satire that Wooler's work was on trial. As would later happen at Hone's trials, when Wooler's texts themselves were read into evidence, "the progress of the Clerk was frequently interrupted by the risibility of the audience below the bar." The trials and legislation aimed to squelch the threat represented by the collective laughter of the courtroom audience. As Wooler's Black Dwarf put it (complete with typical veiled threats), in a pained letter to the defecting William Cobbett,

> A *flock* of sheep may be of service to each other for mutual defence; but a single lamb may be picked up by any stray wolf, and eaten at leisure. . . . All associations are useful to the object they have in view, be it good, or bad. A club of robbers are more secure than a single footpad. And a company of soldiers are more formidable than thrice their number unarmed and separate. Clubs of good men for honest purposes then must be equally effective. (5 March 1817, p. 91)

The potential ability of Wooler's satire to move a wide audience to scoff at power was what made it such a "powerful and destructive engine," and, additionally, was what extended its influence even into the realm of the emergent literary canon.

Radical Satire Within Emergent Romanticism

It would be difficult to overestimate the significance of these prominent trials during 1817. Even the young John Keats was provoked into writing a parodic sonnet based on the Book of Daniel, "Nebuchadnezzar's Dream," provoked in part by the influence of his friend, the satirist Horace Smith. This poem has rightly been characterized as "a gesture of solidarity with Hone and defiance of the Government."[30] In it, Keats has the "scared" king with feet of clay send for the young Daniel, who responds, seditiously enough: "I do not deem / Your sceptre worth a straw, your cushions old door mats."

> A horrid nightmare, similar somewhat,
> Of late has haunted a most valiant crew
> Of loggerheads and chapmen;—we are told
> That any Daniel, though he be a sot,
> Can make their lying lips turn pale of hue,
> By drawling out—"Ye are that head of gold!"

If the king is the regent, the "crew / of loggerheads and chapmen" would seem to be the ministers and their supporters, and "any Daniel" therefore could be Hone or Wooler. Keats remarked at around this time that "Wooler and Hone have done us an essential service." One manuscript shows the variant "belching" for "drawling," which only emphasizes Keats's evident condescension (especially audible in "sot"—line 12) toward the plebeian radicals he supported. If this is a gesture of solidarity with Hone, written in the heat of the moment in 1817, it is instructive to compare its cryptic references and generally oblique style with the rough and direct performances of the radical journalists themselves. But the larger point is that Keats was attuned to the discourse of radicalism, at this moment of historical crisis and at other times in his career, and there is some continuity between his work and the work of Hone and Wooler. Given the position of his mentor, Leigh Hunt, this is not surprising, but critics sometimes lose track of this continuity in treating Keatsian Romanticism.

Hunt had spent time in prison years before for libeling the regent, but as a reformer he worked to distance himself from the plebeian milieu of Wooler, Hone, Carlile, and Henry "Orator" Hunt. Even in his political journalism he carefully staked out a middle ground in the battle for reform, a position culturally higher—more self-consciously educated and refined—than the two-penny or four-penny weeklies. From this position he expressed selective support for the aims of various radicals, and, more important, contempt for the common enemy, the current government. But from the other side this respectable reformer's position is precisely what made the Hunt circle open to Tory satirists' charges of bounding Cockneyism. Caught between the radical and the Romantic, Hunt had to work to make the taste by which he and his circle could be appreciated. Keats's own class- and status-anxieties shaped his attitudes toward the radicals, as seen in his sonnet, and that attitude is also tied to marked cultural and literary differences—for example, an expressed preference for the Romantic tale and symbolic allusion over the direct or "heavy-handed" attack. In terms of diction, language like "sot" and "loggerheads" probably reveals Keats's failed attempt to banter in the rough, "masculine" style he seems to have associated with public satire. But he pulls his foil at the last minute with the opacity of his references; this poem (as has been noted) is not even technically a parody: the biblical text is used only as an analogy, never copied directly.[31] The sonnet is, however, a characteristically self-enfolding satire with countersatire built in, like Keats's later and more substantial experiment, *The Jealousies,* the ambivalence of which I examine in the next chapter.

A similar ambivalence informs the forays into radical satire during 1817–20 of another Leigh Hunt protegé—but from a very different social background—Percy Bysshe Shelley.[32] As Shelley himself originally formulated, he wrote in different modes for different audiences, and from the early days of his career he shared a certain amount of cultural space with writers like Wooler. This goes back at least to 1811 and what may have been a half-parodic political speech at the British Forum, "then a spouting club, in which Gale Jones and other Radicals abused all existing governments." According to the later account of his cousin, John Grove,

Bysshe made so good a speech, complimenting and differing from the previous orators, that when he left the room, there was a rush to find out who
he was, and to induce him to attend there again. He gave them a false name
and address, not caring a farthing about the meeting, or the subjects there
discussed.[33]

Grove's Victorian retrospection probably distorts the events: it seems highly
unlikely, for example, that the young radical cared nothing for the subjects
of the meeting, though it also seems quite likely he was embarrassed or ambivalent about his appearance there. Grove's account seems interested to trivialize the event, to depict the poet as a young man, the rebellious son of a
baronet and M.P., on a condescending lark among the plebeian radicals. But
it seems just as likely, given Shelley's continued commitment to reaching a
popular audience, that giving a false name was a wise caution, his interest
quite serious. He was at this time shortly to compose that notorious mixture
of poetic romance and incendiary footnote-essay, *Queen Mab*. In that regard
Mab stands as a marker of Shelley's dual rhetorical thrust: his transcendent
imagery and strident attack are part of the same poetic aims. It is instructive
to remember that among those radicals also heard in radical debating circles
circa 1811–12 was Thomas Wooler.[34]

Within a year of that speech, Shelley was composing a number of radical
works, including a broadside satire, *The Devil's Walk,* as well as *Queen Mab*.
He traveled to Dublin as an itinerant orator and pamphlet author on behalf
of Catholic Emancipation, and wrote the *Letter to Lord Ellenborough* on the
celebrated trial of Daniel Isaac Eaton. By 1817 (just after *The Black Dwarf*
made its debut), Shelley was engaged in Chancery court in a battle for the
custody of his children. The crucial evidence against him was his own earlier radical publications. Also in early 1817, he set himself up as the anonymous "Hermit of Marlow," intending to produce a new series of Reformist
publications, beginning with the *Proposal for Putting Reform to the Vote
Throughout the Kingdom.* That same year he published his ambitious radical
epic on the French Revolution and Reaction, *The Revolt of Islam,* as well as
a pamphlet on the death of Princess Charlotte, the parodic structure of
which closely mirrors Wooler's obituary page. Shelley's eulogy on the
princess begins tamely but turns gradually into a speech mourning the loss
of the executed radicals and, finally, Liberty herself—the nation's true queen.

In early 1818 Shelley left for Italy, where, against the odds, he continued
to write satires while also producing the more Romantic lyrics and lyrical
dramas for which he was later to be remembered. In 1819 he responded to
Wordsworth and the Tory government with *Peter Bell the Third* and to the
ministerial terror at Peterloo with *The Mask of Anarchy.* Although Hunt
withheld the latter from publication until after the passage of the first Re-

form Bill, it gained a posthumous fame among several new generations of European radicals, from the British Chartists to Bertolt Brecht.

Shelley's career plan, to write for both a "low" and a "high" readership in pursuit of universal social ideals, is well-known.[35] Though John Grove may have been exaggerating his condescension at the British Forum, it is also true that Shelley never was entirely free from the prejudices of his class, the landed aristocracy, as Donald Reiman has shown,[36] and there remains to the end of his career the hint of something opportunistic, even patronizing in his relationship to radical culture. *The Mask of Anarchy*, for example, contains a famous exhortation to the people to "rise like Lions," but in an act of passive resistance, an action dangerously close to mere self-sacrifice given the political climate of 1819. This ambivalence is even more pronounced in the closely related "Song: To the Men of England," which ends with a goading hortative characterization of its working-class audience:

> Shrink to your cellars, holes, and cells;
> In halls ye deck another dwells.
> Why shake the chains ye wrought? Ye see
> The steel ye tempered glance on ye[.] (st. VII)[37]

On a structural level, Shelley's ambivalence informs the *Mask*'s use of the iconography of satiric prints and the pantomime (the opening masque proper could come straight out of Cruikshank and Hone or from popular theatrical masks), all of which are figuratively blown away at the poem's moment of transition, trampled into dust and displaced by a sublime Romantic allegory and the moving final exhortation, a structure resembling the popular theatrical form of pantomime.

Something of the same structure of transformation and displacement is at work in the most recognizably radical production of Shelley's later years: *Oedipus Tyrannus; or, Swellfoot the Tyrant* (published and suppressed in 1820). This theatrical satire is a farce very much out of the dense carnivalesque milieu of London radical culture around Wooler. In it, the low is mixed, in a farrago or generic *satura,* with the high: pigs and ministers, puns and allegories, Aristophanic allusions and bawdy innuendo, Shakespearean lyricism and pantomime tricks, all on one imagined stage. The satire always takes place within a framework of serious political economy. It would be clear from this production alone that Shelley has been reading the work of men like Wooler and Hone, and even that he aspired to address their popular audience.

The first scene contains pigs, potatoes, and paper money, symbols of unstable value that will recur throughout the skit. The opening speeches contrast the gouty corpulence of Swellfoot the Tyrant (George IV) with the poverty of the lean Swine, who "grub / With filthy snouts my red potatoes up / in Allan's rushy bog" (ll. 24–25).[38] But when they call for "hog-wash and clean straw," the monarch replies, "This is sedition, and rank blasphemy!," and calls for the sow-gelding "Jews" of his court, at least two of whom probably point to Malthus and Ricardo, as well as utilitarianism in general, an unfeeling pathway to reform. Swellfoot commands a butcher to "cut / That fat Hog's throat, the brute seems overfed; / Seditious hunks! to whine for want of grains" (ll. 80–82)—a clear reference to the Corn Laws and taxation of the previous five years.

Among all Shelley's works this pamphlet satire best demonstrates Shelley's immersion in radical discourse and the carnivalesque satiric modes that dominated so much of it (in this case, in the work of William Cobbett in particular). And it comes very late in his career, effectively debunking narrative of Shelley's increasing otherworldliness in his final years. But it also evinces a larger fact: the persistence of shared modes available to Romantic poets as much as radical pamphleteers, a public discourse that subsumed canonical and subcanonical works alike. Shelley's satire was written for the occasion of Queen Caroline's 1820 return to England to face divorce proceedings against her, a moment of intense political crisis in which many seriously believed the government would fall, and Shelley seems to have been among them.[39] Like Wooler and other radicals, Shelley saw the royal scandal as a low farce—"Punch and his Wife . . . this mummery"[40]—and then joined the fray with his own theatrical performance, a play tellingly inspired by the grunting of pigs at the raucous Italian fair outside his window in San Giuliano. But unlike Wooler, his class-driven disdain for "this vulgar cookmaid they call a Queen" was almost matched by a disgust with the people and their radical leaders. "Cobbett's euthanasia seems approaching," he wrote to his satiric friend Peacock, "and I suppose you will have some rough festivals at the apotheosis of the Debt."[41]

In the satire, the Queen (Iona Taurina) throws herself into the "Hoggish arms" of the people's protection; this is followed by the final scene, the feast of Famine, in which the swine are eventually metamorphosed, pantomime-like, into John Bull (the Ionian Minotaur) by eating from the emblematic altar symbolic loaves of bread. Not, however, before they offer a frightening obeisance to the goddess Famine:

> Hail to thee, Empress of Earth!
> When thou risest, dividing possessions;
> When thou risest, uprooting oppression,
> In the pride of thy ghastly mirth;
> Over palaces, temples, and graves,
> We will rush as thy minister-slaves,

Trampling behind in thy train,
Till all be made level again.

(ll. 53–60)

Shelley's radical sympathies run deep, it is clear to most readers, but it also seems in such moments that he has frightened himself with his own low sources and potential (and much desired) popular readers; at the same time, he seems to be attempting to turn that fear outward into a satire of terrifying effect. That is why it is so significant that he interrupts this scene of "ghastly mirth" with the theatrical appearance of a highly Romantic, highly Shelleyan countergoddess, Liberty, whose words, however, "are almost drowned in the furious grunting of the PIGS, and the business of the trial" (408). Liberty charges Famine directly: "when thou wake the multitude, / To lead them not upon the paths of blood" (ll. 90–91). With this exhortation, she enters into a "brief alliance" with Famine to bring about a revolution—taking the theatrical form of a pantomimic romp by the Queen and the people in pursuit of the "filthy and ugly animals" who had been the court's ministers. When the satire was published, it is reported that only a few copies were sold before the publisher, Joseph Johnson, agreed to suppress the work—apparently under pressure from the ascendant Society for the Suppression of Vice.[42]

I have rehearsed Shelley's radical and satiric career in this way as a deliberate reminder that Wooler's world was not yet partitioned off from the discursive realm of emergent Romantic literature. As Marcus Wood has suggested, works like Shelley's satires serve as indices to "a common currency for political satire that cut across literary and political barriers and appealed to loyalists, radicals, and major Romantic poets alike."[43] The process of making Romanticism involved partitioning it off from this worldly discourse—and this is the discourse within which much contemporary satire thrived. As Michael Scrivener has said, the partition was originally open at both ends: "the *Black Dwarf* is an unacknowledged early interpreter and popularizer of English Romanticism," having published a fair amount of verse by the now-canonized Romantic poets.[44] I would simply reverse the terms and emphasize the traffic in the other direction. Shelley (and to a different degree, Keats) took seriously and deliberately brought into his own work Wooler's world of radical satire—a reform-minded poet with aspirations to be heard could hardly have done otherwise during 1817–20. Part of my aim in this chapter so far has been to demonstrate how, in its strategically destabilizing mix of satire and sentiment, Shelley's satiric work looks a great deal like Wooler's, and it is one of my key assumptions that it there is no *essential* difference between them, nothing inherently Romantic about Shelley's satire—or un-Romantic about Wooler's.

There are fundamental differences between Wooler's and Shelley's work and their use of mixed modes but these are the effect of their very different cultural and class positions, as well as historical change and the revisionist processes of canonization. In the early Victorian period, when Romanticism as a movement was being constructed at the center of an emerging canon of English literature, what Shelley had in common with Wooler—not only his satire but his politics—was stripped away, dropped like unwanted dross in exchange for Arnoldian angel wings. Shelley's radical-reformist satire was a central part of his *oeuvre*—as everyone from Friedrich Engels to F. R. Leavis well knew—but it was rapidly devalued (in terms of its potential for cultural capital) in favor of the autonomous, high-literary aesthetic of the "Jane" lyrics or *Prometheus Unbound.* It is a great irony of canon history that one of Shelley's most admired and most Romantic works, *The Triumph of Life,* contains unmistakable traces of the scrappy Juvenalian political satire of the reform movement, from its grotesque-comic allegories to its public caricatures in procession. But this worldly referentiality has little to do with the reputation of the poem among readers such as T. S. Eliot or Paul de Man.

The same process of canonization that eclipsed Shelley's satire, in concert with the larger institutionalization of the category of literature (first constructed in the Romantic period), caused writers and editors like T. J. Wooler to drop almost out of sight, at least until recent revisionist studies. To juxtapose the radical journalist and the arch-Romantic on the field defined as "satire" is to contextualize these historical processes, to point to the facts that first, Wooler was the more immediately effective political figure, and second, Shelley borrowed from and aspired to Wooler's discursive milieu at least as much as the other way around. Wooler is more than merely part of the "background" to Romanticism, though that is where the process of canonization places him. He was a prominent and influential figure in the field of nineteenth-century satire, which—it has been my purpose to explain—intersected freely at many key points the developing field of Romantic literature. The definition of that second field as pure and untouched by the first has caused us to lose sight of the pathways through which influences were shared between them.

Wooler was a persecuted printer and satirist. Shelley often figured himself as an outcast, whether he identified with Dante, Tasso, or the Wandering Jew. For his professed atheism and published radicalism, Shelley was indeed something of an outcast from society. But Wooler's was a very different "society," one that Shelley in the end only visited, the way he visited the British Forum debating club to make his youthful speech. Within the larger society and its image of a public sphere, Wooler was paradoxically an active participant, a mover and shaker, and a social pariah. More vividly even than Wooler himself, however, the symbolic persona of the Black Dwarf, created and set loose in the heart of London, remains a more marginal figure than Shelley could ever imagine himself or his projected personae to be.

Understanding these continuities *and* differences helps us to explain the "rhetorical violence" or melodramatic modes in Wooler's satire. When questioned about such writing at his 1817 trial, Wooler said that "nothing but the boldest language" could bring about his radical goal—"to procure the dismissal of Ministers so odious and injurious, and so odious, because injurious." With Shelley he shared a taste for Juvenalian or prophetic righteous indignation that sometimes turned into bitter invective. Shelley could almost have written, for example, Wooler's description of "the hosts of squalid, ragged paupers, that crowd our workhouses, or run after the hand of precarious charity . . . the hardy peasant of past times, destitute of employment, crawling to the door of a parish officer, and supplicating for the means not of *living,* but of prolonging a miserable existence, under every bodily privation, and wracked by every mental anguish" (26 March 1817, p. 131). Also like Shelley, Wooler often applied such language in unholy satiric mixtures whose final effect is the result of the interaction of antithetical modes, the satiric and sentimental. But when Wooler's satire shifts from a relatively comic mode into the violent, performed sincerity of melodrama, when satire fuses with sentiment, the reader is always aware that the shift is temporary and could reverse itself. The unsettling effect of reading the pages of *The Black Dwarf* is the result of such unstable, shifting relations between modes of discourse, self-consciously manipulated to represent and perform instability.

With such instability Shelley begins, in poems like *The Mask of Anarchy* and *Swellfoot the Tyrant,* but then deliberately and earnestly maneuvers his satire into more hopeful, sentimental, Romantic moments, revealing in the process a teleological, Godwinian sense of perfectibility that he never fully abandoned. Shelley's satire makes use of the carnivalesque for strategic purposes, purposes that are always "legislative" in the sense he worked so hard to define. Wooler's satire, by contrast, displays the sentimental or melodramatic as if it were only one show in one booth at the complicated carnival of discourse. Wooler too employs the carnivalesque as part of a deliberate satiric strategy, but his end is less certain, beyond aiming for the destabilization of the current relations of power. Every issue of *The Black Dwarf* carried an epigraph from Pope's imitation of Horace's first satire (Book II):

> Satire's my weapon, but I'm too discreet
> To run amuck and tilt at all I meet,
> I only wear it in a land of Hectors,
> Thieves, Supercargoes, Sharpers, and directors.

The editor may protest too much the discretion of his weapon, that this vision of clear moral targets may belie the deeper uncertainty invoked by the satiric pages themselves. He does not tilt wildly or indiscriminately (on the contrary, his political enemies are usually clear enough); but the larger, centrifugal cultural effects of his satire are anything but sharply directed and calmly, consciously controlled. In this lies their frightening power.

From the perspective of the canon, Wooler, like the topical dross in Shelley, finally had to give way before the ascendant concept of Romanticism—which left only an esoteric and subordinate space for political satire (of any class), turning such public performances into dusty dioramas, of interest only to a handful of literary historians—until the work of revisionist historicist critics.[45] The binary opposition of surviving Romantic poetry versus extinct political satire, however, must give way to richer uncertainties in the face of the complexities of both Shelley's satire and Wooler's Romantic sentiment. In general, it is important to recognize the central role of mixtures of sentimental, Romantic modes *within* the satire of the period. The "Corn Law Rhymer," Ebenezer Elliott, for example (who is the subject of chapter 7 below), was famous for his satiric and sarcastic political rage. But he also wrote his own highly sentimental "Monody on John Keats"—really a monody on Shelley's monody on Keats (itself modeled on many classical precursors)—which celebrates Keats's canonization as just revenge against Gifford's satire and the satirical *Blackwood's:* "He perish'd in his 'scorn of scorn,' / And lowest deem'd, of all was highest." Ultimately, the scorn of satiric reviewers is only part of a larger cultural economy, the judgment of posterity and the canon that determines which performance shall be deemed "low" and which "high."

Chapter 4 ∾

Della Crusca *Redivivus:*
The Revenge of the Satiric Victims

The years just after Waterloo saw a resurgence of radical satire such as Thomas Wooler's and William Hone's. These years also saw the productive peak of second-generation literary Romanticism. The radical writing of this era—like that of the 1790s—provoked conservative, loyalist satires in a resumption of the cultural battles suspended during the war with France. Frequently, Romantic literature emerges from the midst of those battles in these culture wars. Often these conservative satires attempted to resume the traditional, perennial role of enforcer of cultural and political stability in the attempt to exercise disciplinary control over the newly reactivated radical pamphleteers, women authors, and the literature of sensibility. The authors later labeled Romantic were frequently found among their targets: Byron, Hunt, Keats, and Shelley dominate several overlapping constellations of authors and works, none of which is coextensive with canonical Romanticism as a whole, which at any rate was a "posthumous movement" constructed after the fact.[1] Viewed through a parallax effect, these constellations shift to reveal other patterns and groupings, some of which possess considerable revisionary implications for current notions of Romanticism.[2] Sometimes such a shift happens when one revisits and takes seriously the classificatory terms of the historical era in which poetry first appeared—Cockney or Lake School—bracketing the received critical term (Romantic), viewing it as the result of combined perceptions gathered into a gestalt that exceeds the sum of the parts to take on mythic proportions. Once the constellated object is mapped, labeled, and canonized, it overwhelms the significance of other possible patterns of individual works and authors, even those that once seemed more intuitive and direct—other families of objects, movements, modes, and schools.

My purpose in this chapter is to shift the focus to a relatively obscure poetic school seen by many contemporaries (especially satirists) as cognate with an important sentimental strain of Romantic poetry. Robert Merry's Della Cruscan school has come down to literary history as a minor episode by aesthetically inferior precursors to Romanticism. It sometimes seems as if the whole purpose of the Della Cruscans has been historically to serve as a negative touchstone: they are the bad pseudo-Romantics against which to measure the excellence of the true Romantics. But early satiric attacks on Keats, in particular, confused the school of Hunt with the school of Merry, the emergent Romantics with the Della Cruscans, and not accidentally or in ignorance. The satirists deliberately drew attention to Della Cruscan elements in Keats's writing as part of their strategic attempts to depict the author as yet another weak target for their strong satire. What is striking about the exchange is the extent to which, as I will argue, Keats (and Shelley, writing on his behalf) implicitly acknowledged this connection and identified his own work with what deserved satiric discipline and punishment.

Many contemporaries saw Keats as vulgar, Cockney, effeminate, suburban, as a number of critics have shown, including Marjorie Levinson, Susan Wolfson, Nicholas Roe, Alan Bewell, Anne Mellor, Elizabeth Jones, and Jeffrey Cox.[3] Often, by understanding what his attackers found so objectionable and then establishing the connections between gender or class aspersions, style, and political subtexts, for example, or by questioning or even inverting the aesthetic values of the contemporaries, critics historicize Keats's "badness" and hence to some degree redeem it from the condescension of his contemporaries. Along these same lines, Jerome McGann remarks in the introduction to his 1993 anthology, *The New Oxford Book of Romantic Period Verse,* that "In an important sense, Keats is the greatest representative of the Della Cruscan Movement."[4] This provocative remark in effect challenges critics to place Keats in a new, hitherto inconsequential constellation. As McGann argues in *The Poetics of Sensibility* (1996), the Della Cruscans were an important influence in their literary era, a *fin de siècle* that went on to affect, directly and indirectly, the mainstream of nineteenth-century literature.[5] This influential "minor" poetry shaped contemporary views—negative and positive—of the importance of sincerity and sensibility, and its role in this debate was open to contention. While some contemporaries objected to Della Cruscan poetry as artificial and insincere, its satiric critics at the time, on the contrary, attacked it for being (naively) sincere (or sentimental). To a William Gifford, say, or other satirically minded critics of the time who followed in his footsteps, the differences between emergent Romantic (primarily the New School of the Hunt circle, with its tenuous ties to the Lake School) and Della Cruscan verse (the school of Robert Merry) were very slight or even nonexistent. Both groups consisted of sentimental writers and both represented a similar cultural threat to polite letters and public discourse. The differences were less important to the critics than the dangerous family resemblances between the two. If the process of canonization is one of differentiation and speciation, a sorting out of niches and survivors, then it is sometimes necessary to return to the field of the jostling struggle, before a certain naturalized sorting has settled into place. In what follows I look at the socioaesthetic kinship of Romantic and Della Cruscan verse; in order to do this I must place them in the same field, following the example of contemporary critics.

The flamboyant tinseled school of Robert Merry, the founder of the Della Cruscan coterie, arose as part of a general wave of experimental modes at the end of the eighteenth century that led eventually to Romanticism. Recognizing its priority in this way has interesting, indeed paradigm-shifting, results in terms of the symbolic and cultural capital so long and so richly associated with the poetry of Keats and Shelley. Della Cruscan modes are historically significant in their own right, but they also direct attention to important forces that shaped emergent Romantic poetry and conceptions of Romanticism. Often those shaping forces were satiric, or conversely, self-consciously *un*satiric—precisely (and deliberately) the kind of writing the dominant satire of the moment despised (and yet required). Thus the "younger" British Romantics struggled with real and projected satiric enemies in a relational construction of the "Romantic" and the "anti-Romantic," a struggle frequently determined by the terms set during the earlier Della Cruscan controversy of the 1790s. In my reading, both Keats and Shelley collaborate in their own caricatures, offering themselves up as the victims of satire in order to stake out an unsatiric higher ground. "You say that I am"—this is their Promethean reply to their satirists as they undergo a poetic passion to effect their own literary salvation. Literary history, coming later to the struggle, figures their condition of satiric victimage as characteristically, essentially Romantic.

The Della Cruscans and the New School

Lord Byron himself had followed Gifford in attacking the Della Cruscans in *English Bards and Scotch Reviewers* (ll. 759–64). In 1817, Byron wrote to John Murray from Venice that he had met the well-known Italian poet Ippolito Pindemonte, then in his sixties:

—He enquired after his old Cruscan friends Parsons—Greathead—Mrs. Piozzi—and Merry—all of whom he had known in his youth.—I gave him as bad an account of them as I could . . . that they were 'all gone dead,'— & damned by a satire more than twenty years ago—that the name of their extinguisher was Gifford—that they were but a sad set of scribes after all . . . (*BLJ* 5, 233–34)

A few years later, in September 1820, Byron threatened in a letter to his publisher Murray to write, should he return home to England, his own *Baviad* and *Maeviad,* a poem that would rival Gifford's original attacks on the Della Cruscans:

> not as *good* as the old—but even better *merited.*—There never was such a *set* as your ragamuffins—(I mean not yours only but every body's) what with the Cockneys and the Lakers—and the *followers* of Scott and Moore and Byron— you are in the very uttermost decline and degradation of Literature.—I can't think of it without all the remorse of a murderer . . . (*BLJ* 7, 175)

Byron sees this conflation of the Cockney, Lake, and Byronic schools into a single movement of Romanticism as a new wave of Della Cruscanism. (His own professed "remorse" seems to be because his earlier poetry inspired Romantic "followers.") Both waves call for strong satire in the tradition of Gifford or, as he says further on in the letter, Dr. Johnson.

Just over a year later, in December 1821, the pages of the notoriously satiric journal of critical opinion, *Blackwood's,* contained this world-weary cosmopolitan bulletin:

> The *Della Crusca* school has visited us again, but with some slight change of localities. Its verses now transpire at one time from the retreats of Cockney dalliance in the London suburbs; sometimes they visit us by fragments from Venice, and sometimes invade us by wainloads from Pisa.[6]

In this famous review of *Adonais,* William Maginn attacks the Cockney or Suburban School that Shelley's elegy had defended, and exposes inner London and Hampstead as mere outposts for an Italian invasion of licentious yet sentimental "nature poetry." It originates in Pisa, where, as Jeffrey Cox has said, Shelley had attempted to create an expatriate circle extending the New School of Hunt.[7] It also has a Venetian source in Lord Byron himself. As Cox argues, the so-called second generation of Romantics "is not merely a temporal gathering of distinct voices but a self-consciously defined group, an association of intellectuals that centered on Leigh Hunt and that came to be known as the Cockney School" (4–5). The Young Poets, as Hunt himself referred to them, or, alternatively, the New School, are recognized as a group by the critic and, even more than in Byron's comparison, are dismissed as merely the derivative "humble imitators" of an earlier new school—who remained the most obvious and notorious satiric targets of the era, the Della Cruscans.

Keats's *Poems* of 1817 had already received well-known negative reviews making this unflattering comparison. The *Scots Magazine* found his feminized diction "worthy only of the Rosa Matildas whom the strong-handed Gifford put down," and John Gibson Lockhart's familiar attack (signed "Z") "On the Cockney School of Poetry" diagnosed Keats's weakness as "metromanie," suggesting both the female hysteria and a mania for rhyming or scribbling, a malady connected to the French Revolution and originally used in the polemical attacks by William Gifford against the Della Cruscans in the 1790s.[8] The identification became so conventional that one review of *Lamia* found it expedient to argue of Keats that "whatever may be his faults, he is no Della Cruscan poet":

> for, though he is frequently involved in ambiguity, and dressed in the affectation of quaint phrases, we are yet sure that of finding in all that he writes the proof of deep thought and energetic reflection.[9]

This defense reveals the dominant term of attack ("no Della Cruscan") and damns with faint praise. The defining characteristics of Keats's work are clear—"ambiguity" and "the affectation of quaint phrases"—and these are traits that Keats shares with the Della Cruscans. Only the "proof" of his superior "thought" and "reflection" saves him from fully deserving the odious label.

The basic terms of abuse associated with the label "Della Cruscan" are also present in William Hazlitt's remarks on Coleridge's self-parodic gothic ballad *Christabel,* in which he finds "something disgusting at the bottom of his subject, which is but ill glossed over by a veil of Della Cruscan sentiment and fine writing."[10] In another essay Hazlitt tarred Samuel Rogers with the Della Cruscan brush, saying that he is "a very lady-like poet," which is to say an "elegant, but feeble writer."

> He wraps up obvious thoughts in a glittering cover of fine words. . . . This kind of poetry, which is a more minute and inoffensive species of the Della Cruscan, is like the game of asking what one's thoughts are like. It is a tortuous, tottering, wriggling, fidgetty translation of every thing from the vulgar tongue, into all the tantalizing, teasing, tripping, lisping *mimminee-pimminee* of the highest brilliancy and fashion of poetical diction.[11]

Superficial fashion (especially when it comes to experiments with diction), effeminacy, shared introspection, and, interestingly, translations into poetry of demotic or vulgar language—together these constitute the Della Cruscan style. The essence of this style is a fundamental violation of decorum, "asking what one's thoughts are like," as well as mixing high and low for mere effect, which Hazlitt connects with the (undereducated) feminine. "The whole is refined, and frittered away into an appearance of the most evanescent brilliancy and tremulous imbecility" (287).

Keats's harshest critics used these terms, of course, but so did his admirers. In *Adonais*, Shelley depicts the beautiful corpse of the dead poet as a "broken lily" bathed in the tears of the faerylike Dreams:

> See, on the silken fringe of his faint eyes,
> Like dew upon a sleeping flower, there lies
> A tear some Dream has loosened from his Brain.
> (ll. 85–87)[12]

This picture of Keats (and, by extension, of Shelley himself) comes to be popularly accepted as a true likeness and reaches its ironic fulfillment with the 1894 installation of the infamous statue of Shelley by Edward Onslow Ford, erected at the request of Jane, Lady Shelley, in the quad of University College, Oxford. The statue was originally intended as a Victorian monument for Shelley's grave in Rome but, when rejected as too large, found a home in his erstwhile college. The recumbent and languid, long-haired, androgynous or feminized marble nude, surrounded by winged lions and the Muse, represents Shelley's drowned body both as a sexual object and transcendental subject, a sacrifice laid out on a marble altar. Shelley's own lines from *Adonais*, written about Keats, are inscribed on its pedestal. Thus the poem is made to return reflexively to this stylized depiction of its author's own pale corpse, a return that goes back to Mary Shelley's own reading of the text at the time of Shelley's death—"Adonais is not Keats's it is his own elegy"—and to the spirit of the elegy as Shelley originally composed it.[13]

This self-reflexivity is by now well-known to critics of Romantic literature. By coming to Keats's defense in this way in *Adonais*—while deliberately and simultaneously invoking the satiric reviews that supposedly destroyed him—Shelley consciously defines himself, along with Hunt, Byron, and the dead Keats, as a fit target of satire, as "a Power" *strategically* "Girt round with weakness" (ll. 281–82). Shelleyans will recognize in this formula the dynamic of Prometheus's curse on Jupiter (which is reflexively called down on Prometheus himself and those he loves). But in this specific context the Shelleyan trope of the reflexive curse has a wider public significance, because it participates in a specific discourse with a well-known, public history. When Maginn and the other reviewers reenacted Gifford's punishment of Robert Merry, Hannah Cowley, and the rest against this new threat in the new generation, their aggressive allusions invoked a precise range of generic and literary-historical comparisons. Their attacks were opportunistic recapitulations of the politico-culture wars of the 1790s, but they also "constituted an enormously powerful act of cultural definition that still influences our understanding" of Romanticism.[14] The attacks provided a paradigm by which the newest New School (as Leigh Hunt styled the "young poets," the emergent Romantics) began to be constructed in public discourse and literary history, defined in significant measure in opposition to public and powerful, satiric modes of the day.

Keats's example is useful in analyzing the contiguous but jostling and sometimes overlapping positions of "Della Cruscan," "Romantic," and "satiric" during the period, and how—despite the evident crudeness of much of the rhetoric—these terms were first implicated in one another and then strategically differentiated in complex and subtle ways. Nineteenth-century critics use the specter of Della Cruscanism as a scare tactic *and* a real rhetorical weapon against the younger Romantics. Thanks to William Gifford's and T. J. Mathias's strong examples and the collaboration of the Romantics' own self-representations, these attacks took place as a coded war of the satirists against their targets—as a purification of the public sphere by way of an heightened opposition of hostilities between satiric and sentimental modes.

Della Crusca and his Avatars

The monster of Della Cruscanism was at Hester Piozzi's Florence salon in the mid–1780s, a many-headed, effusive poetic monster consisting of the expatriate liberal Robert Merry and his band, including Hannah Cowley, Hester Lynch Piozzi, Mr. Greatheed, Mr. Jerningham, and John Williams. Merry called himself "Della Crusca" for the 1582 academy of which he claimed to be a member, and the name had clear political, even revolutionary, implications in Florence at the time. Using the label was a Romantic-nationalist gesture of opposition to the grand Duke Leopold and current European powers.[15] This political purpose was clear, and Merry was soon to profess an ardent Jacobinism, writing songs for a 1790 pantomime on the fall of the Bastille (see chapter 5 below), and reciting in 1791 an ode celebrating the anniversary of that event, then presenting a poem, "The Laurel of Liberty," to the National Assembly itself, as well as authoring a number of satirical anti-Pitt epigrams, for example.[16] The original *Florence Miscellany* of 1785, to which Merry contributed, was less openly political, but it contained a wide variety of works by Italian authors and English exiles, sometimes with veiled political themes and in encoded public modes—including satire.

Despite this obvious political context, the story of the Della Cruscans resolves itself in traditional literary histories well into the twentieth century as a relatively apolitical battle of style and aesthetics—and of the sexes. Here is the scene of origin in the much-quoted words of William Gifford:

In 1785, a few English of both sexes, whom chance had jumbled together at Florence, took a fancy to while away their time in scribbling high-flown panegyrics on themselves . . . they were unwilling their inimitable productions should be confined to the little circle that produced them; they therefore transmitted them hither. . . . There was a specious brilliancy in these exotics, which dazzled the native grubs. . . . From admiration to imitation is but a step.

This is taken from the introduction to a later edition of Gifford's 1791 *Baviad,* the best-known satiric poem of the Romantic period before Byron.[17] There Gifford relates how Della Cruscan poetry was imported to England in the passionate verse correspondence between Merry (as "Della Crusca") and Hannah Cowley ("Anna Matilda"), which led to a national "epidemic malady":

The fever turned to a frenzy: Laura Maria, Carlos, Orlando, Adelaide, and a thousand other nameless names caught the infection; and from one end of the kingdom to the other, all was nonsense and Della Crusca. . . . the evil grew every day more alarming (for now bed-ridden old women, and girls at their samplers, began to rave).

The extraliterary inflections are clear enough, particularly the class-based, antijacobin fear of the "thousand . . . nameless names . . . from one end of the kingdom to the other" overlaid with a conventional misogyny straight out of Roman satire but newly appropriate to the age of Wollstonecraft and Kotzebue ("of both sexes . . . girls at their samplers"). Victorian and modern literary historians ignored such things, for the most part, following only that part of Gifford (and Mathias and Polwhele) that simply asserted that the Della Cruscans were bad poets—aesthetically insignificant. Literary history as a whole has subsequently treated the school according to the protocols of satiric cliché—as tinseled butterflies broken on Gifford's violent wheel. But then it has ironically displaced Gifford himself (and the satiric tradition in general) in favor of those more substantial sentimentalists, the Romantics.

The dominant metaphor here, tried and true in satire from Juvenal through the Augustans, is disease. Della Cruscanism is, according to the satirists, a mass epidemic begun in the literary, political, and sexual unwholesomeness of individual poets living in close quarters; like the plague, it invades the air of England from foreign—especially southern—countries.

> Now fools and children void their brains by loads,
>   And itching grandams spawl lascivious odes;
>   Now lords and dukes, curs'd with a sickly taste,

While Burns' pure healthful nurture runs to waste,
Lick up the spittle of the bedrid muse,
And riot on the sweepings of the stews . . .
(*Baviad,* ll. 311–16)

The only hope is purification through the quarantine and eventual destruction of those hopelessly infected. At least since Goethe's famous version of the opposition of Romantic and classic, it has become common to think of Romanticism as a disease. But almost immediately upon their appearance in the nineteenth century, the writers who came to be known as the British Romantics were branded as unhealthy, a form of satiric attack going back as far as satire itself, most likely but including prominent examples in Augustan verse. One way this association of satiric cliché with the emergent New School took place was in the redeployment of anti-Della Cruscan weapons, as Gifford's satiric figures were applied to the "modern Della Cruscans," the Cockney School.

In response, Shelley turns the figure of health and disease around and around again in his great pastoral elegy and countersatire, *Adonais.* Shelley may well have literally believed that Keats, whose genius and constitution were "delicate" and "fragile," as well as "beautiful," was killed by those "cankerworms" the critics. While the "savage criticism" he cites was not wholly satirical, satiric attack played the central, generically defining role in the prose reviews Shelley has in mind.

> The savage criticism on his *Endymion,* which appeared in the *Quarterly Review,* produced the most violent effect on his susceptible mind; the agitation thus originated ended in the rupture of a blood-vessel in the lungs; a rapid consumption ensued, and the succeeding acknowledgements from more candid critics, or the true greatness of his powers, were ineffectual to heal the wound thus wantonly inflicted. (Preface to *Adonais*)

This is an account of the critical satiric weapon at its most medically literal. After a paragraph counterattacking the reviewers' own bad taste in poetry, Shelley ends simply: "Nor shall it be your excuse, that, Murderer as you are, you have spoken daggers, but used none." The dagger was Shelley's favorite symbol for satiric wit, the concealed, cloaked weapon of intrigue, assassination, and espionage, which wounds mortally despite its pettiness. Of his own ambivalent and fragmentary "Satire upon Satire" he said that it "was full of *small knives* in the use of which practice would have soon made me very expert." In his "Letter to Maria Gisborne," Shelley praises his satiric friend Peacock's "fine wit," which "Makes such a wound, the knife is lost in it."[18] The "poisoned shafts" and "small knives" of satire led directly to infection and

Keats' consumption, to which, however, he was predisposed, being "suscepti-ble," "delicate and fragile."

The sentimental extravagances of *Adonais* must be understood generi-cally: as part of a deliberately antisatiric display of the corpse of an inno-cent casualty in the culture wars. The critics understood this. *Blackwood's* published in 1829 another counterthrust of a satire in answer to Shelley's countersatire, verse revealing that both sides in this battle understood that the mechanism of martyrdom was being deployed to squelch the vicious ridicule:

> OH! he was great in Cockney Land, the monarch of his kind,
> 'Tis said he died of phthysic by the ignorant and blind;
> 'Twas *we* assassinated him—ah! regicidal deed;
> And he has left Endymion for those who choose to read.
>
> From book to book we hurry us, reviewing as before,
> For Log-books writ in Arctic seas to Log-books writ on shore;
> From arid plains in Afric to the icy Polar main,
> As though we had not murder'd him, the glory of Cockayne.
>
> Remorseless,—nothing heeding the reproaches of his race,
> And martyring King Rimini, who reigneth in his place;
> But he is made of sterner stuff, unsentimental fellow!
> And lives, delighting still to case his nether man in yellow.[19]

Mocking Hunt ("King Rimini") and his yellow breeches is secondary here to mocking the Hunt circle's pose of martyrdom, calling the strategic hand of antisatiric sentiment Shelley had displayed in *Adonais*.

Within that poem, in order to make his position clear, Shelley must make his elegiac sincerity and heightened sensibility diverge as much as possible from the wanton raillery of the murderous reviews. In the elegiac scheme, Keats must be represented as a beautiful but ultimately ineffectual angel—an angel become victim. But for one moment of righteous indignation in the poem, Shelley mixes mourning with counterviolence and turns the weapons of invective satire against his satirists, those "monsters of life's waste." This moment is Urania's speech comparing the critics to unwhole-some scavengers:

> 28
> "The herded wolves, bold only to pursue;
> The obscene ravens, clamorous o'er the dead;
> The vultures to the conqueror's banner true
> Who feed where Desolation first has fed,

> And whose wings rain contagion;—how they fled,
> When like Apollo, from his golden bow,
> The Pythian of the age one arrow sped
> And smiled!—The spoilers tempt no second blow,
> They fawn on the proud feet that spurn them lying low.

Somewhat late in the game, here, Shelley enlists Byron, in his capacity as author of the traditionally Juvenalian *English Bards and Scotch Reviewers,* as a ringer in the discursive battle. Ironically, the reviewers now "rain contagion," while the decadent Lord Byron is all Apollonian health and manly vigor. Here Shelley's allusions attempt to transvalue a satiric cliché. It is usually the dunces and fools, Grub Street hacks and sycophantic courtiers who are described as cormorants and plague-ridden scavengers, and the satiric light of truth/reason or health/authority that disperses them. In several prominent graphic satires of his own period, however, Shelley could have seen just such an inversion: Ministers and officials represented as vermin being driven out by the light of the sun, as in William Hone's *THE POLITICAL SHOW-MAN—AT HOME!,* for example (British Museum no. 14150).

There is also ample precedent for such counterattacks in the elegiac tradition, of course, especially (as critics have noted) in Milton's famous "Blind mouths" passage in *Lycidas.* There, too, wolves and contagion are united in the destruction of delicate and passive victims among the righteous.

> The hungry sheep look up, and are not fed,
> But swoln with wind, and the rank mist they draw,
> Rot inwardly, and foul contagion spread,
> Besides what the grim wolf with privy paw
> Daily devours apace, and nothing said.[20]

Here disease is the effect of poor preaching by the Bishops whose "lean and flashy songs / Grate on their scrannel pipes of wretched straw." In Shelley's poem it is wolfish reviews that "grate" and lead to Keats's destruction. But his prophetic denunciation, superficially like that of his precursor, makes Keats a sacrificial lamb of corrupt public discourse. Like *Lycidas,* Shelley's poem is based on the powerful mechanism of martyrdom. And like the martyr of martyrs, Shelley's Keats makes his own destruction a stumbling block, a reciprocal verbal violence through which Shelley accuses Keats's accusers.

This is a strategy of passive-aggressive resistance, a way of holding up Acteon's shield to satire, saying reflexively in effect: "you say that I am." Shelley experimented with this rhetorical device in almost all of his satiric writings, providing a generic context that helps us make sense of the rhetoric of his pastoral elegy. In *The Mask of Anarchy* the device is transformed by the energy of Peterloo into something like true passive resistance, though ambivalently (the bloodshed seems inevitable, and thus qualifies Shelley's call to the people to "stand"). But martyrdom is its dark underside, and carried to an extreme, as in Byron's "Prometheus," it becomes a resentful strategy for exacting the cold and posthumous revenge of the satiric victim:

> . . . a firm will, and a deep sense,
> Which even in torture can descry
> Its own concentered recompense,
> Triumphant where it dares defy,
> And making Death a Victory.[21]

Adonais first deploys the kind of satire it would counteract, unable finally to escape altogether the taint of the satiric poison in which it deals. The moment of Juvenalian spleen in Urania's speech, like the preacherly denunciation in Milton's elegy, marks an aggressive rupture in the smooth surface of sentimental mourning, a reappearance of the continuing aggression that fuels such antisatiric rhetoric. In order for the rhetoric to work, such satiric aggression must be concealed, projected onto the critics or sublimated in the transcendence of the poem's closing lines. Shelley's speaker, yearning after the stellar eternals, expresses the desire to escape from the "dome of many-coloured glass" and the petty violence of the discursive sphere. But first he fires some opposing shots. In the brilliant gestures of the closing stanzas of *Adonais,* Shelley focuses on the apotheosis of Keats in order to put satire and its petty strife behind him forever; he succeeds so well that many readers forget the satire-driven conflict that occasioned the elegy in the first place and determined its own antisatiric thrust. The poem directs attention above the public sphere to the iconic tableau of two sentimental, sacrificial victims of satire, already well on their way to becoming idealized representatives of the Romantic poet.

Even Maginn's "modern Della Cruscans" review recognizes this transcendental displacement at work in *Adonais,* and it is Maginn's demystification of this poetic mechanism—not his evident disrespect for the dead—that makes his parodic lines in the review seem to us so mean, so venomous. By continuing the satiric onslaught in public, and in the form of yet more satire, Maginn simply ignores Shelley's virtuoso displacement of satire with sublimity, stubbornly continuing the sordid discursive battle, harping on issues of class and breeding, in effect kicking the corpse Shelley had so carefully, ceremoniously prepared and displayed.

> O weep for *Wontner,* for his leg is broke,
> O weep for Wontner, though our pearly tear

Can never cure him. Dark and dimly broke
The thunder cloud o'er Paul's enamelled sphere,
When his black barb, with lion-like career,
Scattered the crowd.—Coquetting Mignionet,
Thou Hyacinth fond, thou Myrtle without fear,
Haughty geranium, in your beaupots set,
Were then our soft and starry eyes unwet?

The pigeons saw it, and on silver wings
Hung in white flutterings, for they could not fly,
Hoar-headed Thames checked all his crystal springs,
Day closed above his pale, imperial eye,
The silken Zephyrs breathed a vermeil sigh.
High Heavens! ye Hours! and thou Ura-ni-a!
Where were ye then? Reclining languidly
Upon some green Isle in the empurpled Sea,
Where laurel-wreathen spirits love eternally.

Come to my arms, &c. (698)

This, it must be admitted, is wickedly funny. It charges Shelley with every Cockney/Della Cruscan defect of style: excessive sentiment, violations of decorum, pretentious coinages, misplaced classicisms. In addition, it gets in barbs about trendy suburban gardening (pigeons and "beaupots") and pedantic floral imagery—which, as Alan Bewell and Elizabeth Jones have shown, were important symbols of what may be theoretically called the Cockney habitus—as well as the feminized eroticism that was associated with the Hunt circle.[22]

What I wish to call attention to is how close Maginn and Shelley are when it comes to their depictions of the basic structure of the conflict. In both, there are sensitive, otherworldly poets at one pole and worldly, violent satirists on the other. The dispute is over what would later be seen as a matter of canonization or, more broadly, competition for dominance of the literary field. Whereas Shelley attempts to place Keats and his circle (including himself) in the space "where the eternals are"—to apotheosize them while making the critics into mere ephemeral insects—Maginn paints the New School poets as nothing new, merely Della Crusca *redivivus* (but, it is to be hoped, not for long). Although the conflict represents a larger culture war of serious proportions then raging in nineteenth-century England, it is remarkable how much, in the opposing depictions, there is tacit agreement that the modern Della Cruscans are destined for a similar fate as their originals—at least until (for Shelley) they are revived by posterity. Both Maginn and Shelley depict them as victims, as in effect already "dead" to the world.

Shelley wishes to invest them with a higher form of cultural value as a result, to shift to the long-term perspective of their ultimate survival; Maginn works to devalue them, to snuff them out as diseased nonwriters. But in both cases, the field, the public world of present discourse, is mostly left to the critics and satirists.

The Della Cruscans were not known for satire but for being the butt of satire.[23] But the members of the coterie did write satire; even the original *Florence Miscellany* included some satires, and two of them were written by Merry himself and directed at the critics. Take for example, this conventional beast-fable ("A Fable"), aimed at past and (especially) future critics:

> Once upon a time an Ass would be
> A Critick upon Melody;
> Tho' when himself began to sing
> Th'affrighted birds were on the wing:
> No more the turtle woo'd his love;
> Each nightingale forsook the grove;
> And scarce a beast upon the plain,
> But mock'd the miserable strain;
> Yet flatt'ring foxes simper'd near,
> And vow'd he had a charming ear.
> Pleas'd with their praise, the strutting brute
> Despis'd the humble shepherd's lute,
> Despis'd the linnet's artless song,
> 'Twas now too weak, and now too strong;
> In spite of all the world might say,
> The only musick was—to bray![24]

Other members of the Della Cruscan coterie wrote satire, especially outside the original circle in Florence. Mary Robinson wrote satiric verse under the pseudonym of "Horace Juvenal." But sentimental modes were more prominently displayed in Della Cruscan verse. Even Merry's satiric strike against the critics depicts the wronged poetry as natural, artless, and sentimental-erotic.

Natural sentiment and civilized satire, as local manifestations of the war between artists and critics, have at least since the early eighteenth century been seen as set in opposition. But in the 1790s and again in the 1820s, this conventional warfare takes on the heightened significance of a struggle for cultural dominance. Merry's kind of "artless song" is appropriated by Keats and Shelley, in their own nightingales and skylarks (and in Maginn's parodic pigeons)—even before its representation in Shelley's pastoral elegy—as a profound threat to the cultural status quo, anything but innocent, "a Power / Girt round with weakness," but a power indeed. This is an instance of what Pierre Bourdieu has described as the process of the aesthetically superior or canonical object differentiating itself from the surrounding mass culture, taking on "a symbolic value inversely proportional to exchange value."[25] In this game played for eventual dominance of the cultural field, as Bourdieu explains it, the "loser wins" by defining himself as superior to the field, relegating his work to the "field of restricted production" in which his values are recognized.

This basic strategy informs Shelley's elegy and, I believe, Keats's appropriation of the sentimentality associated with Della Cruscanism. The strategy and its effects were visible to contemporary reviewers like Maginn.Indeed, the connection and its implications for a protected sentimental practice was an obvious danger to the reborn antijacobins engaged in the very serious culture wars of the post–Waterloo/Peterloo era. This is the context within which Keats can be rightly called a Della Cruscan: he helped to make himself and was also made by his readers—from the reviewers to Shelley to twentieth-century critics—into the quintessential, unsatiric target of satire. The satires that came after were forced by the terms Keats and Shelley established to further the canonization of their intended victims.

Keats as Della Cruscan

On some level, Keats himself understood the dynamic of this identification with the losers who will win in time, the last who shall be first in the canon and "among the English poets." His idea of poetic power was from the start strangely "girt round with weakness," from the famous opening lines in the sonnet "On Seeing the Elgin Marbles," "My spirit is too weak . . . Like a sick eagle looking at the sky" to *Endymion* itself. In the very preface to that poem Keats engages in an extreme example of the conventional self-castigation over the merits of the verse, then offers this strange challenge:

> This may be speaking too presumptuously, and may deserve a punishment: but no feeling man will be forward to inflict it: he will leave me alone, with the conviction that there is not a fiercer hell than the failure in a great object. This is not written with the least atom of purpose to forestall criticisms of course . . . [26]

It is hard to read this now without imagining the effect such remarks would have had on critics already predisposed to punish the young Cockney poet. In the next paragraph it is Keats himself who introduces the term "mawkishness" to describe his "feverish attempt." As Nicholas Roe points out, the term derives from "'mawk,' a maggot, and in this context may also be related to the auxiliary sense of 'maggot,' meaning 'a whimsical fancy'."[27] Quite apart from the poem itself, with its langorous account of the "brain-sick shepherd-prince," this preface offered a wide target to the satirists.

Keats's tendency to confess mawkishness and virtually ask for punishment helps explain his fragmentary, unfinished satire, "The Cap and Bells" or (the title Keats was said to have preferred) "The Jealousies." The poem was drafted only months before Keats's death and therefore only a few months more before Shelley wrote *Adonais.* It has been dismissed as a doomed project well ended, but I believe it deserves greater attention than it has yet received. Its usefulness as evidence for understanding the satiric within Romanticism is difficult to overestimate. In 1970, Carl Woodring referred to the "intricately riddled satire" of the fragment and said no one had yet been able to "say precisely where its lampooning of the Prince Regent becomes a burlesque of Byron in mockery of Keats's own friends."[28] At the very least, the fragment is deeply ambivalent. Robert Gittings, in his 1956 *The Mask of Keats,* argued that the aim of the poem seems to be fundamentally "divided between the public and the personal," that "Keats had intended it primarily as a literary satire, a parody of his brother writers, a fanciful portrayal of the rivalry between Lake Poets and Cockney School."[29] Turning away from the obvious topical and political features of the lines, Gittings believes that it was Keats's "personal obsessions" that fueled and ultimately halted their composition. But as it turns out, even in considering these personal obsessions, the public literary marketplace comes into play. As Gittings himself points out, the poem was begun at a time when Keats was considering for financial reasons (among other options, including the East India Company[30]) entering the "cock pit" of political journalism, which he recognized as the arena of the masculine satiric violence he associated with his mentors William Hazlitt and Leigh Hunt, both of whom eventually wrote satiric counterattacks on William Gifford.[31]

In the letter to Woodhouse containing the draft of "To Autumn" (21, 22 September 1819, *Letters,* II, 219), Keats lays out his plan to turn himself into a liberal journalist:

> —I have determined to take up my abode in a cheap Lodging in town and get employment in some of our elegant Periodical works—I will nc longer live upon hopes . . . I shall enquire of Hazlitt how the figures of the market stand.

Then, tellingly, Keats expands on the very hopes he has just abjured:

> O that I could [write] something agrest rural, pleasant, fountain-vo[i]c'd— not plague you with unconnected nonsense—But things won't leave me *alone.* I shall be in Town as soon as either of you . . .

Material circumstance—"things" and "the market"—drive him into public discourse and away from "agrest [rustic or rural]" poetry like "To Autumn." Indeed, by way of explaining two lines later why he won't publish "Isabella; or the Pot of Basil," Keats has the satiric reviewers of *Endymion* in mind: "It is too smokeable," he says, and then: "I intend to use more finesse with the Public."

As if following the fatal career path of Thomas Chatterton, Keats reluctantly planned in the autumn of 1819 a sacrificial shift in his literary production: from poetic romance to journalistic satire. As Gittings points out, it was just as this plan was failing that Keats composed his conflicted Romantic satire, with its strange mixture of Cockney fairies and Byronic urbanity, its comic-romance plot touching on the Queen Caroline Affair, Byron, and Keats's relationship with Fanny Brawne. The result is symptomatic of Keats's divided loyalties, less between private and public than between Romantic and satiric modes of discourse.

Keats composed it quickly, probably for the periodical venue, and "The Jealousies" is meant to be taken as a spontaneous skit, the monstrous genetic offspring of Pope's *Rape of the Lock* and Hone-Cruikshank pamphlets. It participates in the flood of prints and satires on the scandalous Queen Caroline Affair of 1819–20, but, as critics have noted, Keats uses the occasion of Queen Caroline's mass representation to lob squibs of various kinds in several directions, including at literary targets. There are the expected slapdash allegories—though readers may need to be reminded that Keats is not alone in leaving this type of satirical reference vague or ambiguous. Emperor Elfinian, "famed ev'rywhere / For love of mortal women," is one part Byron and two parts prince regent, just as his bride Bellanaine alludes to Annabella Milbanke as well as Queen Caroline. Keats also names the Princess's nurse with the near-echo of Caroline, "Coralline." Though the stanza is Spenserian rather than ottava rima, *Don Juan* is a target and source, as, for example, in these lines of narrative play:

> 14
> But let us leave this idle tittle tattle
> To waiting-maids, and bed-room coteries,
> Nor till fit time against her fame wage battle.
> Poor Elfinian is very ill at ease—
> Let us resume his subject if you please . . . [32]

This follows close upon Byron's heels in its narrator's self-directed joke, but "The Jealousies" shifts at this point in the general direction of political satire, with the thwarted Prince cursing "*his* House of Commons" (my emphasis):

16

"I'll trounce some of the members," cried the Prince
"I'll put a mark against some rebel names,
I'll make the opposition-benches wince,
I'll show them very soon, to all their shames,
What 'tis to smother up a prince's flames;

. . . .
17

"I'll trounce 'em!—there's the square-cut chancellor,
His son shall never touch that bishopric;
And for the nephew of old Palfior,
I'll show him that his speeches made me sick,
And give the colonelcy to Phalaric;
The tiptoe marquis, moral and gallant,
Shall lodge in shabby taverns upon tick;
And for the Speaker's second cousin's aunt,
She sha'n't be maid of honour,—by heaven that she sha'n't!

18

"I'll shirk the Duke of A.; I'll cut his brother;
I'll give no garter to his eldest son;
I won't speak to his sister or his mother!
The Viscount B. shall live at cut-and-run;
But how in the world can I contrive to stun
That fellow's voice, which plagues me worse than any,
That stubborn fool, that impudent state-dun,
Who sets down ev'ry sovereign as a zany,—
That vulgar commoner, Esquire Biacophany?

Except for Biacophany, who is surely Samuel Whitbread (who so stridently defended Queen Caroline in Parliament), the other names have no obvious specific referents.[33] The general system of corruption and the petty impotence of princes seems as much to the point as local attacks, and literary pretensions—especially of the Romantic or "faery" variety—are targeted as much as are political ambitions.

Rather than attempt to decode all the composite allegories, instead I want to project its generic incongruities against the backdrop of the dispute between Della Cruscanism and satire, hoping thus to gain a perspective on "The Jealousies" not afforded by other readings, however specific their topical references. Most readers of Keats have tended to avoid the most satiric portions of the poem anyway, seeking instead the fragment's "Keatsian" elements—its Romantic similes or stanzas of minute concrete description—and extracting them from the wreckage of tainted, presumably unfunny satire. But by doing so, I am arguing, they miss more complex effects and Keats's ambivalences, which reside in the unholy combination of satiric and sentimental modes.

Despite the fact that the poem was never finished, the basic generic strategy of "The Jealousies" is, I think, discernible. The fragment is a self-parodic experiment with negative results.It cannot finally be completed because Keats is suspended between conflicting desires: to satirize *and* to exemplify its own Cockney Della Cruscanism. In light of the war between the satirists and the Della Cruscans (original and "modern"—with a Cockney accent), "The Jealousies" tries to go both parties one better, attempting compulsively to represent a medley of sentimental, fanciful, Cockneyfied scenes in the form of an ironically self-aware cartoon. Its ironies are, however, only partly conscious, as I have suggested. In the end the fragment attempts a revenge of the satiric victim against his would-be satirists—but also against some part of his own authorial persona.

Take for example the description of the nasty "memoirs" of the author Crafticant (part Wordsworth, part Byron, a bit of Southey):

> 11
> Where, after a long hypocritic howl
> Against the vicious manners of the age,
> He goes on to expose, with heart and soul,
> What vice in this or that year was the rage,
> Backbiting all the world in ev'ry page;
> With special strictures on the horrid crime,
> (Section'd and subsection'd with learning sage,)
> Of faeries stooping on their wings sublime
> To kiss a mortal's lips, when such were in their prime.
> 12
> Turn to the copious index, you will find
> Somewhere in the column headed letter B
> The name of Bellanaine, if you're not blind;
> Then pray refer to the text, and you will see
> An article made up of calumny
> Against this highland princess, rating her
> For giving way, so over fashionably,
> To this new-fangled vice, which seems a burr
> Stuck in his moral throat, no coughing e'er could stir.

If the love of "faeries" for "mortal's lips" sounds at first oddly proleptic of *Adonais,* that is because both Shelley and Keats himself are deliberately echoing the imagery of Keats's earlier poetry—particularly *Endymion* and the "Ode to Psyche." The faery "vice" is in the second quoted stanza, attacked in calumnious satire; this transgression parallels the "new-fangled," "fashionably" Della Cruscan sins against decorum. The central allegorical device of "The Jealousies" is the illicit crossing of faery with

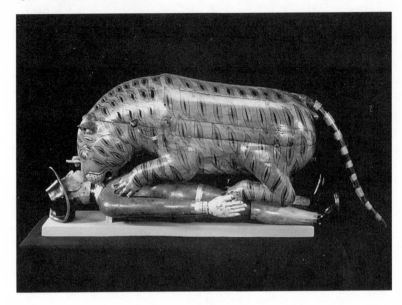

Figure 4.1   "Man-Tiger Organ" (Tipoo's Tiger; Victoria and Albert Museum, V&A Picture Library)

mortal—a fanciful representation of the incongruities of the "Monstrous affair" (l. 164) of the vulgar Queen, but also a literal representation of the literary critique of Keats and the Della Cruscans: they indulged in a promiscuous indecorum that so unnaturally brought down the high and raised up the low.

Critics blamed this transgression, in both the Della Cruscans and Keats, on improper education and a feminized sensibility. Keats plays to this criticism from the start, pretending that "The Jealousies: A Faery Tale" was the production of one "Lucy Vaughan Lloyd of China Walk, Lambeth." One footnote on Cham's being the inventor of magic reports that Lucy (much like the young John Keats) "learnt this from Bayle's Dictionary, and had copied a long Latin note from that work." Partly this persona is a double screen for Keats, allowing for a transparent distancing of the author from unpalatable material. He once remarked, apropos of the charge that his poetry was indecent and offended women,

> there is a tendency to class women in my books with roses and sweetmeats,—they never see themselves dominant. If I ever come to publish "Lucy Vaughan Lloyd," there will be some delicate picking for squeamish stomachs.[34]

Satiric, misogynist representations of female characters may have been the threat implied in this remark, or Keats may have in mind his representations of the Emperor's amorous adventures. But he may also be thinking of jokes like the loud noise heard from Elfinian's chamber, discovered to be made by the "play-thing of the Emperor's choice, / From a Man-Tiger-Organ, prettiest of his toys." The actual mechanical musical instrument to which Keats refers here is the wooden tiger of Tipu Sultan, now in the Victoria and Albert Museum, which is shown devouring an English officer of the East India Company; Keats would have seen the organ in the public reading room of the East India House (figure 4.1).[35] The belows-driven organ emits human screams as well as musical notes and is clearly a violently, inherently satirical object in itself. It was intended by the Sultan to mock the imperial pretensions of the British. But Keats may intend as well to exploit the sexual pun in its name ("man-tiger-organ"). Indeed, this may be one thing he imagined as offending those "squeamish stomachs."

Besides this pun, the erotic elements of the fragment, adjusting for satirical conventions, are less bold than in "The Eve of St. Agnes." Indeed, that poem may be one of several of Keats's own works that are parodied in "The Jealousies," as in these lines on the Romantic decor of the palace.

> 39
> They kiss'd nine times the carpet's velvet face
> Of glossy silk, soft, smooth, and meadow-green,
> Where the close eye in deep rich fur might trace
> A silver tissue, scantly to be seen,
> As daisies lurk'd in June-grass, buds in treen;
> Sudden the music ceased, sudden the hand
> Of majesty, by dint of passion keen,
> Doubled into a common fist, went grand,
> And knock'd down three cut glasses, and his best ink-stand.

This is only one of numerous examples of obvious self-parody in "The Jealousies." But I want to complicate the usual definition of "self-parody" in this case. Neither simply self-abnegation on Keats's part, nor Romantic irony exactly (in the Schlegelian sense discussed in chapter 5 below), these lines seem aimed deliberately to satirize conventional Juvenalian spleen—the public scourging of "unnatural" eroticism—and at the same time, to satirize a vulnerable side of Keats's own authorial persona: the sentimental Endymion or Cockney cupid. In other words, here Keats is simultaneously writing like "Keats" *and* like a *Blackwood's* reviewer, exhibiting a discursive promiscuity to rival the stylistic crossings for which he was ridiculed in the first place and in effect displaying himself as a victim of satire before the fact. No wonder the result should appear to later, sympathetic critics reading biographically as an uncontrolled display of a "tension" between the "personal and the public" spheres of Keats's life. But it is my contention that the fragment is better understood as ironically inscribing the conflict between "manly" public satire and feminized "Della Cruscan" fancy.

The fragment represents the conflict between private and public levels of decorum, but perhaps as a by-product of its Della Cruscanism. Many readers were revolted by the Della Cruscans because they blurred the line between genders and the line between private passion and public rhetoric, thus violating social propriety and literary decorum. In Hazlitt's terms, they had played a "game" of "asking" what each others' "thoughts were like" and then publishing them.[36] One of Gifford's tricks was paradoxically to combine alarm at the public plague of Della Cruscanism with counterimages of sickly, impotent, private scribblers, the follies of an incestuous coterie writing only for itself. "Lo, Della Crusca! In his closet pent, / He toils to give the crude conception vent" (*Baviad*, 9–10). Merry's and Cowley's scandalous 1788 poetic correspondence in the newspaper, *The World,* appeared to its critics as an unholy mixture of erotic epistle and public ode, private intercourse and political discourse. It is possible to see Keats producing a similar medley of private innuendo and public satire in "The Jealousies," but in this case he combines a recognizably Della Cruscan frivolity with its own reflexive satiric remedy.

Defending the Satiric Victims

"The Jealousies" is the product of a moment when satiric discipline was still being effectively applied in public to an emergent Romanticism that was configured by its critics as Della Crusca *redivivus*. Gifford was still being taken as the authority in such matters, the one who had established the use of violent satiric criticism as the moral (and crypto-political) weapon of choice against "the ropy drivel of rheumatic brains," the sentimental erotic verse—particularly with liberal or radical affiliations, a "poetics of dissent" or, in the telling phrase of the satirist of the Cockney School, a stylistic way to "lisp sedition."[37] To look at the process from the other side, one powerful mode of satire after Gifford therefore retrenches in order to present itself as everything its target is not—masculine, disciplined, moral, and public.

For years after, even when the *Baviad* and the *Maeviad* (not to mention lesser lights such as *The Pursuits of Literature*) had left the literary stage, defenses of Gifford's or Mathias's victims took place on the attackers' terms—as chivalric duels over the honor of the weak, particularly the women authors associated with the Della Cruscans. Thomas Campbell's *Life of Mrs. Siddons,* for example, offers a backhanded compliment to the Della Cruscan Hannah

Cowley, "Anna Matilda" herself, but as a dramatist, recommending her comedy particularly "to those who despise her as a *Della Cruscan* poetess. A recognition of her merits as a comic writer is the more due to her, that they were forgotten by the world in her latter years, when the author of the 'Baviad' and 'Maeviad' lashed her under the assumed name of Anna Matilda."[38] While acknowledging that Cowley "deserved admonition" for having published her "cartloads of *Della Cruscan* rhymes," Campbell insists that "her sex and her services to literature ought to have screened her from gross vituperation. Gifford abused his power." Still, the power was his to abuse.

Similarly, Leigh Hunt repeats in his 1850 *Autobiography* what he had made clear in his earlier satire, *Ultra-Crepidarius:* that his antipathy toward Gifford was based at first on the latter's attacks on Mary Robinson and only later on the personal attacks against his own circle.[39] In a transparent gesture of sexist chivalry, Hunt depicts Robinson primarily in her role as "Perdita," the mistress of George IV, as one who "had taken to the stage for a livelihood, was very handsome, wrote verses, and is said to have excited a tender emotion in the bosom of Charles Fox." He then dwells on the aging Robinson's rheumatism, an infirmity that she ameliorated by "writing verses."

> and as her verses turned upon her affections, and she could not discontinue her old vein of love and sentiment, she fell under the lash of this masculine and gallant gentleman, Mr. Gifford, who, in his *Baviad* and *Maeviad,* amused himself with tripping up her "crutches," particularly as he thought her on her way to her last home. This he considered the climax of the fun. (87)

The weakness or lameness Gifford used as a figure for unwholesome poetics and politics becomes literalized in Hunt's supposed defense, turned into a justification for the protection of the satirized victim. As Judith Pascoe observes, Hunt's chivalric defense worked mainly to reinscribe Gifford's negative evaluations, helping to ensure that the Della Cruscan women poets were seen as defenseless, in need of protection (p. 91). Hunt is at great pains to distance himself (and his school) from the Della Cruscans as poets, even as he defends Robinson and Piozzi and attacks Gifford. His point—which was quickly becoming a critical commonplace—was that Della Cruscan poetry was too slight, too bad, to have been worth the trouble:

> The taste was as bad as can be imagined; full of floweriness, conceits, and affectation; and, in attempting to escape from commonplace, it evaporated into nonsense. . . . It was impossible that such absurdities could have had any lasting effect on the public taste. They would have died of inanition. But Mr. Gifford, finding the triumph easy, and the temptation to show his superiority irresistible, chose to think otherwise . . . (88–89)

The strategy is to show Gifford for a bully; its corollary is that Gifford's victims were weak to begin with, never strong enough for the world. Such a defense demands—to some extent, creates—pathetic victims to defend, and what was a literary and cultural battle gets reconfigured as a triumphal rout. While the canon saw to it that Shelley and Keats survived their victimage, it is clear that the Della Cruscans are already in their way to being "evaporated," even in Hunt's defense of them.

What is at stake here becomes clearer when the convention is used to refer to a poet perceived as inherently stronger than his attackers. In an 1824 obituary Sir Walter Scott describes the recently deceased Lord Byron as "the noble victim of the bull-fight . . . maddened by the squibs, darts, and petty annoyances of the unworthy crowd beyond the lists."[40] Like Keats, Byron is attacked by "squibs" or "darts"—common metaphors for satiric writing—in the public ring; unlike Keats, he is "nobler" than either his attackers or the mass audience of spectators that justifies the spectacle of his destruction. That this tableau becomes available as a set piece for an especially Romantic form of death-by-critique is confirmed by the 1834 comment of one of the era's most successful woman authors, one who needed no chivalrous protection in the press, Felicia Hemans. Remarking on an "ungentlemanly review" of her work, she claimed she "scarcely ever read any remarks" on herself, "either in praise of otherwise. Certainly no critic will ever have to boast of inflicting my death-blow."[41] On the other hand, Hemans, it must be remarked, has also not been considered as one of the (canonical) Romantics until very recently (and still is not universally so considered). The quotation above in many respects expresses a very un-Romantic and unsentimental view. The typical Romantic would be more likely to boast, before the fact, of proudly and defiantly receiving his "death blow" from a critic.

Leigh Hunt had first defended Mary Robinson as a noble female victim in 1823, in his own satire on William Gifford, *Ultra-Crepidarius.* There Gifford is improbably caricatured as an impudent shoe, which, in shockingly unchivalric fashion, trips up the goddess Venus and then refuses to apologize to her dandyish escort, Mercury. The suburban-mythological eroticism of the opening setting is pure Hunt; the cartoon image of Gifford as a shoe is pure Cruikshank; the combination of the two in a medley of fairy-tale and topical satire is strikingly like "The Jealousies." In a direct turnabout of Gifford's own class attacks, the shoe joke refers to the social-climbing Tory satirist's own humble background as the son of a cobbler. At Hunt's climax Mercury curses the ungallant, "Vile Soul of a Shoe":

> In ev'ry thing else, thou shalt be as thou art,
> A thing made for dirty ways, hollow at heart.
> Serve an earl, as thou say'st; and, in playing the shoe,

Let the stories told of thee, malicious or true,
Only lead thee hereafter to scandalize too.

(ll. 158–62)[42]

Gifford is to surpass even Pope's dunces in one thing, the curse declares—
his lack of gallantry. As Hunt says in the Preface, he had already struck a retaliatory blow, in his *Feast of the Poets,* at the attacker of Robinson, and "For
this, *and for attacking powerful Princes instead of their discarded Mistresses*"
(Hunt's italics), Gifford had never forgiven *him.*

Hunt then goes on to chastise Gifford for his "unfeeling" and "unchrist-
ian" attacks on Keats and Shelley. In this 1823 satire (only a year after Shelley's death, slightly longer after *Adonais,* a few years after Keats abandoned
"The Jealousies") and then later, in his autobiography, Hunt reveals an assumed connection between the two "generations" of satiric victims: the
Della Cruscans and the younger Romantics. Like Maginn, he sees them as
natural poetic kin. In both cases, a patronizing chivalry defends the sentimental writers in sentimental terms as weak, wounded, vulnerable, feminine
(or feminized) creatures of sensibility, otherworldly victims. In their essential identity, both groups are fit targets of "masculine" satire (though to use
satire in this way is deemed unchivalrous, unmanly). Their only hope is to
be defended by the likes of Hunt (in 1823 at least), by way of countersatire.
Exactly as Campbell does and literary history in general would come to do,
Hunt concedes the basic argument of taste to the Tory satirists and accepts
their caricatures of the victims, though in the case of Shelley and Keats, at
least, he claims that their constitutional weaknesses are allied with, even
somehow consequences of their ineffable "genius."

That shift from one set of victims to another, but with the addition of the
quality of "genius," is part of a process of cultural selection leading to canonization. The Romantics as a "school" are being *produced* in Hunt's account
(and numerous others like it), first by being associated with and then separated from their predecessor-poets, the despised Della Cruscans. In this double move, literary history makes a virtue of victimage, just as Shelley had done
in *Adonais* and as Keats was in part doing in "The Jealousies." The move is
essentially sacrificial, a way of turning a sincere cheek to satiric violence and
appearing to transcend petty literary wars in which satire dominates the
field—first through the vengeance exacted by the survivors and eventually
through the vindication of posterity, culminating in canonization.

Writing just after Keats's death, in a review of Shelley's elegy defending
Keats against his worldly enemies, Maginn had in his satiric review inscribed
Keats and Shelley (and Hunt and Byron, for good measure) into Gifford's
generic opposition. They became what they had participated in making
themselves into by their "massive appropriation" of the Della Cruscan mode:

fit targets of public satire. Victorian literary historians in effect inherited this opposition of satiric and Romantic from the journalists and poets. With the construction of Romanticism as a movement, the opposition survived—but transvalued. The link between Della Cruscanism and nascent Romanticism was forgotten.[43] The Della Cruscans yielded the niche to the emergent Romantics. For the one to ascend and survive, the two tinsel schools needed first to be differentiated and the weaker had to give way to the newly dominant New School. The generically related but aesthetically inferior Della Cruscans became an acceptable collective scapegoat, the sacrifice of which to the gods of taste deflected critical violence away from the Romantics (onetime "modern Della Cruscan[s]"). For this separation of the sheep from the goats to work, however, required that the basic terms of the satirists' denigration of Della Cruscanism be accepted more or less intact, while also requiring a compensatory exclusion of satire from the mainstream tradition of the Romantic period—the process that ironically served to keep William Gifford, as well as Robert Merry, out of the canon.

The satiric scourgings of the Della Cruscans and of the emergent Romantics were an opportunistic coincidence. The Della Cruscans were there as useful precursors and foils; criticism and the larger, collective (and thus to some extent impersonal) forces of canonization merely made use of them, motivated by a diverse set of cultural, ideological, and aesthetic imperatives. But cultural histories are constructed through the telling of relational narratives of contested generic identities, ways of making sense of ongoing competitions for dominance of the literary field and the accumulation of recognized cultural capital. "Satire" in this sense becomes a marker of judgments—sometimes violent—in the process of competing definitions of what matters and is worth preserving. Culture wars are frequently figured as battles of the books, genres, modes, or stances, or of competing media, discourses, or voices. (In the preceding chapter I argued that similar struggles take place at the level of the even more excluded, markedly "low" discourse of radical journalism.) In every case, they are struggles over who will survive in the cultural memory known as the canon. Both major Della Cruscan episodes, in the 1790s and after Waterloo—including the context in which Keats gets draped in the mantle of Della Crusca—are part of the history of paradigmatic identifications and exclusions by which Romanticism was made.

Victorian Postscript

In 1830 Tennyson first published in his *Juvenalia* a brilliantly compressed Theophrastian poem on a friend at Cambridge, Thomas Sunderland, entitled simply "A Character." The object of study is presented as a rigid ideologue who declaims sentimentally on sublime beauty and perfect virtue:

With a half-glance upon the sky
At night he said, 'The wanderings
Of this most intricate Universe
Teach me the nothingness of things.'
Yet could not all creation pierce
Beyond the bottom of his eye.

He spake of beauty: that the dull
Saw no divinity in grass,
Life in dead stones, or spirit in air;
Then looking as 'twere in a glass,
He smoothed his chin and sleeked his hair,
And said the earth was beautiful.

He spake of virtue: not the gods
More purely, when they wish to charm
Pallas and Juno sitting by:
And with a sweeping of the arm,
And a lack-lustre dead-blue eye,
Devolved his rounded periods.

Most delicately hour by hour
He canvassed human mysteries,
And trod on silk, as if the winds
Blew his own praises in his eyes,
And stood aloof from other minds
In impotence of fancied power.

With lips depressed as he were meek,
Himself unto himself he sold:
Upon himself himself did feed:
Quiet, dispassionate, and cold,
And other than his form of creed,
With chiselled features clear and sleek.[44]

Over the course of the stanzas, the youth reveals himself to be utterly beautiful, utterly narcissistic, only superficial in his display of Romantic sensibility. Tinsel here takes on a perfect, amoral, hypocritical sheen, which the satirist reveals by displaying rather than declaiming.

In an 1842 review of Tennyson's *Poems,* none other than Leigh Hunt himself singled out for praise what he called this "poetical satire," and did so in terms of what are now easily recognized as Romantic traits, as exemplifying the egotistical sublime.[45] In a revealing slip, Hunt mistakenly assumes the satire (which he admits shows Tennyson at the peak of his powers) is a portrait of his dead friend, Shelley. What he sees as a satiric anti-elegy for Shelley obviously troubles the reviewer, and, as if in retaliation, Hunt argues that Tennyson at *his* worst writes too much in the stigmatized mode of—and this comes as something of a surprise—Robert Merry ("hight Della Crusca")! In part, it is surprising to find that Merry is remembered at all, still infamous after all those years, the weaver of what Hunt calls "gossamer fantasies."

This provides fascinating evidence of the continued survival of the adjective "Della Cruscan" as an insult—but also as a negative touchstone. It seems to me that it is no accident that the example occurs to Hunt—almost twenty years after his own retaliatory satire on Gifford (*Ultra-Crepidarius*) and fifty years after Gifford's anti-Della Cruscan campaign—in the context of a critical discrimination of satiric and Romantic. Hunt's judgment assumes, I would suggest, what by then had become the norm: that Romantic sentiment, especially when it is linked to Promethean political or religious idealism and lays claim to its own bad eminence, is perfectly suited to be the natural target of satire.

Chapter 5 ~

Byron's Satiric "Blues": Salon Culture and the Literary Marketplace

One of the perennial conventions of satire as a genre has been misogyny, which may help to explain certain similarities in critical reactions to two otherwise widely separated late eighteenth-century coteries: the Della Cruscans in Italy and the Bluestockings in England. In both cases, violent satiric weapons were brought to bear on the perceived threat posed by what were essentially salons, social circles dedicated to literary conversation and more or less dominated by intellectual women. Some were nominal "members" of both groups (notably, Hester Thrale Piozzi and, in some critics' perception, Mary Robinson), and in both cases participants met in mixed company, "both sexes . . . jumbled together" (as William Gifford tellingly said of the Della Cruscans),[1] in the home of a lady for serious and witty conversation on literature and ideas. Members of both circles had literary pretensions and talents of their own: the Della Cruscans wrote infamous sentimental poetry in books and newspapers; many of the Bluestockings produced poetry, plays, essays, translations, or novels. Elizabeth Montagu, the hostess and leader of the original Bluestocking coterie, had written a book of Shakespeare criticism in 1769, and several members of her circle were serious authors—the most famous in the "second generation" being Fanny Burney. This literary production—quite apart from how the works themselves were received—worked to reinforce the further purpose of these gatherings: as critical *conversaziones,* taste-making tribunals that aimed actively to shape the literary canon of the day.

In this light, many of the sometimes disproportionately vicious satires against the bluestockings (I capitalize the term when referring to the original circle of the 1780s, and use the lower case for later, as it were concentric, literary circles in the same tradition) appear as preemptive strikes in the war of taste, counterattacks before the fact of potential judgments. These satires were aimed at what was still seen as a dangerous force in the newly competitive age of the reviews and nascent mass audience, a surviving form of traditional salon culture, which as a matter of course passed literary judgment on texts and authors. But the Revolutionary-era and early nineteenth-century bluestockings passed their judgments in a relatively new environment increasingly dominated by concerns over book sales rather than court opinion. It was widely feared that they also contributed to the growing feminization of literary taste. As it had since the late eighteenth century, later salon culture represented a volatile, fashionable, and potentially humiliating force in literary life. This is vividly represented in the 1996 film by Patrice Leconte, *Ridicule,* in which the fortunes of an entire provincial village turn on the competitive display of wit and verbal aggression in a small circle of influential courtiers. In the early nineteenth century, however, the salon began to play the subtly but significantly different role of helping to make the canon of modern literature, then coming into being dominated by emergent Romanticism.[2] Though they often represented themselves as democracies of talent, and were open to nonaristocrats and wits of various stations, these salons retained something of the aura of the court life of the previous era. Moreover, as literary circles, they possessed the more modern and more imperious power of fashion itself. As Pierre Bourdieu formulates it, this modern form of patronage exercises the power of "peremptory verdicts which, in the name of taste, condemn to ridicule, indignity, shame, silence," works and careers.[3] Such judicial rhetoric and judgmental condemnation, it is worth remarking, has traditionally been the privilege of satire.

In early nineteenth-century England, attitudes toward salon culture were further complicated and politicized in new ways by the perceived connections among such feminine havens, the cult of sensibility, and the French Revolution. Given the fervor of state-sponsored antijacobinism and the general atmosphere during the wars, it is hardly surprising that the less aristocratic and more earnest English literary coteries—even if they showed little affinity with French ideas and self-consciously set themselves apart from them—should be seen by English critics as threatening the status quo, as potential sources of cultural corruption and general leveling. Quite apart from party politics, *femmes savantes* of any political persuasion would have represented a frightening combination of old-regime social power and new-fashioned intellectual aspiration. This combination remained threatening in part because such gatherings had traditionally been the arena of wit and ridicule—before the fashion had shifted to at least *professing* a simpler, more sincere conversation. The potential for satiric verbal aggression within supposedly polite literary society remained an integral feature of salon culture.

This potential is well illustrated in Virginia Woolf's sketch-portrait of Alexander Pope and his social milieu in *Orlando*. On the surface, she represents the stunted satirist as an unwelcome, threatening presence whose malicious wit could shatter the happy illusion of social harmony:

> the door opened and a little gentleman entered whose name Orlando did not catch. Soon a curiously disagreeable sensation came over her. To judge by their faces, the rest began to feel it as well. . . . It was as if their eyes were being slowly opened after a pleasant dream and nothing met them but a cheap wash-stand and a dirty counterpane. It was as if the fumes of some delicious wine were slowly leaving them. . . . No society could survive it.[4]

Feeling Pope's verbal barbs, the salon disperses in horror. The rough satirist shatters the illusion of polite social cohesion, a picture in keeping with Robert C. Elliott's anthropological speculation about the ritualistic power of "primitive" satire.[5] Elliott outlines an ethnographic version of the genre in which the satirist is a borderline figure tainted by the powerful magic he wields, a figure both within and yet always standing outside the circle of civilization, like the "satyr" in the false but popular etymology of "satire." The coherence of certain highly formalized societies, if not civilization as a whole, may depend upon such rough figures—as dark mirrors of their own foundational aggression, ritual scapegoats that make possible the refined group identity.[6] The rhetorical violence just at the edge of the most polite society is frequently embodied and thus contained by the recognizable figure of the "satirist."

Woolf shares this modern view of society and aggression. Pope is a satyr-figure in her sketch, only half civilized. She knows that satire and the salons of civilization are not incompatible; indeed, her own style in this passage is itself satiric, as if she would defend the salon against the satirist who would expose it. But though Pope seems at first her primary satiric target, the supposedly naive illusions and pale witticisms of the imagined salon are also satirized by Woolf. From the ironic perspective of the modern age, the salon is absurd in its illusions and stiff sentimentality. Woolf's sympathies are to some degree with Pope, the outcast author, but my point is that her assumption of the opposition of satirist and society, with the recognition that the satirist is still somehow needed by such circles, is worth remembering when looking at salon culture. In practice, at least in many circles, coveted invitations were likely to go to those guests who, like Pope, possessed a fashionably dangerous wit, those who knew how to infuse social conversation with the spice of satire. On the face of it, it would seem likely that satiric depictions of the obvious absurdities of court or salon—depictions frequently driven by traditional misogyny—would underplay the possibility that satire might emanate from the woman-dominated parlor. For obvious reasons, satire itself would want to mask the degree to which the power to ridicule lay on both sides, the degree to which the coterie and its satirists co-existed, held in a mutual tension of potential humiliation. Historical accounts tend to overlook the power of the threat posed *by* salons, too often taking at face value depictions of these small societies as ineffectual, silly, and unselfconsciously sentimental. From the inside, such devaluation is abetted by self-portraits of the salons as wholly benevolent conversations devoid of party divisions and verbal rancor.

Elizabeth Montagu's salons were in fact powerful generative resources for cultural judgment and changing taste, including producing occasional satiric attacks of their own. Even where direct financial support was not involved, this represented a late form of patronage for (male and female) authors of various stations. Public influence, reputation, and cultural capital—not to mention book sales—were increased or reduced by the coteries. The institution of the salon, like the critical review against which it competed for influence, was an arbiter of taste, as Chauncey Tinker has said, "at once feared and courted by authors who affected at times to despise its pronouncements but never ignored them. The salon mediated between the author and the public."[7] This mediating role of salon culture is an important link in understanding the role of satire in the Romantic era, a time in which the increasing professionalism and vaunted autonomy of literature as a field, aided by the "development of a veritable cultural industry" in conjunction with "the extension of the public, resulting from the expansion of primary education, which turned new classes (including women) into consumers of culture,"[8] was on the other hand met with numerous idealizations of domestic social space. In this era the borderline private/public sphere of the salon began to give way to the press, the nascent mass reading audience, and the critical review.

In this chapter I examine the shifting relations between the salon and the literary marketplace—including booksellers, reviews, and the growing public consumption of fashionable intellectual productions—through the device of Byron's late satire on "The Blues." In the context of the salons this skit appears as a common-enough type of satiric preemptive strike: it ridicules in retaliation for anticipated, imagined ridicule against its own author. Like much satire, it is in part a talismanic gesture meant to ward off potential mortification. But in the specific context of Byron's career and conflicted personae, "The Blues" also demonstrates how the threat of satiric judgment was increasingly felt as coming from the reviews and their shaping of taste as well from within the salons, both of which threatened to affect one's status before the "public" (figured in the skit directly as the lecture circuit). In this complicated way the threat (sometimes realized) of satire emanated from the salons on the one side and the marketplace on the other, both ways of defining what counted as important literature—even at the height of the era of Romantic sentiment and sincerity. "The Blues" will serve my purpose admirably well, despite or even because of its ephemeral nature and "minor" status in Byron's canon, because it openly engages in the sort of squabbles for status that his more canonical satires can merely assume to be settled and thus quietly ignore, or ridicule as beneath contempt. Byron's minor satire wears its marketplace anxieties on its sleeve, whereas *Don Juan* affects an assured success beyond the realm of the tastemakers and book sales. Moreover, the squib is useful because it reveals Byron's homosocial and literary-professional anxieties as he continued, even this late in his career, to stake out an authorial position between the coterie and commercial publishing.

The Birth of the Blues

The term "bluestocking" has a long history with disjunct stages, but as a label for intellectual women it dates to the London Blue Stocking Club of the 1770s and 1780s, centered in the salon of Elizabeth Montagu. The term was used in the 1760s to refer to men who were friends of Montagu's and Elizabeth Vesey's social circle.[9] One etymology suggests it referred to the socially inappropriate dark stockings worn by a male visitor, Benjamin Stillingfleet. By the 1770s, references to bluestockings had begun to focus on women, and by the 1780s the more formal Blue Stocking salon had become well-known, celebrated for example in Hannah More's poem, *Bas Bleu; or Conversation* (1786). This circle included Montagu and Vesey, as well as Frances Boscawen, Elizabeth Carter, Catherine Talbot, Hester Chapone, and secondarily or by association, Hester Thrale Piozzi, Hannah More, Ann Yearsley, and Fanny Burney. By extension, women authors or *savantes* outside this circle were soon being identified as bluestockings.

The type itself was the latest product of the long satiric tradition, a recognizable version of the threatening amazons and society women of numerous Augustan works (in which they often wore the literary mask of one of Juvenal's targets), but with the modern qualities of democratic and intellectual aspiration. Molière had mocked such women long before the birth of the English club, and Montagu was in part inspired by a visit to the French hostesses in 1775; the English Bluestockings developed out of a French social phenomenon.[10] One difference is that the English salons were more socially and politically conservative than the French, and were at least perceived as being (and represented themselves as) more earnest and sincere in their conversational style.[11] More's *Bas Bleu*, for example, holds up the English Bluestockings's "common sense" and "simplicity" over the earlier eighteenth-century fashion for wit and ridicule, offering this encomium to "colloquial wit":

> Our intellectual ore must shine,
> Not slumber idly in the mine.
> Let education's moral mint
> The noblest images imprint;
> Let taste her curious touchstone hold,
> To try if standard be the gold;
> But 'tis thy commerce, Conversation,
> Must give it use by circulation;
>
> (ll. 288–95)[12]

More's modest emphasis here on English "good sense" carries political connotations and it is one reason Richard Polwhele, in his anti-Wollstonecraft diatribe, *The Unsex'd Females* (1798), appeals to Montagu's circle as containing positive alternatives, more properly conservative models for women of letters.[13] The vicious satire on Mary Wollstonecraft, Mary Hays, and Helen Maria Williams is counterbalanced with the conclusion, as if in the voice of More, lifting up the Blue Stocking Circle for praise:

> "Yet woman owns a more extensive sway
> "Where Heaven's own graces pour the living ray:
> "And vast its influence o'er the social ties,
> "By Heaven inform'd, if female genius rise
> "Its power how vast, in critic wisdom sage,
> "If MONTAGUE refine a letter'd age;
> "And CARTER, with a milder air, diffuse
> "The moral precepts of the Grecian Muse;
> "And listening girls perceive a charm unknown
> "In grave advice, as utter'd by CHAPONE;
> "If SEWARD sting with rapture every vein,
> "Or gay PIOZZI sport in lighter strain;
> "If BURNEY mix with sparkling humour chaste
> "Delicious feelings and the purest taste,
> "Or RADCLIFFE wrap in necromantic gloom
> "The impervious forest and the mystic dome;
> "If BEAUCLERK paint Lenora's spectre-horse,
> "The uplifted lance of death, the grisly corse;
> "And e'en a Princess lend poetic grace
> "The pencil's charm, and breathe in every trace.
> She ceas'd and round their MORE the sisters sigh'd!

Soft on each tongue repentant murmurs died.
And sweetly scatter'd (as they glanc'd away)
Their conscious "blushes spoke a brighter day."

(ll. 183–206)

Polwhele finds in one set of women a counterweight to the feminists and radicals quickly becoming prominent in public representations of intellectual women.

There is a structural analogy between the conventional form of the couplet satire, with its litany of proper names, and the structure of salons themselves, both in terms of the architecture of interiors and in terms of sociological rankings of preeminence and subordination within an apparently egalitarian space. As Elizabeth Fay has pointed out,

> Bluestocking salons were carefully yet casually engineered so that participants gathered in select groups within small rooms and areas within the hostess's house, all of these conversational spaces leading effortlessly toward the central space where the hostess reclined with a few select companions. Eventually everyone had to pass through her room. Salon structure, then, orchestrates conversational interaction, directing its flow back to the centering space.[14]

The reader proceeds through Polwhele's satire, "escorted" by the authorial voice as if spatially passing through a salon, encountering conversationalists one at a time, remarking upon them or hearing their own words, judging and dismissing them, and then moving on to the next. The outer circle consists of the bad examples of "unsexed females," but as the poem concludes, the reader is brought into the presence of an inner circle of the original Blue Stockings, listening (it turns out, once the reader is told who is speaking) to Hannah More, thus placed in the core of the "salon" structure of the poem at the place of honor, just as the hostess would be encountered last at the center of a real salon in her home. Polwhele's poem is a useful reminder that "bluestockings" in the 1790s were not strictly associated with jacobinism, because Montagu's original circle was largely conservative, still providing a center and a ruling decorum in female manners.

Eventually, antifeminist attacks on bluestockings came to generalize the type outside this particular group, to include all women of progressive intellectual ambitions, radical or liberal women in particular. By 1826, Sir Walter Scott could feel compelled to defend an acquaintance (Lady Anna Maria Elliot) in these general terms:

> It is the fashion for women and silly men to abuse her as a blue-stocking—If to have wit, good sense and good humour, mixd [*sic*] with a strong power of

observing and an equally strong one of expressing the result, be *blue,* she shall be as blue as they will.

"Such cant," Scott suggests, was usually prompted by the attackers' own fear of ridicule; it "is the refuge of those who fear those they [think] can turn them into ridicule—it is a common trick to revenge supposed raillery with good substantial calumny."[15] I want to return to the wisdom in Scott's apparent commonplace: that ridicule of the bluestockings was often motivated by a perceived threat, a fear of being ridiculed *by* the bluestockings: I think the anti-bluestocking satires have succeeded so well that readers forget how serious such threats seemed at the time. But the rise of salon culture and the recognizable type of the intellectual woman as hostess and conversationalist marks a shift of power, however slight, to woman's traditional sphere, the social-domestic, as a source of public taste—at the same time a nascent mass audience and increasingly autonomous profession of letters were developing as part of the new literary marketplace.

The English Bluestockings of the 1770s and 1780s gave their name to a gendered threat more than merely political in the narrow sense. In later satires against blues, antijacobinism gives way to more generalized antifeminist and misogynist attacks. In part this simply marks the continuation of the "timeless" tradition of misogynist satire, the tradition that includes Juvenal and Swift as well as Gifford. But it is also likely that anti-bluestocking satire was written in part in reaction to the specific threat—namely the feminization of literary taste—posed by the salon in the era of a radically changing profession of letters. Gifford and Wolcot, and (in a different way) Polwhele and Mathias, and the reviews in general, stand for the satiric defense of literary taste as a masculine preserve over and against the women-dominated groups of tastemakers.[16]

Byron aligned himself with such traditionally masculine and satiric taste (in his case often signified by an allegiance to Pope) over and against his own and his contemporaries' sentimental experiments—that is, emergent Romanticism. Even within the texts of his complex corpus of work, the Romantic and the un-Romantic (or satiric) counter and define one another, and, as is often the case with Byron, this is reflected in the text of his personality as well. Lady Blessington's *Conversations* with Byron (recorded in 1823) include this pithy observation on his famous mobility:

> Byron seems to take a peculiar pleasure in ridiculing sentiment and romantic feelings; and yet the day after will betray both, to an extent that appears impossible to be sincere, to those who had heard his previous sarcasms: that he is sincere, is evident, as his eyes fill with tears, his voice becomes tremulous, and his whole manner evinces that he feels what he says.[17]

And yet, only the day before he had been ridiculing such "romantic" senti-ment. Such "inconsistent" attitudes, as Lady Blessington refers to them, are more than a personality quirk; they feed into the generic mobility of Byron's work, as well, and become a characteristic feature of his style. The young au-thor who in the public eye *was* the sentimental Childe Harold had also pro-duced *English Bards and Scotch Reviewers*. Byron always wished to be identified with the school of Pope as it was carried on in William Gifford's satire, and in the Preface to *English Bards* he attacks the "perverted powers" of his generation of authors and says that he would draft William Gifford to expose them, but in his absence will himself take the satirist's place, a "coun-try practitioner" taking over for the "regular physician."[18]

Besides serving as the scourge of the Della Cruscans in *The Baviad* (1791) and *The Maeviad* (1795), Gifford was also editor of the Tory *Quar-terly Review* from 1809 to 1824. His authority on satire, however, was re-inforced by his edition of Juvenal's *Satires*, which first appeared in 1802, then in a second edition of 1806 and a third in 1817. In part because Gif-ford was already well known as a practicing satirist, the edition was widely anticipated before publication, even, for example, by the radical William Cobbett.[19] As had become traditional since Casaubon and Dryden, the edi-tion was prefaced by a substantial "Essay on the Roman Satirists," in which Gifford defines the Juvenalian satire as a mode of "energy, passion, and in-dignation"(liii).[20] Though Byron's style is usually identified with the Hora-tian conversational mode, he was also obviously attracted to the idea of Juvenal's *genus grande* as the passionate style of moral outrage. (*English Bards and Scotch Reviewers* was after all directly modeled on Juvenal's First Satire.)[21] Byron admired Gifford because he saw him as a modern Juvenal scourging the age with fearless, *feeling* truth-telling. In *Don Juan*, for ex-ample, violent anger directed at Castlereagh sits adjacent to haughty irony and nostalgic sentimentality over his own lost youth. Even within his satiric oeuvre, then, mixed tones prevail, and the Byronic version of Romanticism as a whole is based on conflicts between subtle variations on the sentimen-tal and satiric modes.

When Byron writes "The Blues," he is still fighting a rear-guard action against all-but-accomplished changes in English literary values—changes he feared he had helped to effect in his earlier sentimental work. But he is doing so in "a mere buffoonery." This makes his fantasies of salon culture all the more interesting, since it is clear—in his satire and also in his letters—that Byron proves Scott's point: he ridiculed the blues largely our of fear of being ridiculed, of being himself ridiculous, even if after the fact, in his earlier in-carnation as the darling of the salons. Despite the historical setting for the satire, in the halcyon days of the Regency, the generalized category of the bluestockings still represented in 1821 a power for the making of literary reputations and the canon that Byron could not quite ignore, even as he ridiculed it as a thing of the past.

The Byronic "Blues"

In 1821 Byron was established in Italian exile, an expatriate involved with the Liberal Carbonari in Ravenna and with the Countess Teresa Guiccoli, but still keeping one eye on English politics, literature, and gossip, and producing a remarkable list of literary works of his own. In that year he continued *Don Juan* and published *Marino Faliero, Sardanapalus,* and *Two Foscari,* as well as engaging in the ongoing controversy with Bowles over the merits of Pope. On 7 August, he mailed to John Murray a short satiric skit apparently set in the era of his earliest literary fame, circa 1812–14, titled "The Blues: A Literary Eclogue." His note to Murray calls it simply

> a thing which I scratched off lately—a mere buffoonery—to quiz "the Blues" in two literary eclogues.—If published it must be *anonymously*—but it is too short for a separate publication—and *you* have no miscellany that I know of— for the reception of such things.—You may send me a proof if you think it worth the trouble—but don't let *my* name out—for the present—or I shall have all the old women in London about my ears—since it sneers at the so- lace of their antient Spinsterstry.[22]

On 20 September he told Murray that he never intended to publish the satire, but despite this–and despite the conventional dismissiveness of the first letter—Byron took the time to mail and consider publishing this "buf- foonery" (apparently in some journalistic venue). It sat at Murray's until Byron recalled it less than two years later and published it in the third number (23–26 April 1823) of the literary journal he had started with Leigh Hunt, *The Liberal.*[23] Moreover, he expected it to be controversial, at least among the now-aged bluestockings of the earlier decade: he joked, at least, about what they might do to him in retaliation for its quizzing. What they were most likely to do was *talk* about him and thus expose him to fur- ther ridicule at a time when his way of life in Italy and the publication of the first cantos of *Don Juan* left him highly vulnerable to such exposure. On the basis of this contextual history, it seems to me worth paying closer at- tention to this satire than has been common in Byron studies.[24] "The Blues" offers a useful way in to Byron's surviving attitudes toward the blue- stockings. But it is also an interesting focal point for questions surrounding then-established salon culture and the modern profession of letters, as well as the imminent threat—in the public arena whose borders these two spheres demarcated—of critical, judgmental ridicule, one of the primary ingredients of satire.

The setting of "The Blues" is fashionable literary London around 1812–14, in the overlapping spheres of lecture hall, bookseller, and salon. Tellingly, the bluestockings themselves make only a brief appearance in Eclogue II. Mostly the spotlight is on the two central male characters, Inkel and Tracy, probably based on Byron and Tom Moore respectively, and their talk about the bluestockings but also about publishing and reviewing. Byron's sympathies are finally with the miserable husband of a bluestocking hostess, Sir Richard Bluebottle (who may be based on Lord Holland but also somewhat resembles Sheridan's Old Sir Peter in *The School for Scandal*). Sir Richard is given the final words of the play: "I wish all these people were d——d with *my* marriage!"

As the satire opens, Inkel and Tracy are standing "Before the Door of a Lecture Room," in which their acquaintance Scamp is holding forth to the gathered, paying public. Jerome McGann reasonably suggests that the lecturer Scamp may be Coleridge, perhaps combined with the Hazlitt of 1818.[25] While Byron surely would have had these famous fashionable lecturers in mind (Hazlitt's interest in literary "schools" seems especially relevant), it also seems possible that Scamp is partly based on Byron and Moore's mutual friend from the London *says*, Campbell (whose name may be embedded in the name "S*camp*"). In his journal entry of 1 December 1813, Byron notes that "C[ampbell] talks of lecturing next spring; his last lectures were eminently successful. Moore thought of it, but gave it up" (*BLJ* 3, 232). At any rate, the setting of the lecture hall reinforces the nostalgia of the satire, its act of recollection of Byron's old male club of worldly writers, along with their ambivalent involvement with the bluestocking coterie. Everyone who was anyone in the literary world of 1812 was familiar with the institution or genre of the fashionable tastemaking lecture, a dramatization of the author as a performer before the paying public. The salon is a meeting in private space of the fashionable and influential, but the lecture takes place in the physical embodiment of the public sphere, a modern parody of the agora of the ancients, a literal marketplace of ideas commodified and consumed by an audience. Scamp's audience is apparently made up largely of "the pride of our belles,"

> who have made it the fashion;
> So, instead of "beaux arts," we may say "la *belle* passion"
> For learning, which lately has taken the lead in
> The world, and set all the fine gentlemen reading.
>
> (I.3–6)

But the focus remains significantly *outside* the hall, with Inkel and Tracy, who linger at the door and make fun of the proceedings while noting how crowded the hall has become. Setting themselves apart, they say they are not "fine gentlemen" but worldly literary men, most at home on Paternoster Row among the booksellers. Their initial exchange about the lecture in progress soon gives way to talk of the writing profession, sales, and reviews. From this serious business the lecture is merely an annoying distraction. Tracy has just come from a publisher's shop, where he had been "skimming a charming critique, / So studded with wit, and so sprinkled with Greek!"— a ferocious attack on an unnamed friend of Inkel's, whose reply reveals the pull of such writing, even for those who claim to ignore it:

> So they've cut up our friend then?
> *Tracy.*   Not left him a tatter—
> Not a rag of is present or past reputation,
> Which they call a disgrace to the age and the nation.
> *Inkel.* I'm sorry to hear this; for friendship, you know—
> Our poor friend!—but I thought it would terminate so.
> Our friendship is such, I'll read nothing to shock it.
> You don't happen to have the Review in your pocket?
>
> (I.29–35)

Thus from the opening lines Byron comically plays upon very real anxieties surrounding authorship in the age of the reviews and the new patronage of the booksellers. Critiques like the one under discussion—as found in the *Quarterly Review,* for example—fall under the broad generic rubric of satire. In most cases they ridicule their target, even indulge in personal invective, in order to demean and discredit it. This is especially the case with the *Quarterly* or *Blackwood's,* journals whose weapons of choice in the culture wars of the early nineteenth century were so often the tropes of vitriolic satire, and whose reviews (as for example in the attacks on Hunt, Keats, and Shelley as "modern Della Cruscans") frequently included poetic parodies as part of their arsenal.[26] In this opening scene of Byron's skit, the threat posed by such destructive reviews is transparently matched by the threat posed on the distaff side, as it were, from the "belles" and their subversion of artistic taste. Indeed, the blues take the reviews too seriously, borrowing from them too solemnly, thus increasing the power of the former.

This is also the danger of literary lectures, whose opinions are magnified in effect by the patronage of the coteries. The fashionable lecturer Scamp (whom Inkel and Tracy disdain to hear) has also been co-opted by the ladies, made a pet and a fool of the salon. Inkel confesses that he is "engaged to the Lady Bluebottle's collation,"

To partake of a luncheon and learn'd conversation:
'Tis a sort of re-union for Scamp, on the days
Of his lecture, to treat him with cold tongue and praise.
And I own, for my own part, that 'tis not unpleasant.

(I.137–41)

Tracy agrees to go in order to see one Miss Lilac (probably based on Annabella Milbanke), a bluestocking he is pursuing. He is not in search of "cold tongue" or "praise." As he has just reminded us, speaking from behind the mask that is more or less in the voice of Byron, his "own grand romance"

> *Tracy.*   Had its full share of praise.
> I myself saw it puffed in the "Old Girl's Review."
>
> (I. 124–25)

This clear self-allusion to the popular and critical success of *Childe Harold's Pilgrimage* works as a witty charm against Byron's appearing to care one way or another what any salon says. Inkel's share of praise comes straight from the masculine public sphere of the reviews, which he only pretends not to want to read. Never mind that Byron's fame in the earlier decade, largely as a result of that "grand romance," was as much a function of fashionable society's collective opinion, the judgment of *ton,* as it was of public journalism; the two forms of opinion fed one another in making the myth of "Byron." The skit, however, projects a practical separation of these spheres of influence in order to trivialize the one in (relative) favor of the other, at least to hold out the possibility of a separation of the world of action (including publishing) from the world of fashion ("*le beau monde*").

This is more than nostalgia. In the autumn of 1821, just after having written "The Blues," Byron was still very much interested in what the reviews had to say in their "praise" and its opposite, so interested that he found it necessary to cut himself off from their pernicious influence on his confidence and creativity. On 24 September—just days after telling Murray not to bother returning "The Blues"—he asked him to send a more restricted list of literary works by selected authors, and absolutely no periodicals. This, he confessed, was "to keep my mind *free and* unbiased—by all paltry and personal irritabilities of praise or censure":

—if they regard *myself*—they tend to increase *Egotism,*—if favourable—I do not deny that the praise *elates*—and if unfavourable that the abuse *irritates*—the latter may conduct me to inflict a species of Satire—which would neither do good to you nor to your friends—*they* may smile *now,* and so may *you* but if I took you all in hand—it would not be difficult to cut you up like gourds. . . . Therefore let me hear none of your provocations—(*BLJ* 8, 219–21).

Besides being sensitive to the praise and censure of the reviews, Byron also possessed a strong reflex for satiric retaliation, a willingness to threaten cutting satire as revenge before the fact, a preemptive measure against "provocations."

Praise and censure, the threat of satire in making taste and its tyrannies—these are the serious topics behind Byron's seemingly trivial skit. "The Blues" is a decidedly male literary fantasy. It is far less about the bluestockings per se (except as scapegoats and foils) than it is about projecting an ideal of the modern literary profession as an autonomous, public, masculine, and rational arena, one free of the vicissitudes of coterie tastemaking and of the newly powerful forces of the competitive market for literary commodities. The not-so-hidden truth of the skit, however, is that these spheres remain deeply entangled and that in the face of the triumphal marketplace, Byron's satire can only imagine and project the modern profession of letters in the form of an alternative coterie, as a masculine, homosocial mirror of the blues.

Refusing Invitations from the "Inviting Ones"

In that legendary season just after *Childe Harold*'s first appearance, when Byron awoke to find himself famous, his appearances in society—including at the collations of various bluestockings—were many and frequent. His journal from 17 November 1813 gives a sense of this social activity, and mentions many of the actual names who end up as characters in "The Blues":

> * * [Sotheby] is a *Littérateur*, the Oracle of the Coteries, of the * *s [?Berry sisters] L[ydia] W[hite] (Sydney Smith's "Tory Virgin"), Mrs. Wilmot (she, at least, is a swan, and might frequent a purer stream,) Lady B[eaumont,] and all the Blues, with Lady C[harlemont] at their head—
> ... M[oor]e has a peculiarity of talent, or rather talents,—poetry, music, voice, all his own. ... In society, he is gentlemanly, gentle, and, altogether more pleasing than any individual with whom I am acquainted. ... He has but one fault—and that one I daily regret—he is not *here*. (*BLJ* 3, 214–15)

Byron remembered himself and Moore as comrades only superficially caught up in the social whirl at the time, but they were obviously caught up nonetheless. His erotic life had been especially complicated at this season; he encountered both Lady Caroline Lamb and that ultimate (and for Byron fatally attractive) bluestocking, Annabella Milbanke, at these very *conversaziones*. But this earlier letter to Moore shows how Byron represented all this social activity as something secondary to the bond between the two of them, an excuse for reinforcing that bond:

I should have answered your note yesterday, but I hoped to have seen you this morning. I must consult with you about the day we dine with Sir Francis. I suppose we shall meet at Lady Spencer's to-night. I did not know that you were at Miss Berry's the other night, or I should have certainly gone there. (*BLJ* 2, 173–74)

Miss Mary Berry—probably also alluded to in the journal entry—was a well-known bluestocking hostess. Byron and Moore would have made impressive trophy-guests at her salon. Significantly, in the weeks that followed this letter, such social memoranda are matched by numerous queries to John Murray about critical reviews of *Childe Harold,* a strangely negative foreshadowing—and the logical flip-side—of Byron's refusal of reviews in 1821. (One goes so far out of one's way *not* to read only writing that has mattered and still might matter a great deal.) Again, the coteries and the reviews are parts of one powerful system of tastemaking, reputation-building or -destroying, held in tension between the masculine world and the feminine salon. This tension is the background—and is more or less successfully relegated *to* the background—of "The Blues."

What exactly prompted Byron to begin the satire when he did remains unclear. It may have been the same nostalgia for his own youth and the fashionable Regency world—"that microcosm on stilts," *le monde* (*DJ* XII.56)— that would soon show up in the English cantos of *Don Juan.* As Jerome McGann points out, he wrote the famous lament in *Don Juan* XI for the passing of this world ("'tis gone, a globe of glass" [st. 76]) in October 1822, and "The Blues" was part of Byron's "large recollective writing project" in that same period.[27] And I would suggest it is at least possible that the skit could have been planned for the projected weekly newspaper he discussed with Tom Moore at the end of 1820 and considered returning to England to publish.

I have been thinking of a project for you and me, in case we both get to London again, which (if Neapolitan war don't suscitate) may be calculated as possible for one of us about the spring of 1821. I presume that you, too, will be back by that time, or never; but on that you will give me some index. The project, then, is for you and me to set up jointly a *newspaper*—nothing more or less—weekly, or so, with some improvement or modifications upon the plan of the present scoundrels, who degrade that department,—but a *newspaper*— which we will edite [*sic*] in due form, and, nevertheless, with some attention.

There must always be in it a piece of poesy from one or other of us *two,* leaving room, however, for such dilettanti writers as may be deemed worthy of appearing in the same column: but *this* must be a *sine qua non;* and also as much prose as we can compass. We will take an *office*—our names *not* announced, but suspected—and, by the blessing of Providence, give the age some new lights upon policy, poesy, biography, criticism, morality, theology, and all other *ism, ality,* and *ology* whatsoever. (*BLJ* 7, 253–54)

He closes the letter intriguingly enough, "If you think this worth a thought, let me know, and I will begin to lay in a small literary capital of composition for the occasion." Though the satire was not written until later in 1821, after the plan to return to England seems to have been more or less abandoned, it is possible that Byron conceived of the *idea* for "The Blues"—a self-mocking return to his and Moore's salad days with characters based on the two of them—as a work for the ill-fated periodical. Either way, the plan for a newspaper makes it clear that he was aware of and concerned with the public arena as a competitive space requiring "literary capital" for success.

The connection between "The Blues" and Tom Moore is significant for several reasons. Byron's London life around 1812 represented for him a moment in which the social whirl of London *conversaziones,* the companionship of Moore (the model for Tracy), and his own rising literary career overlapped as daily preoccupations. Moore's own more topical and timely comic opera on this social world, *M.P.; or the Blue-stocking,* had been performed the previous autumn (September 1811). It lampoons the follies of one Lady Bab Blue and her male friends and juxtaposes the fashionably intellectual salon with the publishing enterprise (represented by Leatherhead the bookseller); there is also a silly male coxcomb who serves as the pet of the blues (Davy). As Sir Charles Canvas remarks, "I never yet knew a learned lady, that did not delight in having a booby to shew off upon.—whether it be in the shape of a servant, lover, or husband, these curious copies of Sappho generally have a calf-skin at their backs" (I.i). (Byron's Botherby belongs in this same category.) The moral of Moore's opera is put in the mouth of Mr. Hartigan: "learn as much as you please, but learn also to conceal it.—I could even bear a little peep at the blue-stockings, but save me from the woman who shews them up to her knees!" It isn't surprising that Byron's own skit on this same topic should return to Moore (and base a main character on him). It is set in the era of his social heyday with Moore, the time when Moore's own opera was produced.

According to the later recollections of Lady Blessington, herself a salon hostess and traveler who recorded her conversations with Byron in Italy in the spring of 1823, Byron still had a great deal to say in those latter years about bluestockings and literary men—and especially his friend Moore.[28] James Soderholm rightly cautions that Lady Blessington is likely to have performed her own distortions on Byron's conversation, but the particular remarks in which I am interested are consonant with other reports and texts by Byron, and generally ring true.[29] In recording and publishing her conversations with the famous poet, Blessington was playing the Boswell-like role associated with that famous bluestocking, Hester Thrale Piozzi; in Leigh Hunt's very late poem, "Blue-Stocking Revelries," Blessington makes a dramatic appearance before Apollo as one of the famous "blues."[30] In this case the publication of her conversations with Lord Byron amounts to exactly the sort of "gossip," exposure, and potential ridicule (as Soderholm says [12]) that Byron feared from his affiliation with "the Blues" as a group—and feared in general. As Blessington's *Conversations* report, Byron "had an extreme susceptibility to censorious observations. . . ."

> He winces under castigation, and writhes in agony under the infliction of ridicule, yet gives rise to attack every day. Ridicule is, however, the weapon he most dreads, perhaps because it is the one he wields with most power; and I observe he is sensitively alive to its slightest approach. (109–110)

Or, to turn it around, Byron's tendency to ridicule was surely in part a self-protective measure based on his sensitivity to being ridiculed. The poet was drawn to Lady Blessington's ad hoc salons in Genoa, where he shone and apparently willingly exposed himself in some of his remarks (even assuming that some of the particular language was creatively reconstructed). It is an ironically appropriate accident that "The Blues" was finally being published in *The Liberal* at around the same time that Byron was conversing with this expert hostess and latter-day bluestocking—who apparently had designs on helping to make Byron's reputation.

According to Lady Blessington, Byron supposedly said that, while it was a mistake for "clever men" to marry women "destitute of abilities," nevertheless, "*une femme savante* is apt to be a bore." His own "*beau ideal*," he remarked, "would be a woman with talent enough to be able to understand and value mine, but not sufficient to be able to shine herself" (162). But in general, Byron asserted, "Society and genius are incompatible" (106). Lady Blessington recalls his continued improvisation on the topic, to the effect that poetic geniuses should live in utter solitude and in particular should never do anything so coarse as to dine in company (a clever enough remark for a poet to make in company, probably at dinner). The one exception to this rule, the poet admits, is his good friend Tom Moore, who "can certainly pass the ordeal of dinners without losing any of his poetical reputation, since the brilliant things that come from his lips reconcile one to the solid things that go into them" (164). Despite the virtuoso effervescence of this *bon mot,* the remark touches on a recurrent theme in these conversations, Byron's concern that the society he was obviously still enjoying was somehow threatening to his genius. This was a matter of friendly competition with his fellow (male) poet, Moore, especially during those earlier years in London. Still there is perhaps a hint of professional as well as social anxiety in Byron's remark. It echoes his infamous claim that women lost their allure when seen dining in public (unless it be on lobster salad and champagne).

> I always felt, with Moore, the desire Johnson expressed, to be shut up in a post-chaise, *tête-à-tête* with a pleasant companion, to be quite sure of him. He must be delightful in a country-house, at a safe distance from any other inviting one, when one could have him really to one's self, and enjoy his conversation and his singing, without the perpetual fear that he is expected at Lady This or Lady That's, or the being reminded that he promised to look in at Lansdowne House or Grosvenor Square . . . (pp. 292–93)

There may be a pun in the phrase "inviting one" and a note of erotic possessive jealousy behind the surface jocularity of the remark.

Byron's personal relationship with Moore is not my point; rather, I am interested in the way his experiences with salon society and the poetic career get personalized and reconfigured such that women's social invitations were seen to pose a threat to the integrity and unity of the brotherhood of male genius. These reported remarks indicate a homosocial (if not openly homoerotic)[31] interest in Moore that was both mediated and threatened by the women whose invitations both men accepted. Most important for my purposes: this triangulated competition for attention in the salons was itself competitive with the related competition for literary fame in the "world." As Inkel and Tracy affirm their bond in "The Blues," it is with a recognition of this double marketplace in which they both participate but also with a clear recognition of which "triumph" really matters in the end:

> *Tracy.*   I know what is what:
> And you, who're a man of the gay world, no less
> Than a poet of t'other, may easily guess
> That I never could mean, by a word, to offend
> A genius like you, and moreover my friend.
> *Inkel.* No doubt; you by this time should know what is due
> To a man of—but come—let us shake hands.
> *Tracy.*   You knew,
> And you *know,* my dear fellow, how heartily I,
> Whatever you publish, am ready to buy.
>
>   (I.112–20)

Though the Byronic character immediately denies any interest in anything so vulgar as sales, it is clear that the two authorial characters have shared an important—almost serious—moment in the farce. Their dispute had originally arisen over Tracy's Cyrano-like request for some lines of verse from

Inkel, the better to woo a young bluestocking (whose literary taste demands some expertise).

> In these times, there's no lure
> For the heart of the fair like a stanza or two;
> And so, as I can't, will you furnish a few?
> *Inkel.* In your name?
>> *Tracy.* In my name. I will copy them out,
> To slip into her hand at the very next rout.
>> (l. 90–94)

In passing, he makes an offhand remark competitively comparing their two styles, suggesting that his prose is "as sublime" as his friend's poetry. After some verbal sparring over that marker word denoting the supreme Romantic aesthetic virtue, they make up in the scene just quoted. The bluestocking has very nearly come between them but is put in her place in the nick of time. In this comic triangular scene they in effect reaffirm their homosocial bond as men and as authors—and this in tacit opposition to "other inviting one[s]."[32]

In another (and better-known) satire from this period, Byron made the stakes of this opposition clear. In the midst of the *buffo* marriage farce of *Beppo,* Byron the narrator, apparently just beginning to feel his strength in the ottava rima, remarks on the virtues of Turkish women:

> 72.
> They cannot read, and so don't lisp in criticism;
>> Nor write, and so they don't affect the muse;
> Were never caught in epigram or witticism,
>> Have no romances, sermons, plays, reviews,—
> In harams learning soon would make a pretty schism!
>> But luckily these beauties are no 'blues,'
> No bustling Botherbys have they to show 'em
> 'That charming passage in the last new poem.'
> 73.
> No solemn, antique gentleman of rhyme,
>> Who having angled all his life for fame,
> And getting but a nibble at a time,
>> Still fussily keeps fishing on, the same
> Small 'Triton of the minnows,' the sublime
>> Of mediocrity, the furious tame,
> The echo's echo, usher of the school
> Of female wits, boy bards—in short, a fool!
> 74.
> A stalking oracle of awful phrase,
>> The approving '*Good!*' (By no means GOOD in law)

Humming like flies around the newest blaze,
    The bluest of bluebottles you e'er saw,
Teasing with blame, excruciating with praise,
    Gorging the little fame he gets all raw,
Translating tongues he knows not even by letter,
And sweating plays so middling, bad were better.[33]

Botherby is William Sotheby, a classicist and playwright who was indeed popular in the salons. Byron became convinced he was the author of a letter criticizing "The Prisoner of Chillon," and he never thereafter missed an opportunity to include him in satiric attacks. But in this case more specific typecasting is going on. He repeatedly referred to Sotheby as a "blue" or "blue-bore" and seems to have fixed him in his satiric bestiary as the quintessential male bluestocking.

He plays much the same role in "The Blues," where, true to from, he remarks "very good!" at just the wrong moment and makes a ridiculous speech on the buoyancy of spirits:

'Tis the Vision of Heaven upon Earth: 'tis the gas
Of the soul: 'tis the seizing of shades as they pass,
And making them substance: 'tis something divine:—
Inkel. Shall I help you, my friend, to a little more wine?
Botherby. I thank you: not any more, sir, till I dine.
                                                    (II.139–43)

From Montagu's joke on Stillingfleet's blue stockings, through Moore's sycophantic Davy, the feminized male author or poetaster who accepts too readily the patronage of the salon is a perennial figure of ridicule. One could say that for Byron, Sotheby represents the polar opposite of Moore and the other "better brothers": instead of being a man of the world who can resist the seductions of the salon, he is the male bluestocking, bluer than the blues. In *Beppo,* however, this is strangely equated with taking one's professional status as "author" too seriously—too professionally.

75.
One hates an author that's *all author,* fellows
    In foolscap uniforms turned up with ink,
So very anxious, clever, fine, and jealous,
    One don't know what to say to them, or think,
Unless to puff them with a pair of bellows;
    Of coxcombry's worst coxcombs even the pink
Are preferable to these shreds of paper,
These unquenched snuffings of the midnight taper.

76.
Of these same we see several, and of others,
  Men of the world, who know the world like men,
S[cot]t, R[oger]s, M[oor]e, and all the better brothers,
  Who think of something else besides the pen;
But for the children of the 'mighty mother's,'
  The would-be wits, and can't-be gentlemen,
I leave them to their daily 'tea is ready,'
Smug coterie, and literary lady.

The way to true professional status is the way of sprezzatura, of casual non-chalance. The worldly men "who think of something else besides the pen" (but something symbolically suggested by the pen) are exactly those who used to meet with Byron at Murray's shop; indeed, they form a counter-coterie, an autonomous men's club of professional authors who are safely above New Grub Street and beyond any dependency on the patronage of the women-dominated salon. At Murray's—where, to the publisher's annoyance, the young Byron used to drop in and fence with his swordstick at the bookshelves while listening to the latest reports of the critics—Byron had something closer to his private all-male, post-chaise conversation, a way to counter the seductive but socially and personally dangerous attractions of the salon. During these years of fame, it should be remembered, Byron made a point of balancing his teas and *conversaziones* with more robust drinking bouts with the dandies and the members of the hypermasculine Pugilistic Club.[34] The fights he undertook against reviewers, critics, and fellow authors were similarly situated in opposition to his time in society. Participating in the emerging commercial publishing world of the new literary marketplace may have exposed him to the pains of the reviews, but it also partially exempted him from the feminizing judgments—and, potentially, the ridicule—of bluestocking culture. This included the ridicule of being embraced by and too closely associated with this culture.

The *Witlings* and the Dangers of Ridicule

For deepening the historical perspective of these issues, I turn briefly to Fanny Burney's suppressed play, *The Witlings*. This work and its history provide another perspective on this dynamic of ridicule, satire, and the salon. A satiric-comic drama on the bluestockings written by an insider and directed against Montagu and the original Blue Stocking Club, *The Witlings* was composed in 1779 at the urging of Burney's advisors and friends, including Dr. Johnson. The play is all about the ridiculous, the dangers of ridicule, and the power of the mere anticipation or fear of ridicule. Its Lady Smatter is probably based on Elizabeth Montagu herself, the "Queen of the Blues," and this fairly unflattering portrait is the most likely reason Burney's father led her to suppress the play. Lady Smatter's nephew Beaufort characterizes her coterie near the beginning of the play:

> My good aunt has established a kind of club at her House, professedly for the discussion of literary Subjects; & the Set who compose it are about as well qualified for the Purpose, as so many dirty Cabin Boys would be to find out the Longitude. To a very little reading, they join less Understanding, & no Judgement, yet they decide upon Books & Authors with the most confirmed confidence in their abilities for the Task. And this club they have had the modesty to nominate the Esprit Party. (I.228ff.)

The plot concerns the mutual flatteries of this coterie and the "Poet of Fashion," Dabler, follies that are ridiculed and threatened with exposure by the worldly Censor. Censor is the dark interpreter of the scenes, the Tiresias always about to blow everyone's cover with a withering truth. He is the quintessential satirist.

In act 2, Cecilia worries about Censor's propensity for raillery and Beaufort replies, "The Sting of a professed Satirest [*sic*] only proves poisonous to fresh Subjects; those who have often felt it are merely tickled by the Wound" (II.311ff.). But if this is true, then the play is peopled with "fresh Subjects." The plot turns in the end on Lady Smatter's fear of satire. Censor has engineered the potential threat as a blackmail to further the marriage plot, to force the capitulation of Lady Smatter. After the machinery is in motion, Dabler remarks blandly in act 5 that "We men do not suffer in the World by Lampoons as the poor Ladies do;—they, indeed, may be quite—quite ruined by them" (V.846ff.). This unwitting threat terrifies Lady Smatter, as does the deliberate scare-tactic of Censor's offhand "one satire will but be the prelude to another. . . ." The waiting landslide of contagious aggression—satires and lampoons, epigrams, libels, farces—is the weapon Censor tells Lady Smatter in private that he will unleash, "drop in every Coffee-House." In the equivalent of a generic good cop/bad cop routine, he holds out the alternative promise of panegyrics, triumphs, and so on. "You have but one moment for reflection," he tells her coldly, "either to establish your Fame upon the firmest foundation, or to consign yourself for life to Irony & Contempt." She is persuaded to allow the marriage of Cecilia and Beaufort.

It is a brilliant coincidental accident of literary history in this case that Fanny Burney's own threat of satiric ridicule proved to be too much to allow publication of her farce. Then again, this suppression is no accident, since Burney was part of a real literary coterie subject to these same kinds of fears and threats. Montagu was already the subject of much public ridicule, and Burney's social and literary dependence on the Blue Stocking Club was at that time more pressing than it later became for her, as her father well recognized. Burney herself, when once referred to in a pamphlet satire, reacted in a telling panic: "May God avert my becoming a public theme of ridicule!"[35] Beaufort's reassurance to Cecilia about "fresh Subjects" being the only truly vulnerable satiric victims amounts to directive advice. Burney's writing *The Witlings* can itself be seen as a self-protective countermeasure, an attempt to join with Johnson and others on the side of ridicule rather than find herself by association on the side of the satirized Bluestockings. Dabler's remark about the ability of lampoons to ruin women was essentially true, or at least was an operative social assumption, and young women with protective fathers were well directed "for their own good" away from satire (even if toward novel-writing).

Burney's artistic ability and wit are unquestionable, and the work suggests that she took a simple wicked delight in her own satiric performance, even indulging in a certain playful fun involved in writing the play. But the act of writing such a coterie satire from within the Bluestocking Circle appears, nonetheless, as something of a self-protective act. Such a satire works as a homeopathic inoculation against the poison of other satire, proof by demonstrated raillery that one is anything but a "fresh Subject." This is not a psychoanalytic interpretation of Burney or her text. On the contrary, the dynamic is written on the surface of literary and cultural history. A great deal of social satire—as is often said about acerbic stand-up comedy—is written out of the anxiety that one is vulnerable to ridicule in the first place. The best defense is a quick offense. In a world of satirists, no one wants to appear ripe for ridicule.

The Salon and the Profession of Letters

Byron reportedly told Lady Blessington that ridicule was the only weapon the English climate could not rust.[36] "The Blues" finds him still wielding it (and still concerned that he might suffer it). Though "The Blues" was influenced by satires such as Anstey's *New Bath Guide* (1766) and *Election Ball,* and in general by the Menippean satires of Thomas Love Peacock,[37] it can also be aligned with Burney's *Witlings* (though Byron would not have known the text) and works like it in the eighteenth-century dramatic tradition. Byron was well aware of that larger tradition, which includes Molière, English Restoration comedies, and Sheridan, for example, and even popular farce and comic opera like Moore's *M.P.* Like many works in this tradition, especially from the later era, Byron's "Blues" suggests that the world of publishing offers either a more powerful alternative or a dependent adjunct to the tastemaking of the salon. In the face of these conditions, it attempts to strike the first satiric blow, to protect its author from ridicule—however slight he might imagine it to be, coming from women in their "Spinsterstry"—including especially the ridicule of being associated with the bluestockings at all.

It is a proverb (originally self-generated) that the earnest English Blue-stockings banished harsh talk of politics and scandal, along with refreshments, at their literary and intellectual salons. Hannah More's *Bas Bleu* says as much, if not in so many words. In the preface she asserts that the Blue Stockings were a circle "in which learning was as little disfigured by pedantry, good taste as little tinctured by affectation, and general conversation as little disgraced by calumny, levity, and the other censurable errors with which it is too commonly tainted, as has perhaps been known in any society." I take this as part of a general program to "English" the earlier French style of witty society, making conversation less formal and also less threateningly corrosive, more "improving." They may not have been successful in controlling such wit, but that satiric ridicule comes to be figured as a force to be held at bay, the predatory beast recently banned and now just outside the firelit circle of civilization. The nineteenth-century shift from the French to the English model of bluestocking culture—more earnest, pedantic, feminine, sentimental, and romantic—would have meant increasingly self-conscious representations of salon society as incompatible with satire. Such representations must be read with skepticism. More was herself a graceful and effective satirist. *The Bas Bleu* praises simplicity and common sense in part by setting these virtues against their opposite through satire. More mocks her own pretense to learning, but also, for example, the competing style of eighteenth-century society party:

> Where the dire *Circle* keeps its station,
> Each common phrase is an oration;
> And cracking fans, and whisp'ring Misses,
> Compose their Conversation blisses.
> The matron marks the goodly show,
> While the tall daughter eyes the Beau—
> The frigid Beau! Ah! luckless fair,
> 'Tis not for you that studied air;
> Ah! not for you that sidelong glance,
> And all that charming nonchalance;
> Ah! not for you the three long hours
> He worshipp'd the Cosmetic powers;
> That finish'd head which breathes perfume,
> And kills the nerves of half the room;
> And all the murders meant to lie
> In that large, languishing, grey eye;

> Desist:—less wild th' attempt would be,
> To warm the snows of Rhodope:
> Too cold to feel, too proud to feign,
> For him you're wise and fair in vain;
> In vain to charm him you intend,
> Self is his object, aim, and end.
> Chill shade of that affected Peer,
> Who dreaded Mirth, come safely here!
> For here no vulgar joy effaces
> Thy rage for polish, ton, and graces.
> Cold Ceremony's leaden hand
> Waves o'er the room her poppy wand. . . .
>
> (ll. 100–127)

Against such outdated formality, the substantive conversation of the blues can only shine. But such constructions of English salons as earnest and (to their critics) pedantic, rather than witty in the old way, are in the early nineteenth century on their way to becoming the clichés that Woolf's satire on Pope can simply assume. Byron's "Blues" provides evidence of this opposition between salon and satire as it was in the process of being established. Byron's own allegiance was characteristically dual. As in the old joke, he couldn't help but satirize the club that had wanted to celebrate him as a member.

One of the things these salons were busy celebrating was emergent Romantic poetry and its attendant ideology of feeling, sincerity, and nature. In "The Blues" Lady Bluebottle defends the Lake poets ("Wordswords" and "Mouthey") as ahead of their time and the common taste:

>   time and posterity
> Will right these great men, and this age's severity
> Become its reproach.
> *Inkel.*   I've no sort of objection,
> So I am not of the party to take the infection.
> *Lady Bluebottle.* Perhaps you have doubt that they ever will *take?*
> *Ink.* Not at all; on the contrary, those of the lake
> Have taken already, and still will continue
> To take—what they can, from a groat to a guinea,
> Of pension or place;—but the subject's a bore.
>
> (II.99–107)

To this highly Byronic judgment, the hostess, Lady Bluebottle, replies,

> Come, a truce with all tartness;—the joy of my heart
> Is to see Nature's triumph o'er all that is art.
> Wild Nature!—Grand Shakespeare!" (II. 113–15)

As the banter continues, she interjects again—"A truce with remark"—and encourages instead rhapsodic expressions of Romantic sentiment (like Botherby's wild "entusimusy," as Byron liked to call such displays, already quoted above). Tracy and Inkel continue to the end to slip deflating witticisms into the conversation, however, as when Botherby praises supper as the meal at which "our true feelings most genuinely—feel."

> *Inkel.* True; feeling is truest *then,* far beyond question:
> I wish to the gods 'twas the same with digestion!
> *Lady Bluebottle.* Pshaw!—never mind that; for one moment of feeling
> Is worth—God knows what.
> *Inkel*   'Tis at least worth concealing
> For itself, or what follows—But here comes your carriage.
> *Sir Richard* [*aside*]. I wish all these people were d——d with *my* marriage! [*Exeunt.*
>
> (II. 160–65).

The rush of the comic conclusion may divert readers from the significance of Byron's depiction of tastemaking by the blues. The silly salon is in this instance making and banking on the "literary capital" accruing to the emergent Romantic canon. The tone of the conversation from the Blues' side is itself in imitation of Romantic sentiment. True feeling is set against "tartness" and "remark," transcendent intellect against critical rhetoric.

Byron, who had written himself famous with *Childe Harold*, was in 1821 taking part in the famous "Pope controversy," defending the Augustan satirist over and against the newer Romantic modes. Murray published Byron's initial *Letter* on the subject in that year. William Lisle Bowles followed the general opinion of Joseph Warton's earlier influential literary history in denigrating Pope's wit and "artificial" style in favor of the "natural" virtues of imagination and feeling. Byron blamed English "cant" for this lapse in taste, praising instead Pope as the supreme "moral poet of all civilization."[38] He also continued to write *Don Juan,* which included a great deal of its own *soi-disant* moral poetry and plenty of pointed anti-Romantic satire. Produced during these same months, "The Blues," with its couplets and its subject matter, was in its limited way (and with limited success) one more attempt to align Byron with an ideal of worldly, satiric literary energy and *against* his own tendency and the tendency of the age to produce and valorize sentimental and sublime Romanticism. Byron was attempting at this point in his career to renegotiate the terms of his earlier established fame, to align his own practice with what he saw as the standards of the school of Pope. Hence his interest in returning to the scene of 1812 and the reign of the bluestockings.

After a long and serious meditation on fame in *Don Juan* IV, a passage written at around the same time as "The Blues," Byron connects the theme to the bluestockings—and to his own career:

> 108
> Oh! ye, who make the fortunes of all books!
>   Benign ceruleans of the second sex!
> Who advertise new poems by your looks,
>   Your 'imprimatur' will ye not annex?
> What, must I go to the oblivious cooks?
>   Those Cornish plunderers of Parnassian wrecks?
> Ah! must I then the only minstrel be,
> Proscribed from tasting your Castalian tea!
>   109
> What! can I prove 'a lion' then no more?
>   A ball-room bard, a foolscap, hot-press darling?
> To bear the compliments of many a bore,
>   And sigh, 'I can't get out,' like Yorick's starling;
> Why then I'll swear, as poet Wordy swore,
>   (Because the world won't read him, always snarling)
> That taste is gone, that fame is but a lottery,
> Drawn by the blue-coat misses of a coterie.

Despite their mockery these lines reveal Byron's serious frustration with the arbitrariness of tastemaking in his age, the "lottery" of fame versus true "taste," and his feeling that there was no refuge in the end from, on the one hand, the vicissitudes of the literary marketplace (becoming a "foolscap, hot-press darling") and, on the other hand, the whims of the coterie.

Only Wordsworthian Romantic disdain remains an option—but not for Byron. The salon members are depicted with comic horror as ignorant or unwitting arbiters, more or less unconsciously drawing the names of those authors who will live and die. But Byron tacitly acknowledges that book sales increasingly depended on such coteries and their boon of fame, and by the early nineteenth century depended increasingly on the commercial patronage of the bookseller in league with the reading public. Besides, he cannot quite take seriously Romantic aesthetic transcendence and the dismissal of contemporary fame it implies. No wonder then that in the stanzas that follow he seems almost wistful about his former centrality in such tastemaking circles, while simultaneously reducing the bluestockings to sexual objects rather than anything like intellectual conversationalists and potential critics:

110

Oh! 'darkly, deeply, beautifully blue,'
   As some one somewhere sings about the sky,
And I, ye learned ladies, say of you;
   They say your stockings are so (Heaven knows why,
I have examined few pair of that hue);
   Blue as the garters which serenely lie
Round the Patrician left-legs, which adorn
The festal midnight, and the levee morn.

111

Yet some of you are most seraphic creatures—
   But times are alter'd since, a rhyming lover,
You read my stanzas, and I read your features:
   And—but no matter, all those things are over;
Still I have no dislike to learned natures,
   For sometimes such a world of virtues cover;
I know one woman of that purple school,
The loveliest, chastest, best, but quite a fool.

The key phrase here, for Byron's program of career revisionism, is "all those things are over," a wish as much as a regret. As for the blues in general, like individual intellectual women in particular, the type is for Byron an object of both desire and fear. Their patronage by opinion was something his fame could not have lived without; but this fact galls. In 1821, the fact is something he cannot happily live with.

Using The "Blues"

Shortly after talking to Lady Blessington in Genoa, Byron began writing the English cantos of *Don Juan,* the centerpiece of his "recollective project" looking back at the England of the Regency. His elegiac mode in 1822–23 included producing "The Age of Bronze," a poem mourning the passing of the Napoleonic era, and at the same time satires like *The Vision of Judgment,* settling old scores. This is more than personal nostalgia. It is almost as if Byron must return (somewhat sentimentally) to his years of fame in order to re-make himself as the unsentimental satiric author and citizen of the world who writes his final dry-eyed poems and, eventually, departs for Missolonghi. Paul Trueblood is I think quite right to detect in Byron's late work "an increasing inclination toward social satire" as well as toward political intervention, and to sense in *Don Juan* a "growth . . . in satiric seriousness."[39] As part of this self-refashioning project, Byron needed, among other things, to return again (and more than once) to the stock target, the bluestockings, in order to define himself as free of their judgments once and for all.

Thus, when Juan comes England in the late cantos, he must encounter the bluestockings. Interestingly enough, when he does so (canto XI) he reveals again the troubled connection between the opinions of the blues and of the reviews:

> 50
> The Blues, that tender tribe, who sigh o'er sonnets,
>   And with the pages of the last Review
> Line the interior of their heads or bonnets,
>   Advanced in all their azure's highest hue:
> They talked bad French of Spanish, and upon its
>   Late authors asked him for a hint or two;
> And which was softest, Russian or Castilian?
> And whether in his travels he saw Ilion? (XI.50)

In "The Blues," the coterie and the "Row" (where books actually get sold and reviewed) are set up as worlds apart. The mobile male authors move freely between them but are ultimately (ideally) free from the constraints of either. Though Tracy and Inkel are secretly interested in gossiping about satiric reviews, they strike a pose beyond the reach of such tastemaking—just as they remain aloof from the bluestockings but still partake of their tea and company. The blues, on the other hand, are shown in this passage from *Don Juan* to consume the reviews uncritically, to accept these published opinions by the sheet and fill their empty heads with them. This "learned and especial / Jury of matrons" (st. 51), which includes further caricatures—"Lady Fitz-Frisky" and "Maevia Mannish," for example—is thus demoted in Byron's scheme from tastemakers to mere followers of fashion. They buy their literary opinions like the latest hats (a sonnet's as good as a bonnet) from those who dictate taste and pull the strings of culture.

Byron declares his own independence from this empty fashion system. Against the "ten thousand living authors" who pass through the coteries and literary parties, he famously defines himself as larger than (social) life: "the grand Napoleon of the realms of rhyme" (st. 55). Thus he claims to have transcended public taste. The toast of the town in 1812–14 now in 1821 projects himself as a literary emperor, making the taste (and the myth) by which he is to be appreciated by posterity. That myth, however, remains stubbornly grounded in the fame that was celebrated in and partly created by the coteries of 1811–12. He knew this well enough to make the effort to satirize the ghosts of bluestockings past, even at the late date of 1821. Byron still needed the *idea* of the blues as a foil for the man of action and the man of the world he wished to become.

Byron's attitudes toward the "blues," while complicated by his personal history, were in large measure based on fear of their tastemaking judgments, the resultant potential public ridicule, and the taint of association with fashionable modes and their new marketplace. Against such a threat, it has been my purpose in this chapter to suggest, he felt the need for preemptive satiric strikes—even long after the event of his actual performance before the salons. This involved mocking the site of his own early poetic reputation. To reverse the terms of Scott's remark about the bluestockings ("it is a common trick to revenge supposed raillery with good substantial calumny"), Byron employed "raillery" against the threat of "calumny" in order to revise the terms of his Romantic fame. That self-revision was his attempted revenge. The salons and, increasingly as the nineteenth century wore on, the marketplace itself, were beginning to recognize the canonical role of the new Romantic writing, in the process further institutionalizing the opposition of satiric and sentimental modes. Certain famous Byronic self-contradictions are best understood as falling in the ambiguous space between these two modes, as acts of partial resistance to his own fame. In the next chapter I examine one form in which the contradictory tensions between the sentimental and the satiric get expressed in Byron's late work: the pantomimic satire of *Don Juan,* and one way literary criticism has subsequently overwritten the influence of this popular satiric mode with the idea of philosophical Romantic irony, thus making its energies seem more amenable to a generically unified construction of Romanticism as a movement.

Chapter 6 〜

Turning What Was Once
Burlesque into Romantic:
Byron's Pantomimic Satire

> *I have never written but for the solitary* reader—*and require no experiments for applause beyond his silent approbation. . . . I claim my right as an author to prevent what I have written from being turned into a Stageplay.—I have too much respect for the Public to permit this of my own free will.—Had I sought their favour it would have been by a Pantomime.*[1]

In this excerpt of a letter from Ravenna, Byron complains about losing control of *Marino Faliero,* thus documenting both his authorial intentions and the frustrating limits of those intentions. Byron had heard from John Murray that the closet drama was to be taken out of the closet and produced for the stage. This he vehemently opposed; instead he put forth a highly Romantic formulation of his ideal reader—as "solitary" and wholly apart from the collective "Public" who went to plays. That amorphous mass, he suggests, would be best reached (if that were one's goal) through that most popular of all popular and spectacular theatrical forms, the pantomime. The "Public" has a taste for the masks, big heads, type characters, slapsticks, pursuits, pratfalls, and illusionistic stage tricks of the form. Byron means that he is above such pandering. In *English Bards and Scotch Reviewers* he had bemoaned the popularity of pantomime and other popular forms, including farce and sentimental tragedy, in this apostrophe to Richard Brinsley Sheridan:

> If aught can move thy pen,
> Let Comedy assume her throne again;
> Abjure the mummery of German schools;

Leave new Pizarros to translating fools;
Give, as thy last memorial to the age,
On classic drama, and reform the stage.
Gods! O'er those boards shall Folly rear her head,
Where Garrick trod, and Siddons lives to tread?
On those shall Farce display Buffoon'ry's mask,
And Hook conceal his heroes in a cask?
Shall sapient managers new scenes produce
From Cherry, Skeffington, and Mother Goose?

(ll. 580–91)[2]

Thus in 1809 Byron affects Popean horror at what it has all come down to: Mother Goose, the central figure in one of the most popular of all popular pantomime plots by Thomas Dibdin. He goes on to see the proof of this "pollution" in the taste for an Italian import, the ultimate source for pantomime in turn being the *commedia dell'arte,* just recently experiencing a revival in Italy:

Degenerate Britons! Are ye dead to shame,
Or, kind to dulness, do you fear to blame?
Well may the nobles of our present race
Watch each distortion of a Naldi's face;
Well may they smile on Italy's buffoons,
And worship Catalani's pantaloons,
Since their own drama yields no fairer trace
Of wit than puns, of humour than grimace.

(ll. 610–17)

These are conventional enough complaints about sensationalism and the debased national taste. But Byron's characteristic ambivalence, a form of which runs throughout this maiden satire, reveals itself in his own more amused note to the lines: "Naldi and Catalani require little notice; for the visage of the one, and the salary of the other, will enable us long to recollect these amusing vagabonds. Besides, we are still black and blue from the squeeze on the first night of the lady's appearance in trousers."

This gossipy note is a reminder that Byron was there among the crush, and Byron himself participated in the fashion for popular theater. As Peter W. Graham points out, quoting a fascinating account, Byron later recalled actually going onstage at one pantomime at Drury Lane in 1815–16.[3] This particular performance, *Harlequin and Fancy; or the Poet's Last Shilling,* staged an imitation of a masquerade held in 1814 at which Byron had been present. At the pantomime, Byron and Douglas Kinnaird went onstage, "amongst the [*hoi polloi*]—

to see the effect of a theatre from the Stage.—It is very grand.—Douglas danced amongst the figuranti too—& they were puzzled to find out who we were—as being more than their number.—It was odd enough that D. K. & I should have been both at the *real* Masquerade—& afterwards in the Mimic one of the same—on the stage of the D. L. Theatre.

As this story suggests, through contextual invocation of Byron's style and way of life, the young satirist of *English Bards* protests a bit too much in 1809; at any rate he is not literally setting himself beyond the influence of popular theatricals. The older Byron's claims, in the letter of 1821 quoted above, to possess only antitheatrical intentions are even more suspect. Even his closet dramas are inherently theatrical. They require their solitary reader to play the role of audience at a performance, based on previous experience with the stage and its conventions, a translation of the theatrical over into the purely "literary" experience. Besides, the letter only says that had he wished to seek the favor of the "Public" (in this particular instance), he would have known very well how to do it. It can be read as a threat or promise as much as a denial, and it expresses the belief that the newly powerful popular or mass audience *could* be won by strategic application of the right generic mixture. Byron knew how to mix genres effectively, and was fully aware of the still-current fashion for the pantomime. By the 1820s he was also a frequenter of *carnivale* theatricals, a fan of the renown *improvisatore,* Sgricci, and an admirer and acquaintance of Joseph Grimaldi, the most famous English Clown in the history of the pantomime. He commissioned special carnival masks for himself and the Countess Guiccoli in Ravenna. Byron's restored mask is both Romantic and carnivalesque; it may represent a grotesque bearded pirate, like Conrad the Corsair and, in later works, Beppo and Lambro (see figure 6.1).[4] But such carnival masks, in use since the middle ages, commonly represented Harlequin and the other characters from the *commedia.* He was at the same time writing a sprawling epic satire—his signature work—whose picaresque hero was taken from that very popular tradition, whom, Byron could assume in the opening lines, all of his readers had seen "in the pantomime."

It is my purpose in this chapter to make something more—significantly more than has previously been made—of that declared (and yet only incompletely declared) lineage: to show precisely how Byron's *Don Juan* has a family connection to the popular pantomime.[5] The character of the Don had appeared in pantomimes, and some of these served as sources or influences for Byron's satire. But there is a deeper generic family resemblance between Byron's poem and the pantomime, one that had a profound effect on the stance and tone of the poem, its fundamental ambivalence, tensions, and artistic ironies. The greatest (and certainly by consensus the most solidly

Figure 6.1   Byron's Carnival Mask (Ravenna; Keats-Shelly House, Rome)

canonical) satire of the Romantic period drew important structures and modes from, and thus bears serious critical comparison with, what Leigh Hunt called "the best medium of dramatic satire" in his day—the English pantomime. The pantomime was not the only or even the most common source of generic conventions incorporated into Byron's famously mixed-genre poem. Italian comic epic, for example, is surely a more significant source on the whole. But pantomime conventions are vitally important in *Don Juan,* in part because they are directly connected to the idealist tradition of Romantic irony. In the hands of the theorists who constructed it, from the eighteenth to the twentieth centuries, Romantic irony is the intersection where the dialectical opposition of romance and satire produces a higher synthesis: a paradoxical, transcendental perspective that came to be seen by some as the essence of Romanticism itself. In recent versions, pantomime and its theatrical cousins have disappeared, and the "irony" has been subsumed in the dominant term, "Romantic." In the latter portion of this chapter I will attempt to reground Romantic irony in the pantomimic tradition, thereby specifying more precisely than heretofore how the construction of Byronic Romanticism is historically dependent on satiric wit (*Witz*), on the material performance of illusion in pantomime trickwork, an effect based on technology in which the wires remain visible to the audience. I offer this look at pantomime, a "low" satiric graft that produces one important scion of "high" canonical Romanticism, as an antidote to overly philosophical notions of Romantic irony—which tend to idealize the very poetic modes they were meant to explain. They do so largely by forgetting what was, historically, performatively satiric in Romantic-ironic theories of art.

Pantomime in the Air

The first thing to be said about the pantomime is that it was everywhere in late eighteenth- and early nineteenth-century English culture, a form so common it was, as we say, in the air, or (more accurately) in the available repertoire of almost any author who cared to draw upon it. Pantomime came close to being what is now called a mass entertainment, in the sense that it attracted at holiday time a mix of demotic and elite audiences, who would have been familiar with its forms and conventions. Pierre Bourdieu has asserted that such popular theatricals—he specifically names the closely related forms of "melodrama and vaudeville"—were among the new genres produced in the era of "quasi-industrial methods," in which the newly ascendant press and the emergent field of literature worked together to make products for the consumption of a mass audience, now extended by education and mobility to include women, for example.[6] This fact of the growing marketplace is one reason Byron disdained to write for this audience directly and openly, preferring instead to imagine a lone reader as his interlocutor.

It is important to remember that this mixed-class audience for the pantomime was extremely heterogeneous, anything but uniformly "low." On 27 December 1823 the *Times* noted that "Every body 'pooh-poohs' the pantomime, but every body goes to see it." This "everybody" included royalty and a diverse range of middling types, including almost every major writer of the era. Looking back on the Georgian period, William Thackeray turns this taste against the court, telling us that the vulgar George III preferred farces and pantomimes to Shakespeare or tragedy, "especially when clown swallowed a carrot or a string of sausages, he would laugh so outrageously that the lovely Princess by his side would have to say, 'My gracious monarch, do compose yourself.'"[7] Thackeray goes on to represent the Hanoverian court in terms of the pantomime scene:

> What a strange Court! What a queer privacy of morals and manners do we look into! Shall we regard it as preachers and moralists, and cry Woe, against

the open vice and selfishness and corruption; or look at it as we do at the king in a pantomime, with his pantomime wife and pantomime courtiers, whose big heads he knocks together, whom he pokes with his pantomime sceptre, whom he orders to prison under the guard of his pantomime beefeaters, as he sits down to dine on his pantomime pudding? (*Four Georges*, 101–102)

This association of the Georges with the pantomime was conventional. In later decades the people's favorite, Princess Charlotte, was popularly identified with Columbine, the beautiful daughter of a tyrannical Pantaloon.[8]

Indeed, during the Regency the pantomime was one of the identifying features of English popular culture. It was represented in countless prints and regularly referred to by journalists. As it did for Thackeray, so in the earlier era it provided a set of allegories or types for categorizing public figures or fictional characters. It influenced even unlikely authors to some extent and was, for example, a favorite diversion of the famously earnest Percy Bysshe Shelley, who was generally no fan of theatrical comedy. Shelley attended pantomimes in London and, as I suggest below, seems to have drawn on its structures in composing his popular satires, *Swellfoot the Tyrant* and *The Mask of Anarchy*. Representative Romantic-era critics Leigh Hunt and William Hazlitt reported on the pantomime—and so did John Keats (who used it as a suggestive metaphor for a certain mental outlook, as I show later in this chapter).

By the Victorian era, the pantomime was most closely associated with the Christmas season, but in the early nineteenth century it could be seen at holidays around the calendar.[9] Although part of its rise to popularity was based on its ability to evade English theatrical restrictions (since its parts were mostly sung or mimed rather than spoken), during the height of its vogue pantomimes could be seen in the patent houses as well as unlicensed theaters, and the two competed for the most lavish productions and most famous performers. The pantomime form itself was derived from the Italian *commedia dell'arte,* with its regionally inspired type-characters or "masks"— Harlequin, Pantaloon, Columbine, Clown, et al.—and its basic knockabout plot of the lovers' elopement and their pursuit by an authoritarian father (or father-figure). The improvised business filling in that plot was the heart of the *commedia* and became the mainstay of the derivative English form.

There were imported versions of the *commedia* characters in England as early as the seventeenth century, but the adaptation that came to be known in England as the pantomime dates from the late eighteenth century, and its inception has been pinpointed to the staging of Sheridan's 1781 "Grand Pantomime" of *Robinson Crusoe; or, Harlequin Friday.*[10] This work may have been responsible for establishing the conventional two-part structure for the one-act form: first a serious or sentimental (and usually fabulous) opening part; followed by a second, raucously comic and burlesque part, the Harlequinade. In Sheridan these two parts were connected thematically and the characters of the first part are at a crucial moment transformed into the type-characters (from the *commedia*) of the second part. And "this was the pattern that pantomime was to follow for the next century and more, with structural change being limited to altering the relative lengths of the two parts."[11] David Mayer, the most thorough historian of the form, explains that the opening "often gave the pantomime its title," and was frequently based on familiar folk material, fairy tales, chapbooks, ballads, or classical mythology; it tended toward romantic or sentimental narratives, either traditional tales or original stories "with authentically remote or exotically imaginary settings peopled by dwarfs, giants, fairies, good or evil magicians, genii, or kings" (23).

The basic plot revolved around the authoritarian father, his daughter, and her lover. The conflict that arises as the father attempts to force a separation of the young lovers is resolved by the supernatural intervention of a "benevolent agent," usually female, for example, Mother Goose or Queen Mab, who divides the play in two by enacting the "transformation scene" and magically changing the lover into Harlequin, the daughter into Columbine, the father into Pantaloon, a servant into the Clown, and other characters into other "masks." Harlequin is then usually sent on a quest and given a magic sword or slapstick bat, with which he will enact further transformations as the plot unfolds. But to be transformed into these stock "masks," some of the characters of the opening often must take off their comic "big heads" or full masks (beneath which are their costumes for Harlequinade).

> When, at each wave of the benevolent agent's wand the characters of the opening are transformed, the big heads are snatched away by stagehands, and the costumes, loosely held, are stripped away to reveal the comic types that populate the "harlequinade," the larger portion of the pantomime. (Mayer, 28)

The main action of the second part, the Harlequinade, is the elopement of the lovers and their pursuit by authority. Harlequin works his magic to try to thwart the pursuers and further the elopement of the lovers. People jump through windows or trapdoors, hide and tumble in very physical chases and comic pratfalls, panoramic backgrounds roll behind the actors, suggesting travel through exotic locales. After a time, there is usually a climactic, penultimate "dark scene," a gothic moment in a cave or grotto; then the benevolent agent again intervenes to reconcile the generations and sometimes to re-transform some of the characters, ushering in and presiding over a grand finale and concluding spectacle. Everything in the performance hinges on the initial transition from serious to burlesque, folktale to farce, romance to satire.

These transformations are the result of magic, but are experienced by the audience as the practical, illusionistic, even materialist "magic" of stage tricks. As Tom Dibdin himself admitted, "the best pantomime ever constructed depends upon strings, and flaps, and traps; and, if machinery does not work, the pantomime must fail."[12] No form of theater in this age of competitively elaborate spectacle was more dependent on theatrical technology than the pantomime. One contemporary review gives a sense of how elaborate this could be, mentioning only some such devices, those among "the best tricks" of a pantomime:

> the transformation of an old woman into a table and a couple of chairs. The transformation of a chest into a sofa, on which the Clown seats himself, and which is immediately afterwards converted into a kitchen-grate, with a fire briskly burning in it, which gives the Clown an unpleasing hint, *a posteriori,* was also cleverly executed.[13]

The pantomime did not conceal its technology behind a naturalistic plot, but instead thematized its machinery in a self-conscious fashion as magical transformations effected by characters within the play and by more or less invisible stagehands. These tricks often supplanted the dramatic action as the audience watched the flaps fall or the traps open and shut.

Harlequin's bat, like a magician's wand, became a symbol of all magical special effects. Isaac Disraeli later marked this as a result of the translation of the pantomime characters from the Italian to English stage:

> we have turned Harlequin into a magician, and this produces the surprise of sudden changes of scenery, whose splendour and curious correctness have rarely been equaled: while in the metamorphosis of the scene, a certain sort of wit to the eye, "mechanic wit," as it has been termed, has originated; as when a surgeon's shop is turned into a laundry, with the inscription "Mangling done here;" or counsellors at the bar changed into fish-women.[14]

Like multimedia experiments in almost every historical era, pantomime stage-tricks called attention to themselves. They were often even the main draw or selling point of the show: the medium in this case became the theatrical message. This foregrounding of formal artifice, the technological magic or "visual wit" of pantomime, quickly became central to its sensational effect on and appeal to the audience. Many spectators, immersed as they were in other forms of special-effect entertainment of the era (from layered transparencies to sublime panoramas and impressive magic lantern shows), must have attended the pantomime at least in part to witness the latest tricks.

But the line between this fashion for sensational trickwork and the larger fashion for the sentimental special effects of acting was a fine one. From the 1780s, Paula Backscheider suggests, actors in popular gothic melodrama drew upon pantomime conventions and style, and this fed into the high tragedy of the day: Edmund Kean himself, she reminds us, had performed as a Harlequin.[15] The general connection between the taste for sentiment and popular theatricals including pantomime persisted. One prose satire in 1801 specifically connected this thirst for spectacle with the Romantic fashion for sentiment and imagination:

> The success of pantomime is a proof that the people, who had long been accustomed to *feel* gradually became satisfied with *feeling;* a sort of *second childishness,* or indolence of mind, preferred shew to sentiment; and the love of noble entertainments was refined into a desire to behold a glittering pageant, which, by filling the imagination, prevented the toil of thinking.[16]

The same sentimental and fantastic qualities were beginning to be associated with Romantic modes of writing, and in this sense the pantomime is a truly Romantic form of theater.

In January 1808, Leigh Hunt appended to his review of *Much Ado About Nothing* a short notice on the Christmas pantomimes at Drury Lane and Covent Garden. On the face of it, this is a patronizing, even dismissive article, especially when it comes to the typical knockabout comic business of the form: "I do not mean to criticise that indescribable species of drama which consists in mere legerdemain, in a continued bustle of fiddles and feet, and in giving people huge slaps on the face."[17] But Hunt's criticism continues in a less sarcastic (if still condescending) vein:

> The modern pantomime appears to me to be capable of great improvement without losing any of its essential qualities. *Harlequin* is a very merry personage; his many-coloured habit, his fantastic dances, his disjointed jumps and postures, his conjurations with wooden sword, and his utter contempt of ease and rest, not to mention that gradual spin of his pericranium which is so alarmingly facetious, present an inexhaustible fund of merriment to all my little masters.(8)

Hunt goes on to suggest, absurdly but in keeping with his poetic predilections, that Harlequin take off his mask and emote more directly, through pure facial expressions. He then closes with an anecdote of the pantomime in the classical Augustan age. It is an awkward, somewhat embarrassed essay, serving in part to display the reviewer's learning and taste as well as align him with the currently fashionable school of acting as emotive expression. But on the other hand, in contrast with the attacks on pantomime quoted above, Hunt demonstrates an essential sympathy with the appeals of pantomime to the audience's sentiment and imagination along with his nervous ambivalence about the status of the form.

Nine years later, in January 1817, Hunt adopts a somewhat more magnanimous (or even confessional) editorial persona: "We must indulge ourselves a little this season on the subject of Pantomimes—a species of drama, for which, at whatever hazard of our critical reputation, we must acknowledge a great predilection"(140). Hunt's ultimate intention in this essay seems to involve borrowing the tone of pantomime for his own Romantic-satiric purposes. In the absence of any good comedy, he says, "Pantomime flourishes as much as ever, and makes all parties comfortable";

> It enchants the little holiday folks; it draws tenfold applauding thunder from the gods; it makes giggle all those who can afford to be made giggle; and finally, it brings out the real abilities of our dramatic writers, who would be very pleasant fellows if they would not write comedy. (140)

Hunt might be seen here as indulging in reverse snobbery or camp criticism, praising pantomime—for containing something "*real,*" an enchanting "animal spirit"—at the expense of legitimate alternatives in his day. The point is to call attention to his own position as a champion, even if an ironic champion, of the popular form. But the criticism also serves as a pretext for more literary-philosophical speculations. Hunt really is the champion of art that "enchants" its audience, and this makes the form especially suited for instruction, in his view. Running through the stock characters, he acknowledges the origins of the pantomime in Italian comedy and focuses on Clown as "a delightful fellow to tickle our self-love with. He is very stupid, mischievous, gluttonous, and cowardly, none of which, of course, any of us are, especially the first . . ."(141). Spectators are fully entitled to enjoy the theatrical illusion of superiority, Hunt says, which is harmless enough. The point is to offer a gently satiric reminder that, if spectators are made to "giggle," they must ask themselves if they can "afford to be made giggle" (140).

When the essay concludes in the next number (26 January 1817), Hunt names the main pleasures of the pantomime as a form: "its bustle, its variety, and its sudden changes." But then he remarks on a more sociological virtue: "a Pantomime, at present," he asserts, "is also the best medium of dramatic satire" (144). On the face of it, this is a strange claim. Comedies and farces of the day, he makes clear, are too badly written to be effective, so in a tone of irony he suggests that the laurel must go to the sung and silent form, "which leaves the spectators, according to their several powers, to imagine what supplement they please to the mute caricatures before them" (144). But it may also be the case that Hunt is here seriously answering the attacks on the sentimental spectacle of pantomime. He may be asserting simply that unheard melodies are sweeter even in popular theatricals; the Romantic fascination with the reader's imagination as interpretive supplement shows up here as the spectator's ability to "half-create" the satiric meaning of the spectacle. This too seems at first a strange thing for Hunt to claim when it comes to satire, which is traditionally regarded as a topical genre. Topicality requires public, shared references, the in-joke or knowing wink interpreted within a given social context as ridiculing or passing judgment on something both the satirist and audience understands as deserving of judgment. Any survey of nineteenth-century pantomimes reveals a great deal of satire on fashions and manners—dandyism for example, or the rage for urban "improvements"—but very little topical political satire.

David Mayer argues that Hunt's claim for pantomime as the "best medium of dramatic satire" was simply wrong, unsupported by the evidence, and that it was a claim made in the period "before royal inertia and intransigence made political reform so desperate a necessity, and when Grimaldi's vigor and wit still dominated the shape and tenor of pantomime spirit," that at bottom, "the particular capacity of the pantomime for satire leads us to expect more than we find" (268–69). He sees the form as resorting to "escapism" in the face of pressures, including especially censorship on the part of the Lord Chamberlain's Examiner of Plays from 1778 to 1824, John Larpent, who frequently suppressed scripts in which the topical allusions were too topical, too blatantly political (Mayer, 238ff.) Despite this, there were topical political references in some pantomimes during the period, especially during the years of the French Revolution, as Mayer himself documents. And some limited degree of political satire undoubtedly was seen on the stage, particularly since the performances were based on schematic scripts on which the actors improvised. As Mayer suggests, Grimaldi was famous for his subtle satiric gestures as Clown, none of which are recoverable from scripts alone (and may not have been mentioned in contemporary reviews, even where those exist).

One example comes to us from none other than Robert Merry, the chief Della Cruscan. He wrote a pantomime, *The Picture of Paris,* and saw it performed in Covent Garden in 1790.[18] Its opening contains a Silversmith (Harlequin), along with a Painter and a Stone Carver, who have been commissioned by the National Assembly to destroy armorial bearings and badges of nobility in a Parisian home of a Marquis. The Marquis's daughter is Columbine before her transformation, and a servant is the Clown. Thus the family plot is mapped onto the conflict of aristocrat and artisan-worker. (A "Petit Maitre" is the father's preferred suitor for his daughter.) The surviving script is as usual only schematic, but painted scenes include The Jacobins' Convent, The Temple of Concord, a "Partial view of the *Champs de Mars,* including the Pavillion preparatory to the Festival . . . and The Grand Illuminated Platform, prepared on the Ruins of the Bastille, and named the Temple of Liberty, &c. &c." The sketch includes a paragraph setting each scene and general stage directions, as well as several "airs," some political and some sentimental love songs. In the third scene, during the Harlequinade, Columbine asks Harlequin to intervene in an execution underway in the street, led by vicious Poissard forces, begging him to "exert his transforming power on the occasion," and he then "converts the three magistrates into the emblematical Figures of *Justice, Mercy,* and *Truth.*" Later, he also transforms a scene of the "Grand Assembly in debate" into "The Temple of Concord," to be followed by an Air and Duet. These songs by Della Crusca himself demonstrate the fusion of sentiment and Jacobinism that so terrified Edmund Burke and William Gifford. As the nightingale—"the tuneful, am'rous bird"—and his mate sing to one another: "Their transports, balmy breezes bless, / And passion glows with fond excess; / For sacred night and concord join / To make the peaceful scene divine." This is followed by "A GRAND DANCE" to end the first act. The appropriateness of French Revolutionary pageantry and theatrical spectacle to this form is obvious, and this is an extreme example. After 1793, it became increasingly unlikely one would see such things on the pantomime stage. And yet this reminds us that politics and topical allusion were not inherently antithetical to the form—on the contrary.

Marilyn Gaull has described the cumulative subversive effect of Grimaldi's famous performances:

> Grimaldi's Clown, supposedly in pusuit of Colinett but often in escape from everyone else, violated both human and natural law, a saucy, resourceful, mercurial fellow, clever, silly, dancing, weeping, singing, fencing, howling, fiddling, juggling, lusting after women, stealing and then devouring huge quantities of food, throwing furninture, dishes, and small children in the paths of his pursuers. If he mutilated his adversaries, they recovered, and so did he—his nose is glued on, his arms repaired by carpenters. Even the dead revived, for in pantomime evil has no power, nor is there shame, guilt, or repentance. His irreverence, his defiance of authority, decorum, manners, pieties, and social conventions provided a viarious satisfaction for the unappeased appetites of the lower classes, a vicarious release from the self-imposed restrictions of the middle classes, restrictions that simultaneously beset individuals and guaranteed their survival, a vicarious expression for their hostility, frustration, and anxieties.[19]

This promiscuous, cross-class subversive appeal is surely one of the strongest attractions of the pantomime. Moreover, as Moyra Haslett argues, the political impact of popular theatrical performance must be measured at the metatheatrical and contextual levels, as well, by the complex set of cues and effects set in motion by the very form and its popularity, effects of audiences and their responses as much as speeches and actions on the stage. Even during the years of stringent censorship, the pantomime remained political, but more in its representations of plebeian and middling taste onstage (to meet the demands of the audience) than in direct topical commentary. The Don Juan pantomimes, in particular, had a political impact, as Haslett suggests, simply because they took place within a popular, low form of entertainment: "the popularity of the Don Juan theme was tainted by its association with the lower classes" (134). The reception of Byron's pantomimic epic satire was shaped by these same associations, and many reviewers were especially troubled by the working-class readership of the poem—a problem exacerbated by cheap piracies, which Murray attempted to combat with his expensive editions.[20]

In the end, Hunt's claims for pantomime as a satiric form must be explained according to these more than topical features of the form. Larpent's censorship of pantomimes is only one particular example of a widespread phenomenon, especially during the French wars. The organized political reaction in England at the time, which led to very real pressures of legal and quasi-legal censorship, created a climate that, Terence Hoagwood has argued,[21] helped produce the kinds of indirection and symbolism, and an open-ended emphasis on the reader's responsibility to make meaning, that characterizes High Romanticism. Hunt identifies pantomime as a form with kinship ties to emergent Romantic literature. His notion of mute satire assumes a relatively apolitical or strictly moral purpose, and depends upon the individuation and internalization of the audience's response, with the traditionally public effects of "satire" giving way to an occasion for private self-examination, something like the individual spectator's "restless casuistry" that Percy Bysshe Shelley said in the Preface to *The Cenci* that he hoped to provoke.

As the essay proceeds, it becomes clear that Hunt is also writing satire in this very review, satire on the types of human folly.

> Harlequin's sword also, besides being a thing very pleasant to the imagination to handle, is excellent at satirical strokes. Lissom as a cane, and furnishing all that little supply of conscious power which a nervous mind requires, and which is the secret of all button-pulling, switch-carrying, seal-twirling, and glove-twirling, it is not possible to witness its additional possession of a magic power without envy. We always think, when we see it, what precious thumps we should like to give some persons—that is to say, provided we could forget

our own infirmities for the occasion. We would have a whole train of them go by at proper distances, like boys coming to be confirmed—the worldly, the hypocritical, the selfish, the self-sufficient, the gossiping, the traitorous, the ungrateful, the vile-tempered, the ostentatious, the canting, the oppressing, the envious, the sulky, the money-scraping, the prodigiously sweet-voiced, the over-cold, the over-squeezing, the furious, the resenter of inconvenience who has inconvenienced, the cloaker of conscious ill by accusation, the insolent in return for sparing. What fine work for a winter's morning, with a good broad set of backs to operate upon! (144–45)

This is a highly conventional encyclopedia of universal vices for satire to scourge, but in context this list is the work of a political reformer of the Regency, which inevitably colors interpretation of the vices of "the selfish, the self-sufficient," "the canting, the oppressing," and "the money-scraping." And eventually, the imagined Swiftian scourge gives way to the more "Shelleyan" remedy, the pseudo-medical, philosophical mirror:

We would have looking-glasses put before the patients, in order that they might know themselves when transformed into their essential shapes; after which they might recover; and then the wisest. The least presuming, and most generous person among the spectators, such a one as was agreed by his most veracious companions to know himself best, and to be the most able to bear objection, should set the glass before ourselves, and give us a thump equally informing. (145)

Indeed, this calls to mind the fragment of an unfinished "Satire upon Satire" by Hunt's protégé Percy Bysshe Shelley, a text that imagines scourging the Tory turncoat, Laureate Robert Southey, and subjecting him to a "looking glass" of sorts:

> And from the mirror of truths sunlike shield
> shafts of the
> From which the Parthian [arrows fall, like snow]
> Flash on his sight the spectres of the past
> Which his mind's eye will paint thereon—[22]

Reform rather than punishment shapes this attempted Romanticization of satire as a genre, and the tensions between the reformer's goal and the violence of satiric modes make Shelley's inchoate satire a fascinating case study.

Shelley's and Hunt's ideas of the definitions and goals of satire surely influenced one another, and were generalized to all those in Hunt's circle, becoming the shared ideal of the New School of so-called younger Romantics. This essay on pantomime is valuable in part for what it tells us about those generic definitions and goals. Ideally, Hunt makes clear, satiric targets are not to be scourged but "transformed into their essential shapes," which is somewhat like the effect of the *Dunciad,* say, or of any caricature, properly defined, but with this difference: in Hunt's ideal this transformation is a metaphor for the ultimately salutary psychological process of a Godwinian, internalized re-formation of the self. How fortunate, then, that in pantomimic satire the act of transformation itself is foregrounded as an essential human truth and sign of open-ended potential. Compare Shelley's turn, in the satire fragment quoted above, toward conversing with Southey as an alternative to satire proper, simply and sincerely telling him "how incorrect his conduct is."

Like Shelley, Hunt emphasizes the reflexive imagination of the viewers of the spectacle. To apply the terms of Shelley's *Defence of Poetry,* even the "visual similes" of the pantomime are to some degree "vitally metaphorical"— that is, they work to stimulate the metaphor-making, imaginative capacity of the spectators, to accustom them to "previously unapprehended combinations" of identities and ideas.[23] The trope of transformation embodied in Harlequin's tricks is a self-consciously comic figure of figuration, a figure for the ability of the mind to alter its perception of reality by way of metaphor, to imagine (even effect) transformations. The satiric intent, Hunt would say, is to be didactic and reforming, but by being ultimately constructive, self-revelatory and educational, despite a few harmless thumps and diversionary giggles. This reformist satire—a *Romantic* kind of satire—is to be self-reflexive, including in its sights the satiric reviewer himself.

Hunt's generic ideal here is based in part on his Romantic reading of Aristophanes, always one of his and Shelley's favorite Greek authors. Hunt was serious in his playful praise of pantomime, as confirmed in his later remarks on the decline of pantomime in the early Victorian era:

> Pantomime used formerly to be the representative of the Old Comedy, and gave us some good Aristophanic satire on events of the day. It attempts this but sparely now, and but seldom does it well. . . . Pantomimes seem to have become partakers of the serious spirit of the age, and to be waiting for the settlement of certain great questions and heavy national accounts, to know when they are to laugh and be merry again.[24]

The legendary connection of pantomime to Aristophanes is to Hunt high praise for the former, a way of legitimizing pantomime (and his own effort to write about it) by connecting it to classical drama—but in an author and form that still carried the stigma of low comedy in the nineteenth century (when Plato was bowdlerized for university students). This association of pantomime and Old Comedy tells us a great deal about the critical seriousness with which

Hunt regarded the "best medium of dramatic satire." It also connects Hunt—via the roots of pantomime in the *commedia*—to the German Romantic theorists who were influential in the construction of the notion of Romantic irony, as I argue below.

Hunt's opinions on these matters directly influenced Percy Bysshe Shelley, who wrote a blatantly pantomimic farce on the Queen Caroline Affair in 1820, *Oedipus Tyrannus; or, Swellfoot the Tyrant.* Shelley's chorus of hogs openly parodies *The Frogs* and, as I have suggested elsewhere,[25] the Queen Caroline Affair provided him with the plot of a threatened civil war, an oracle's prophecy, public sexual desire, and bad marriage—all found in the *Lysistrata,* which Shelley read in 1818. Like Aristophanes's play, Shelley's burlesque is also about the vulgarity of the mob, a "masculine" woman and gender role-reversal, the virtues of peace, and the senselessness of violence. Its humor mixes sacred and profane, double entendre with high allegory, and at its climax (II.ii), a semi-veiled nude female figure of Liberty appears as a pantomimic "benevolent agent" on a central altar, a scene that invokes both the pantomimic transformation and Aristophanic comedy. The stage direction reads: "A graceful figure in a semi-transparent veil passes unnoticed through the Temple; the word LIBERTY is seen through the veil, as if it were written in fire upon its forehead. Its words are almost drowned in the furious grunting of the PIGS, and the business of the trial."[26] The goddess of Famine confronts the graceful figure of Liberty, rises, and then abruptly disappears (significantly, as if through a trickwork stage-trap), and Liberty makes a rousing speech in effect to the reformers: "when thou wake the multitude, / Lead them not upon the path of blood."

This moment is familiar to readers of Shelley and echoes, for example, the crisis of *The Mask of Anarchy,* another pantomimically structured work, in which the first part, the satirical masque procession, contains caricatures of contemporary politicians and allegorical evils, all of which are wiped away in a sudden transformation scene enacted by Hope and a benevolent agent, the illuminating "shape." The second part of the *Mask* follows, an exhortative speech to the people of England ("They are many, ye are few"). So again, a revelatory scene of unmasking is effected by a fairylike benevolent agent, who makes possible a direct address to Shelley's intended audience, much like Liberty's speech to the reformers in *Swellfoot the Tyrant.*

Both the speech of Liberty in *Swellfoot* and the final exhortation in the *Mask* resemble the pantomimic transformation scene, which in turn resembles the Aristophanic parabasis, a sometimes satirical but also didactic device of the Old Comedy in which a character would break the frame of the play at a key moment in order to address the audience directly, often speaking on behalf of the playwright himself. Topical and political references were common features of these speeches, expressed rhetorically in a mixed mode at once "monitory/abusive/didactic."[27] The parabasis of Shelley's Liberty is almost ignored in the raucous business of the slapstick ending (so reminiscent of the knockabout Harlequinade), but one of her incantations seems to work well enough: "Be what thou art not!" she says, and like Mother Goose's wand or Harlequin's bat, Liberty's speech causes a transformation, as the pigs are turned into free-born English "Bulls," the conniving ministers who had led the conspiracy against the injured Queen are transformed into their essential shapes, "vermin," and the "Ionian Minotaur" becomes JOHN BULL, a hunter who can "leap any gate . . . even the palings of the royal park" (II.ii.109–11). Queen Iona (Caroline as the heroic representative of John Bull) is metamorphosed into a powerful Artemis-like huntress, who rides down the king and his verminous ministry to the play's conclusion, shouting "Hey for a whipper-in!" and "Tallyho!"

Even this concluding hunt would have invoked pantomime's trickwork, including the use of animals onstage, along with cobbled-together "Nondescript" absurd animals, as well as driving and riding in general. In *Harlequin and the Red Dwarf* (1812), there is even a ludicrous parodic hunt, using incongruities to burlesque the code of the best-known aristocratic sport according to an established tradition.[28] The pantomime was based on a real-life stag hunt held in Epping Forest at Easter, in which the lower orders joined, a license for masking or mumming in which "merchants and tradesmen from the City played at being country gentlemen" (Mayer, 103). In the pantomime the Harlequinade simply runs into the Epping Hunt in progress and the type-characters take part in hunting a llama instead of the stag. Columbine rides alone (Harlequin being comically ungallant and afraid of the chase), and Pantaloon rides a small pony. As one contemporary account reports, "the whole motley group . . . passed across the stage three times, with dogs in pursuit; but the hissings and applause of the audience so terrified the animals on the first night of the performance, that the hunt went off badly" (quoted in Mayer, 102). Later in the run the production improved.

Shelley's final burlesque hunt belongs to this same carnivalesque theatrical tradition, and his satire is obviously toying with the overlapping of the (high) Old Comedy and (low) pantomime and farce in its conventions and allusions. At the intersection of Aristophanes and the pantomime more than one contemporary author and critic discerned a rich vein of satiric (and sentimental or Romantic) possibilities in the early nineteenth century. Shelley is one of these authors, and, as I argue below, so is Byron; Leigh Hunt is one of the formative critics—but so, for example, is Friedrich Schlegel.

Pantomime, *Commedia,* and Romantic Irony

The connection between the Old Comedy and Italian popular theater (not Regency pantomime per se, but its predecessor and source, the *commedia dell'arte*) was much discussed by Friedrich Schlegel in the context of his musings on ancient and modern poetry and "Romantic irony." Romantic irony is a crucial heuristic idea for literary criticism, especially as a conceptual bridge from history-of-ideas to historicist constructions of Romanticism.

The metacritical method of reading Romanticism's self-contradictory ideological formations—associated with American deconstruction and postructuralism in the 1970s—first entered mainstream criticism with the publication of two books: David Simpson's *Irony and Authority in English Romantic Poetry* and Anne K. Mellor's *English Romantic Irony.* Explaining the satirical Byron and his absence from M. H. Abrams's account of the spirit of the age was particularly important to Mellor's project, which applied Schlegel's theories to English poetry. Whereas Simpson tends to stress features of Romantic irony that resonated with postructuralism, the "avoidance of determinate meanings," for example, "the incorporation of any potentially available 'metacomment' within the primary language of the text," and even a "free" or "slipping linguistic sign," Mellor tends to stress the plenitude, enthusiasm, creativity, and synthesis, the self-constructing and self-transcending qualities of Romantic irony.[29] As a result, Mellor's extended readings of Byron can at times make his texts seem more comprehensively comic, more synthesizing than they are. As Jerome McGann's critical-theoretical study of Romantic ideology suggests, a certain Romantic idealism gets translated from the German into some accounts of English Romantic irony.[30]

The real question is: what's so ironic about English Romantic irony? (Its Romanticism seems clear enough.) In context, Schlegel's own transcendentalism is frequently and interestingly offset by his emphasis on the dialectical process of Romantic irony, including the sustained paradoxes of *der Witz* and, most notably, the performative buffoonery of his ideal Romantic artist. Despite the near mysticism of his theory, it is grounded in the example of the pantomimic theater—especially the practice of Ludwig Tieck—and this theatricality often plays out as setting a material boundary to Schlegel's transcendence. To return to Schlegel in the present context, then, is to attempt to put the pantomime back into the critical notion of Romantic irony—as Schlegel theorized it and as it was further constructed by twentieth-century critics, down to more recent formulations of Romanticism. The pantomime points toward the central place of a form of satire—a particularly *romantische* form—in this "ironic" construction of the Romantic.

Look at the particular examples Schlegel uses in making his points, beginning with Aristophanes. Irving Babbitt, speaking for much of early twentieth-century criticism, would later remark that the German Romantics' attempts to compare Tieck's drama to Aristophanic comedy were particularly "absurd."[31] But in Schlegel at least, Aristophanes is mediated by "modern" artists practicing pantomimic forms of drama. For example, in several of the *Athenaeum Fragments* he compares the popular fairy dramas (*fiabe*) of the Venetian satirist Carlo Gozzi to Aristophanes; while the comparison is usually unfavorable to Gozzi, the very comparison itself shows that Schlegel recognized an important generic family resemblance. Schlegel observes that "The comedies of Aristophanes are works of art that can be viewed from all sides. Gozzi's plays have one point of view,"[32] and then offers a prescription for bringing modern and ancient comedic forms together:

> Magic, caricature, and materialism are the means by which modern comedy can become inwardly similar to the old Aristophanic comedy, just as demagogic popularity is the outward means. Gozzi has succeeded here to the extent of reminding us of it. But the essence of comic art will always remain enthusiastic spirit and classical form. (*AF* 246, p. 197)

Magic (a characteristic feature of "romance" itself), caricature (dialectical/satiric distortion and reduction), and materialism (including philosophical skepticism, but more immediately the very theatricality of performance)—these are important observations about what a "modern," Romantic-ironic poetry might be like, according to Schlegel. The link thus created between the revival of *commedia dell'arte* and Romantic poetry derived from it is extremely significant for any understanding of Romantic-era satire. I would suggest that it is more significant for Byron's practice than any philosophical exposition of German theory.

It turns out that Carlo Gozzi (1720–1806) makes a useful intermediary figure for connecting German notions of the "Romantic" (including the key concept of Romantic irony) with their sources in the practices of popular Italian theater, which in turn lead directly into the English pantomime. A biting satirist and reactionary polemicist, Gozzi championed the ancient *commedia,* with its masks and structural conventions, against the reformist criticisms of Goldoni and Chiari.[33] As part of his campaign he wrote a series of satiric dramas for the local Sacchi troupe to perform, whose characters were the masked types of the *commedia*—Pantalone, Arlecchino (Harlequin), Pulcinella, Truffaldino, et al.—but whose plots were based on legendary or popular fairy tales; the most famous was the *Love of Three Oranges,* performed at *carnivale* in 1761. Deliberately adapted from the simplest and most absurd folk tale Gozzi could think of, these plays were political demonstrations and satiric volleys in the theater wars then raging locally in Venice. But these fairy dramas or *fiabe* are also close cousins to the pantomime just then becoming extremely popular in England. Both develop modern forms of satiric entertainment by grafting traditional *commedia* types and conventions onto fairy tales and folk material, and both use the result for social, literary, and (less often) political satire.

In the final decades of the eighteenth century Germany experienced a Gozzi vogue, as the *fiabe* were staged and discussed by the foremost critics of the day, including Lessing and Goethe, as well as Schlegel.[34] E.T.A. Hoffmann was an admirer of Gozzi, and Ludwig Tieck was inspired to imitate Gozzi's "method of literary satire" in his famous satirical fairy-tale adaptation of "Puss in Boots," *Gestiefelt Kater,* as well as in *Prinz Zerbino* (Rusack, 122). Tieck was very much in favor of returning to the use of the *commedia* masks in modern theater, but also made the following satiric comment:

> Only, to be sure, if they are to have speaking parts, one could never exempt this grotesque, yet poetic task from the use of real wit, extravagant, mad sallies, and pertinent satire—in one word—the truly poetic; and that might be very difficult for the authors of the present day. (*Dramaturgische Blatter,* IV.3; quoted in Rusack, 137)

The constellation of manifestos and epigrams now, thanks to critical arguments, grouped together as the theory of Romantic irony has been extremely influential on modern literary criticism, especially of Byron. But at its inception, this theory had recourse again and again to a set of satirical theatrical examples. Tieck and the Schlegels, in particular, were the source of one of the most influential set of definitions of the "Romantic" style of modern poetry over and against the "classic" but also as possessing an "ironic"— or satiric—element at its core.[35] Even admitting Madame de Staël's *De l'Allemagne* and various writings by Samuel Taylor Coleridge, for example, as local intermediaries for the English reception of these definitions, it remains clear that the definitions had a wide-reaching influence on ideas of what united certain early nineteenth-century English authors and works. Hence, important theories of the "Romantic," from the inception of the term in its modern critical sense, ultimately and to some degree share a set of historically specific paradigms, sources not usually considered in formulations of English High Romanticism: the Old Comedy, the *commedia dell'arte,* and the modern pantomime. The low reputation of the pantomime—and the proof of its deserving that low reputation, its wide popularity—may have prevented our acknowledging the centrality of pantomimic modes to emerging ideas of Romanticism itself. "The pantomimes of the ancients no longer exist," Schlegel portentously remarks, "But in compensation, all modern poetry resembles pantomimes" (*AF* 69, p. 169).

Byron did not read this in Schlegel, so far as is known, though he may have gleaned some of it from de Staël's writings and conversation; but the present argument is not about direct influence. The German Romantic tradition and Byron shared a common interest in certain forms of theater as models for ways of writing a new kind of poetry. Byron's use of the models differs from Schlegel's—and differs as well from Leigh Hunt's. Still, though Byron would not have approved of the label, these sources in popular theater are part of what makes the satire of *Don Juan* "Romantic" in the strictly literary-historical sense. "To become popular with the masses, a poem or drama has to have a little of everything, has to be a kind of microcosm" (*AF* 245, pp. 196–97), Schlegel writes, and this works very well as a summary of *Don Juan*—especially as it has been read in the light of a critical heritage, a line extending from German theory, through de Staël, Coleridge, Carlyle, to M. H. Abrams and Simpson and Mellor. But when placed in the context of pantomimic theater, this description sounds less like ontology and more like genre theory: Schlegel's observation accompanies remarks on Aristophanes and Gozzi, the Old Comedy and the revival of the *commedia*. It is a recipe for Romantic satire.

Like Schlegel, Byron recognized the dialectical basis and poetic potential of the idea of "Romantic irony." Such a dialectic was one of his noticeable personal traits. Recall Lady Blessington's remark (cited in the previous chapter) that Byron seemed to "take a peculiar pleasure in ridiculing sentiment and Romantic feelings," but then also in turning the tables on his own ridicule, such that "the day after" he would "betray both."[36] Schlegel's theory is dialectical, melding fantastic sentiment with philosophical irony. Romantic irony considered through the lens of pantomime offers another, more materially performative, way to characterize the play of contradictions at the heart of Byron and his work.

More immediately than the primary philosophical German theorists literary history has usually cited, the example of Romantic irony closest to hand, in the air, for *English* Romantic-period authors would have been the popular pantomime. And this is especially true for Byron, who also knew the Italian and Spanish popular traditions at first hand—including the very Venetian *carnivale* characters and street performances on which Schlegel draws for his examples (witness his carnival mask). The lowly theatrical entertainment is a form of Romantic irony performed—and for the widest popular audience. In this sense, the pantomimic theater is the missing link between high theories of Romantic irony and Byron's poetic practice. This is the thickly layered context for Byron's loaded opening remark, that everyone had seen "Don Juan"—not only the character but, I am arguing, much of the generic conventions of Byron's greatest satire—"in the pantomime."

Byron's Pantomimic Satire

Byron had easy recourse to many of the huge number of popular theatrical—and especially pantomime—representations of the Don Juan myth as
he was inventing his own epic satire.[37] His work on the Drury Lane Com-
mittee alone helps establish as much, but he also knew and admired Joseph
Grimaldi, the famous pantomime clown (Byron visited him backstage and
gave him a silver snuffbox), as well as Thomas Dibdin, the theater manager
and popular author of farces and pantomimes. Byron's early years of fame
in London "coincided with performances of the pantomime of *Don Juan* at
the Lyceum Theatre in October-December 1811; August-September 1813;
and July 1814."[38] And this is to speak just of one known Don Juan pantomime, the "Grand Pantomimical Ballet," *Don Juan; or the Libertine Destroyed.* This pantomime shared the bill on 23 October 1811 with Tom
Moore's comic opera, *M.P.; or the Blue-stocking,* which, as I suggested in the
previous chapter, Byron would have remembered (Haslett, 110). Interestingly, Moore went to see a pantomime version of the Don Juan myth on 10
July 1819.

Byron would have encountered many more pantomime performances at
other times and on other themes. No one in England with even a casual interest in the theater could have escaped some form of the pantomime, at
least as tailpieces and interludes. And Shelley, whose interest in the pantomime is quite clear, might have talked with him about the form. *Don Juan*
makes several direct allusions to the pantomime besides the opening remark
naming it as a source for the hero. Contemporary readers were quicker than
many recent critics to notice the family resemblance of Byron's satire to the
pantomime and its theatrical cousins. For example, as Haslett points out, a
September 1821 review of *Don Juan* in the *Monthly Magazine* classified the
poem as a "serio-comic melo-dramatic harlequinade" and referred to Juan's
"prototype in the pantomime"(cited in Haslett, 60, 146n).

The general resemblance is clear enough. Byron's poem shares a number
of qualities with the pantomime, as Peter Graham says; it is

> improvisational, topical, eclectic, accumulative, volatile, characterized by
> rapid and formulaic inversions and transformations, and dominated by the re-
> sourceful and potent being (shall we say actor?) who serves as transformer and
> who constructs what order there is. In offering Byron a precedent and method
> for assimilating diverse materials (among the poem's many and varied other
> influences) through transformation and construction, spectacular theater
> might even be seen as the poem's ultimate influence. (Graham, 64)

The likelihood of this influence is reinforced by the dual English and Italian
sources, the pantomime and *commedia dell'arte,* which together would have

symbolized for Byron "the sort of cosmopolitanism" his poem celebrates (Graham, 64).

I would add that the Romantic-ironic ideal is embodied in both these sources and *Don Juan* and provides a way to understand Byron's Romantic satire in generic terms, beyond questions of borrowed characters, plots, or local structural devices. Pantomime particulars are often the details through which Byron's Romantic satire also gets "performed," but this involves the total generic effect of the form, its outrageous claims to satirize its own transcendence as often as—more often than—it transcends its own satire. It is worth remembering that, as James Chandler says, Byron's jokes in *Don Juan* are "characteristically 'antiphilosophical,' which is to say 'materialist' in orientation."[39] This is where I believe Byron's Romantic satire subtly but significantly differs from Schlegel's brand of Romantic irony. Closer to home, Byron's views differ even more significantly from Hunt's lighthearted stress on the imaginative potential of pantomime; instead, he emphasizes the bathetic and corrosively satiric potential of the form. As it differs from Schlegel's transcendence, Byron's poetic practice of Romantic irony also differs a great deal from most twentieth-century critical constructions of Romantic irony as positively "creative" and self-transcendent, I would argue. It is instead heavily weighted on the side of the irony in the equation, the unresolved skepticism and dialectical play that refuses any final transcendence. It is also likely to fall into what Schlegel identifies as the "materialism" of Old Comedy—including especially a self-conscious reveling in the limits of its inherited forms.

This "materialism" was only one ingredient of Schlegel's (ironic) recipe for producing Aristophanic-pantomimic poetry in the modern age: "magic, caricature, and materialism." It turns out that these terms work quite well to describe the mixtures and contradictions of the Romantic satire *Don Juan* exemplifies: the "magic" is of the imagination, especially as it conceives of romance and the fantastic: exotic locales and events, improbable transformations. Bu this magic is effected by way of a self-conscious, formalist focus on special effects—everything from the famous ottava rima devices to narrative digressions and authorial intrusions, a "materialism" that reveals the puppets' strings and the puppeteer pulling them. This "materialism" has its philosophical foundation in the "antiphilosphical" outlook and generally corrosive skepticism of the poem. And "caricature" is the technique of distorted representation in order to satirize what is represented—another way of foregrounding the formal process and critical point of view of the act of representation itself.

Don Juan is characterized by those moments when the narrative suddenly gives way to general commentary or a personal apostrophe by the narrator, who then metamorphoses into "Byron" and back into our narrator ("return we to our story"). Its topical caricatures take place at the narrative level (in Catherine of Russia, say) but also within the discursive "digressions" (as

Byron satirizes Southey) or both: as the narrative represents satiric versions of the English bluestockings, then Byron comments on intellectual women he has known. The poem's own form takes center stage, not as a display of generic conventions but rather as a matter of "chewing up the scenery" in performance, pushing the "thingness" of words and even print conventions like the stanza to their most obviously material limits: sometimes until they collapse in a pratfall. The poem is about its own machinery, the trapdoors of comic rhymes giving way, the masks and improbable costumes being put on and stripped away, the picaresque mobility of characters quickly transported from Spain to Greece to Turkey to Russia to England, like the rolling of a panoramic backdrop. *Don Juan* is pantomimic in precisely these ways. This amounts to very nearly the same thing as saying it exemplifies Romantic irony: but in a way that is actually closer to the spirit of Schlegel's *commedia*-inspired theory than most twentieth-century criticism has yet realized.

On the simple level of its narrative or plot elements, *Don Juan* resembles pantomime—or several pantomimes rolled into one. Peter Graham suggests that the seraglio episode in canto V is "the most clearly pantomimic interlude" in the poem, including in its use of cross-dressing for comic and magical effect (80). Haslett reads several scenes as drawing upon popular mythic material associated with *Don Juan* in pantomimes and other forms, including the moment in canto II when Juan is washed ashore on an exotic beach, saved and nursed in a picturesque cave by two young women. This, she points out, is "strictly in accordance with the Spanish/pantomime tradition," and may even be the most explicit allusion to the traditional Don Juan story in the poem.[40] I would suggest in an even simpler way that the basic plot in cantos II-IV, the story of Juan and Haidée and Lambro echoes the conventional triangle found in every pantomime opening. The idealized young love of a youth (Harlequin) and girl (Columbine) thwarted by her authoritarian father-figure (Pantaloon) has obvious parallels here. In the pantomime, the youth is often kidnapped or the father-figure sets out to have him killed, but usually through the magical intervention of the benevolent agent, the Harlequinade is set in motion when the masks come off and the three are revealed as the type characters and Harlequin is sent on a quest or journey.

After Juan and Haidée have fallen in love at the end of canto II, and have begun a sexual relationship in a setting of domestic "oriental" luxury in canto III, Lambro the pirate returns home to discover his house celebrating rather than mourning. The sentimental orientalism and lushly operatic "sets," here, along with the balletic dancing and shifting panoramic scenes within the scene, are characteristically pantomimic.

30
And further on a troop of Grecian girls,
    The first and tallest her white kerchief waving,

Were strung together like a row of pearls;
  Link'd hand in hand, and dancing; each too having
Down her white neck long floating auburn curls—
  (The least of which would set ten poets raving);
Their leader sang—and bounded to her song,
With choral step and voice, the virgin throng.
     31
And here, assembled cross-legg'd round their trays,
  Small social parties just begun to dine;
Pilaus and meats of all sorts met the gaze,
  And flasks of Samian and of Chian wine,
And sherbet cooling in the porous vase;
  Above them their dessert grew on its vine,
The orange and pomegranate nodding o'er,
Dropp'd in their laps, scarce pluck'd, their mellow store.

The set-piece song, "The Isles of Greece," interpolated (after stanza 86) as if made for reprinting in pamphlet form, could have come from any number of popular theatricals. Even the allusions to the *Odyssey* in this passage— Lambro as the returning voyager finding his house has come under siege in his absence—are loosely and opportunistically borrowed, much the way such material (or, more often, a fairy tale) would be lightly borrowed for the opening of a pantomime. And the clusters of "extras" posed in various tableaux would be right at home on the pantomimic stage.

     34
Afar, a dwarf buffoon stood telling tales
  To a sedate grey circle of old smokers
Of secret treasures found in hidden vales,
  Of wonderful replies from Arab jokers,
Of charms to make good gold, and cure bad ails,
  Of rocks bewitch'd that open to the knockers,
Of magic ladies who, by one sole act,
Transform'd their lords to beasts, (but that's a fact).

The *Arabian Nights*-style exoticism here, dwarf-buffoonery and all, is pantomimic, down to the secret doorways, animals, and magic ladies (suggesting stock benevolent agents) and their transformations. But just as Byron's ottava rima collapses their magic into marital conflict (and nudges the audience to make it notice this collapse), so the pantomimic episode of Juan and Haidée is rendered something more shocking by the explicit sexuality of their love. What was in pantomime Romantic is transformed in *Don Juan* into burlesque—a trick to top conventional transformation tricks. Byron's Romanticism in this poem is almost always a mask, a transparent special effect. On the other hand, the earlier stanzas on the youthful animal passion of Juan and Haidée are the most celebratory in the poem. Just as the boy Juan's highly Romantic meditations on nature and poetry in canto I give way to sexual fantasy and "Donna Julia's eyes," so in general romance is unmasked in the poem as displaced desire, and Byron delights wickedly in waving the wand to transform the one into the other over and over again.

When she discovers him half-drowned, Haidée nurses Juan in a cave, another Odyssean allusion but also an allusion to the many caves in pantomimic "dark scenes," in which Harlequin conventionally undergoes a gothic descent and harrowing before the final climax and reunions of the conclusion. But the true parallel with the pantomime plot makes the idyll on Lambro's island the "opening" and everything that comes afterwards Juan's raucous Harlequinade. Haidée dreams her own short "dark scene" in IV.31–33, which first connects her to Ariosto's Angelica "Chain'd to a rock," then transforms the scene into yet another gothic cave, "its walls / Were hung with marble icicles; the work / Of ages on its water-fretted halls. . . ." When she awakes, Lambro has returned to stand "High and inscrutable" like every tyrannical father/Pantaloon and finally order Juan bound and sold into slavery. "The world is full of strange vicissitudes," Byron drily tells us (IV.51). This is the moment he chooses to leave his hero and leave his readers in suspense—especially if they have seen the pantomime—because it is at this moment they would expect a sensational transformation scene through the intervention of Queen Mab or some other benevolent agent.

There is no such character, and no such supernatural magic in this poem, and this is where Byron's divergence from the pantomime conventions is most obvious. Instead of a transformation scene, Byron gives us the actual (and highly sentimental) death of his Columbine, Haidée. Then the poem simply rejoins Juan onboard the slave ship, where he encounters an Italian opera *buffa* troupe:

> 80
> He saw some fellow captives, who appear'd
>   To be Italians, as they were in fact;
> From them, at least, *their* destiny he heard,
>   Which was an odd one; a troop going to act
> In Sicily—all singers, duly rear'd
>   In their vocation; had not been attack'd
> In sailing from Livorno by the pirate,
> But sold by the impresario at no high rate.
>
> 81
> By one of these, the buffo of the party,
>   Juan was told about their curious case;
> For although destined to the Turkish mart, he
>   Still kept his spirits up—at least his face;

> The little fellow really look'd quite hearty,
>   And bore him with some gaiety and grace,
> Showing a much more reconciled demeanour
> Than did the prima donna and the tenor.
>
> (IV.80–81)

The *buffo* then goes on for eight stanzas to tell Juan and us all about the troupe, appealing to his evident cosmopolitanism and "travelled air," assuming him a fan of the opera. Thus the transition is under way.

Byron—as himself and/or the narrator—serves as the real transforming agent at such moments in the poem. His manipulation of mood and generic convention, at this blatantly stitched seam in the narrative, calls our attention to this role, as do his long digressions and frame-breaking apostrophes to the audience, descended from the satiric and topical parabasis of the Old Comedy. The wand Byron waves is the power of narrative control, but it is always set against the force of circumstance. This is his version of Schlegel's "transcendental buffoonery," the Romantic-ironic puppetry that reveals itself at work behind the curtain, punctures its own created illusions, and imitates "the mimic style of an averagely gifted Italian *buffo*,"[41] a figure like the one represented in this scene onboard the slave ship. The proper way to survive the "vicissitudes" of life, the lesson is clear, is with the "face" or mask of the *buffo*, whose sense of Romantic irony (with an emphasis on the irony) reinforces his resiliency. Schlegel writes that (Romantic) irony consists in "the clear consciousness of eternal agility, of an infinitely teeming chaos."[42] But Byron's view in *Don Juan* is, I think, considerably darker. For Byron this is not simply a question of "self-creation and self-transcendence."[43] It is something more like a seriously ironic diversion in the face of the "nothingness of Life" (VII.6). Everything comes down to a succession of "transformation scenes" in the end, Byron's carefully placed *buffo* (in chains, the reader can't help but notice) implies, and only a satiric reduction to the materialist conditions of "the vicissitudes of life" can preserve the possibility of a limited (because openly theatrical) and "anti-philosophical" sort of "magic" in the face of those conditions.

Transformation Scene:
Burlesque Becomes Romantic

In December 1817 John Keats attended the Christmas pantomime and on the way home discussed with his companion Dilke "various subjects":

> several things dovetailed in my mind, & at once it struck me, what quality went to form a Man of Achievement especially in Literature & which Shakespeare

> posessed so enormously—I mean *Negative Capability,* that is when man is capable of being in uncertainties, Mysteries, doubts, without any irritable reaching after fact & reason.[44]

This is a touchstone moment, one of the key canonical passages in all of High Romanticism. Notice how Keats, coming home from the pantomime, articulates one of the foundational Romantic artistic ideals—and in theatrical terms. There is no direct evidence in this letter that the pantomime Keats had just witnessed was one of those "several things" that "dovetailed" in his mind to influence his articulation of the idea of negative capability, but it is possible. Even the coincidental juxtaposition, if that is all it is, of pantomime and negative capability prompts a re-examination of the Keatsian idea, usually glossed in relation to Shakespeare and Kean, in relation to the lower theatrical form. But pantomimic theatricality—the "best means of dramatic satire" of Keats's age—may also have helped him to shape his own version of Romantic irony. Keats's equanimity of the artist in the face of "uncertainties, Mysteries, doubts," can usefully be juxtaposed with Schlegel's "clear consciousness of . . . an infinitely teeming chaos"—but also with Byron's satiric mobility.

Consider the following use of the pantomime by Keats, in the journal letter of 14–31 October 1818, in which he is writing about a young woman, a "Charmian" he has recently noticed:

> Yet she is a fine thing speaking in a worldly way: for there are two distinct tempers of mind in which we judge things—the worldly, theatrical and pantomimical; and the unearthly, spiritual and ethereal—in the former Buonaparte, Lord Byron and this Charmian hold the first place in our Minds; in the latter John Howard, Bishop Hooker rocking his child's cradle and you my dear Sister are the conquering feelings. As a Man of the world I love the rich talk of a Charmian; as an eternal Being I love the thought of you. I should like her to ruin me, and I should like you to save me.[45]

In Keats's half-playful dichotomy, the "pantomimical" is in apposition with the "worldly" frame of mind, with the essentially satirical perspective associated with Byron. The pantomimical is the dialectical opposite of sentimental sincerity and Romantic transcendence. But the "theatrical" is associated in Keats's earlier letter with negative capability, which, I wish to suggest, is closely related to Romantic irony. Like Romantic irony, negative capability is an attempt to achieve sympathetic representation while acknowledging and preserving an ironic perspective—essentially an attempt to *manufacture* the effect of artistic "sincerity" through the device of ironic detachment. Magic, caricature, materialism: transcendental buffoonery, but no ultimate transcendence.

Now my sere fancy 'falls into the yellow
  Leaf,' and imagination droops her pinion,
And the sad truth which hovers o'er my desk
Turns what was once romantic to burlesque.

(*DJ* IV.3)

Like the shift in countless pantomimes from enchanted fairy tale to knock-about slapstick, Byron's movement here is downward toward the burlesque. In the cause of canonical coherence, critical constructions of Romanticism (including constructions based on theories of Romantic irony) have tended to reverse his direction, to turn what was once burlesque in his satire into something recognizably Romantic, to subsume stubbornly ironic and satiric effects in larger plots of ultimate sincerity, higher synthesis, and self-transcendence. Reading the pantomime as a source and model for Romantic modes of satire would help critics to resist this trend, because doing so foregrounds the burlesque elements found within some canonical Romantic works. The dialectic of Romantic irony—or what I would rather call in this particular set of cases Romantic satire—toggles in both directions and depends upon a materialist aesthetic. There is no teleological progression from irony to sincerity, and in Byron's practice, at least, readers are very often left with the opposite of such progress ("down we tend"[IV.1]). But the narrative openness and tonal complexities of *Don Juan* do suggest at least the dark hope of an infinitely teeming chaos. In the pantomime, when the big-head masks of romance are removed, the magic continues unabated. In pantomimical Romantic satire, readers are given a glimpse of the "truth in masquerade," shown that all things are a "show," and yet are asked to lose themselves in a spectacle transparently constructed as folding romance into its satire, satire into its romance. This mutual dialectical enfolding may be the most effective (it has proved the most enduring) Romantic stage-trick of all.

Chapter 7 ∽

The Wheat from the Chaff: Ebenezer Elliott and the Canon

I conclude this study of satire and Romanticism with a brief look at a nearly forgotten poet, Ebenezer Elliott. Once widely known and respected as the "Corn Law Rhymer," he was in his strongest and most characteristic work a political satirist. When read as political satire rather than as the curious productions of an "uneducated poet" or the failed attempts of a "minor" late Romantic, Elliott's verse shows its real power, as part of an alternative tradition reaching from Burns through "Junius" and "Peter Pindar" (Wolcot), to Hone and Wooler, incorporating parts of Shelley's corpus, and to Chartist verse and other labor poetry.[1] *The Corn Law Rhymes* appeared in 1830 and in several editions over the next few years, during the phase of the reform movement leading up to the legislation of 1832, a pragmatic intervention of a very specific kind. In part because of this topicality and in part because he was defined (and defined himself) as a satirist in terms that carried specific class connotations, Elliott's work—otherwise highly regarded—simply found no place in the developing nineteenth-century canon. This chapter examines Elliott's satire and the public perception of it, particularly as exemplified in a key 1832 review by Thomas Carlyle, whose ideas of Romanticism and what should come after it turned out to be so lastingly influential. Carlyle is especially interesting in this regard because he was at the same time that the wrote the review of Elliott working out his own counter-Romantic mode, producing the "Satirical Extravaganza on Things in General," *Sartor Resartus,* a work that satirizes its own Romanticism. For Carlyle, Elliott appears on the horizon as an ephemeral presence, a potential alternative to Romanticism; but literary history reveals that he was bound by the standards of taste already established along Romantic lines to remain outside the emerging canon.

Elliott is only one among the legion of writers who cannot survive their time, but as a satirist writing at the culmination of the Romantic period, at a moment when the canon was consolidating and ensconcing an idea of Romanticism at its center, he offers an especially compelling example of the kinds of writings left behind in the process. The so-called Romantic ideology assumes that the greatest and most fully "literary" of texts are free to transcend the material limitations of their own era.[2] One corollary to be derived from this assumption is that topical satire, with its culturally embedded and tendentious rhetoric, is inherently un-literary, that the best such topical poetry can claim is a momentary victory based on its claims of referentiality, a victory sure to fade with time. Elliott's work is from the start a strong candidate for just this brief fame and ultimate fading. In his case, the topical nature of his satire was compounded by his working-class background and the deliberately class-inflected voice of his verse, and there is no question that he has suffered from the typical condescension of posterity as a result. Nevertheless, I argue in what follows that Elliott's work became a casualty of literary history not so much because of the difficulty of recovering its topical references (a brief introduction to the Corn Laws renders his poetry as accessible as most nineteenth-century texts), or primarily because of its working-class perspective, but because it was not valued highly enough in its own *generic* terms. Even to a sympathetic critic such as Carlyle, Elliott's verse too often appeared to be argumentative rhetoric rather than "literature" proper, essentially and unredeemably satiric in an age that had established countersatiric modes as the touchstones of the canon.

The Corn Law Rhymer as a Satirist

Elliott came to public attention during a late stage of the early nineteenth-century reform movement. Though he wrote sentimental rural poetry in the manner of George Crabbe, including for example the well-known *Village Patriarch* (1829), it was for the collection of *Corn Law Rhymes* that he was best known. The book contained works in a variety of mixed genres: sentimental, melodramatic tales of hardship, prophetic denunciations, and indignant satiric invectives. Coming during the buildup to the Reform Bill of 1832, the reviews were mostly positive, especially in their praise of Elliott's honesty and sincerity, his "genuine feeling" and economic and political independence. But Elliott himself said in response that this critical praise "ought to make Gifford, in his coffin, shake the worms from the brow of a dead slave," thus revealing that he saw the *Corn Law Rhymes* as a direct literary competitor with the most famous Tory satirist of the age and placing his work within the generic field of public, moral satire.

The son of an eighteenth-century radical, an old-style Jacobin known as "Devil Elliott" who worked at a Sheffield ironworks, Ebenezer Elliott was a laborer, a blacksmith and a mechanic; in his own words he was of "the lower, little removed from the lowest class."[3] He was eminently suited, therefore, for the public role he came to play. The titular subject of *The Corn Law Rhymes* is the series of protectionist bills leveling tariffs on imported corn (primarily wheat) in the attempt to control the price in favor of English farmers. The most significant legislation in Elliott's time was the Corn Law of 1815, which actually made illegal the sale of foreign wheat to millers so long as the domestic price remained below 80s./quarter. This was surely "intended to preserve for the agriculturalists a structure of prices and rents that had been created by the war,"[4] to offset the natural tendency of the economy to slump after Waterloo, but it served only to outrage the public outside the special interests of the farmers. There were petitions, protests, and riots on the eve of and just after the passage of the Bill.

> When the Corn Laws were passed in 1815, the Houses of Parliament had to be defended from the populace by troops. "NO CORN LAWS" was prominent among the banners at Peterloo, and remained so (especially at Lancaster) until the anti-Corn Law agitation of the 1840s.[5]

The law served only to make the cost of bread too high, therefore causing deleterious ripple effects felt throughout the agricultural economy. In addition, prices failed to stabilize and fluctuated wildly, driven in part by speculators who exploited the tariffs. Another law in 1828 was no more successful or popular, and the Reform Bill of 1832 focused dissatisfaction that led to the creation of the Anti–Corn Law League was in 1839. It was 1846 before the Corn Laws were repealed by Peel.

When Elliott's poetry came before the public in response to these laws, he was often automatically fitted into the category of "uneducated poet," the same group that included for example Stephen Duck and Mary Collier, even Robert Burns (whose popularity and critical reputation, however, allowed him ultimately to transcend the category). Rusticity of a sort, as depicted in a "rough" style of balladic simplicity and poems on village and farm life, is central to Elliott's work; and he owes much to the tradition of "realistic" counterpastoral culminating in Goldsmith and Crabbe, as he himself admitted: "I am called, as I expected to be, an unsuccessful imitator of the pauper-poetry of Wordsworth; I might be truly called an unfortunate imitator of Crabbe."[6]

His invocation of the by-now familiar critical opposition of Crabbe and Wordsworth—and his use of the term "unfortunate"—suggests that he already anticipates and understands the relative canonical fortunes of both poets in relation to his own work. The implication is that his verse is too closely allied with Crabbe's species of satire at a time when Wordsworthian Romanticism had effectively displaced it from the niche (of rural poetry or modern pastoral) both kinds of poetry had for a brief time shared. But the implication is that either way, whether aligned with Wordsworth or Crabbe, Elliott's own verse is simply unable to compete with the two stronger contenders. Wordsworth actually admired Elliott's poetry; he requested a copy in 1833 and eventually asserted that "None of us have done better than he has at his best."[7] Elliott owed a debt to Romanticism—and not only to Wordsworth's "pauper-poetry"—but he is correct in asserting his ultimately deeper connection to Crabbe (to apply the terms of the opposition as he used them). What Elliott and Crabbe primarily have in common, and what differentiates them both from Wordsworth, is a preference and reputation for satire. By the 1830s it was clear to most observers that the canon and the future belonged to Wordsworth's Romantic sincerity rather than to Crabbe's satiric realism. Identified in the popular mind with Romantic verse, with which he felt he could not compete, and attempting himself to imitate Crabbean satire, which as a species of writing had become displaced by Romanticism, Elliott is caught between changing modes at a crucial moment in literary history.

The most recognizable kind of satiric poem in the *Corn Law Rhymes,* the kind the public would have immediately identified as Elliott's, is the "popular song." This is a self-consciously literary imitation of the sort of popular satire found in William Hone's pamphlets or Thomas Wooler's *Black Dwarf,* or in the newspaper verse of innumerable, often anonymous, correspondents.

> THE FOUR DEARS
> Dear Sugar, dear Tea, and dear Corn
> Conspired with dear Representation,
> To laugh worth and honour to scorn,
> And beggar the whole British nation.
> Let us bribe the dear sharks, said dear Tea;
> Bribe, bribe, said dear Representation;
> Then buy with their own dear humbugg'd and be
> The bulwarks of Tory dictation.
>
> Dear Sugar and Tea, said dear Corn,
> Be true to dear Representation;
> And then the dear crown will be worn,
> But to dignify dearest taxation.
>
> Dear Sugar, dear Corn, and dear Tea,
> Stick to me, said dear Representation;

> Let us still pull together, and we
> Shall still rob the dear British nation.[8]

The short lines and epigrammatically simple diction, but especially the rough-and-ready allegory, mark this as deliberately of the broad popular tradition grounded in *Pilgrim's Progress* and seventeenth-century Dissenters' pamphlets as well as nineteenth-century political cartoons and reformist ballads. The same tradition informs the opening of Shelley's *Mask of Anarchy,* for example, with its triumphal procession of Murder, Fraud, and Anarchy, and of Coleridge's "Fire, Famine and Slaughter," in which the hellish allegories are made the friends of Pitt. The point is to label common enemies—whether actual persons or abstractions—as if with cartoon captions, the better to ridicule them and cast them out.

The rhetorical stance is one of deliberate ironic insubordination going back to civil-war tracts, or as found later in Burns, for example, a sign of Elliott's self-conscious rootedness in radical journalism and its traditions, notwithstanding the evidence of the more respectable, bookish venue of his own poetic productions. The direct pun on "dear" and the flippant tone are defiantly childlike in their simplicity, like the Hone-Cruikshank nursery-rhyme satire, *The Political House that Jack Built.* The choice of that key term, "dear," and the way Elliott manipulates it from line to line, is self-consciously effective, more subtle than it at first appears, suggesting first that the cost—just in terms of taxes and tariffs—of the current form of representation is too "dear," an unprofitable transaction. Virtual (and corrupt) representation means giving up too much for too little in return. The song ends, however, by glancing at serious, even loyal-sounding sentiment in the reminder that what is truly held "dear," in the sense of valuable and worthy, is the British nation herself, which is in danger of being destroyed by the economic manipulations of a "virtually" representative parliament and a crown that is merely a figurehead. Both, Elliott says, cost too much—come too "dear"—and like other dear commodities, namely the bread made from taxed corn, merely cheat the people. The most radical thing about the song, in the forward-looking, mid-nineteenth-century meaning of the term, is its implicit exhortation to its readers rationally to count the utilitarian cost of the current system. It manages this rhetorical exhortation through a series of modulations between sarcastic and serious, even sentimental inflections on the word "dear."

The Corn Law Rhymer as a Sentimentalist

That hint of a sentimental love of country contained in "the dear British nation" is part of Elliott's original appeal to contemporary readers. The implied undercurrent of moral seriousness, the stirring expression of deep feeling mixed with bitter satire, despite the apparent lightness of tone, is characteristic of his work as a whole. He himself best describes his passionate motivation to satire. When faced with the Corn Laws and the social structures they represent (including economic inequality in general), Elliott applies homegrown imagery straight from the forge, saying that his "feelings are *hammered* till they are 'cold-short'—habit can no longer bend them to courtesy; they snap—and fly off in a sarcasm."[9] In this figure, his feelings are an essential ore, a steely substance at the heart of his work; but they are also vulnerable to being "worked" and worked upon. The break or "snap" that leads to his "sarcasm" is a violent provocation that morally justifies strong satiric language in retort, what Blake would call the voice of honest indignation. Thus Elliott characterizes himself as a victim in angry, vocal sympathy with other victims. Under better conditions, the remark suggests, he might well be inclined to "bend" his naturally ductile feelings "to courtesy." But unnatural oppression has made his passions brittle. This is a metallurgical variation on the most conventional of satiric *topoi,* going back to Juvenal's claim that in his corrupt time it is difficult *not* to write satire, but there is also something of a new emphasis here—which is reflected in the laudatory reviews of Elliott—on the author's "feelings" as the justification and aesthetic touchstone for his satire.

This touchstone of sentiment more obviously measures the effect of Elliott's prophetic laments, such as "Oh Lord, How Long?" which ends with a conventionally vengeful rejection of vengeance, or "The Jacobin's Prayer," with its recognizable parodic echo of Milton's echoes of biblical prophecies:

> Avenge the plunder'd poor, oh Lord!
> But not with fire, but not with sword,
> Not as at Peterloo they died,
> Beneath the hoofs of coward pride.
>
> . . . . .
>
> Lord, let them feel thy heavier ire,
> Whip them, oh Lord! with poverty!
>
> . . . . .
>
> Yon yeoman used, in better days,
> When "D—n the French" was pray'r and praise,
> To teach us thrice a year or so,
> From Tory-rule what blessings flow:
>
> . . . . .
>
> For wool-tax now, and parish pay,
> He prays in curses every day,
> And bans the liberals and the peace.
> Lord, let him take his farm on lease!

That he may feel the growing pain
Which they endure who toil in vain.

Elliott's poem "prays in curses" of its own, magical incantations of satiric vengeance. The poem wishes for punishment but also for a forced sympathy where there is no natural sympathy. It performs this wish in the tones of prophetic anger.

Some form of this prophetic ire makes its way into many of Elliott's satires. His mockery is usually fueled by a sense of moral outrage with biblical overtones, audible even as a rumbling beneath the surface of his less serious songs, as in the following example of Elliottic "pauper-poetry":

> HOW DIFFERENT!
> Poor weaver, with the hopeless brow,
> And bare woe-whiten'd head;
> Thou art a pauper, all allow,
> All see thou begg'st thy bread;
> And yet thou dost not plunder slaves,
> Then tell them they are free;
> Nor hast thou join'd with tax-fed knaves,
> To corn-bill mine and me.
>
> What borough dost thou represent?
> Whom bid'st thou toil and pay?
> Why sitt'st not thou in pauperment,
> If baser beggar may?
> Where are thy hounds, thy palaced w—e,
> To feed on mine and me?
> Thy reverend pimp, thy coach and four,
> Thy thieves in livery?
>
> No house hast thou, no food, no fire;
> None bow to thee, alas
> A beggar! Yet not lord, nor squire?
> Say how comes this to pass?
> While yon proud pauper, dead to shame,
> Is fed by mine and me?
> And yet behind the rascal's name
> The scoundrel writes M.P!

(92)

The apparently middling-rank singer is situated *between* the pauper and the M. P., both of whose livelihoods he freely compares. From his vantage he can pity the pauper and accuse with authority the corrupt representative, who is busy "beggaring" the nation, thriving through structural pauperism or dependency on the wealth produced by others. The name-calling—"scoundrel," "rascal," and, implicitly, "whoremonger"—and partly deleted expletives are supported by Elliott's effective analysis of the politics of "different" stations. In this way it resembles the songs of Robert Burns:

> Ye see you birkie ca'd a lord
> Wha struts, and stares, and a' that,
> Though hundreds worship at his word,
> He's but a coof for a' that.
> For a' that, and a' that,
> His ribband, star and a' that,
> The man of independant mind,
> He looks and laughs at a' that.—[10]

The *Corn Law Rhymes* contains a ballad specifically giving voice to "Burns, from the Dead"—"But his voice—oh! Its tones were the music of scorn, / The laugh of the trumpet, impatient for morn!"(66–69; ll. 13–14). Despite this willed identification with Burns's independent stance, however, times have changed. Elliott's song is significantly less universal than Burns's, much further removed from the cosmopolitan spirit of the "Marseillaise." In its own particular way, however, it taps into similarly universal feelings and is both accessible and yet highly skilled, the sort of sharply honed satiric poetry Shelley wished to publish. Like Shelley's political writings, this song would teach its audience to recognize the potential inversions of meaning inherent in words like "representation" or "pauper." Less esoteric and more in the mainstream of party politics than William Blake's songs (to invoke another comparison), Elliott's rhetoric nonetheless wishes to promote a related linguistic nonconformity, a cantankerous propensity to question and reinterpret inherited differences.

The same play on the malleable meaning of pauperism, with similar ironic inversions, governs "Squire Leech," which, like Shelley's "England in 1819," argues that the powerful are the true leeches and the true paupers because they live off the lifeblood of the laboring poor.

> COME, Lord Pauper! pay my bill
> For radish-tops and fire;
> Ploughman Joe, and Weaver Bill,
> Keep Robert Leech, Esquire.
> You say, shares are fairly shared
> Between the high and low;
> While we starve, this joke runs hard

On bread-tax'd Will and Joe. . . .

(90–91)

Simplicity is more than style here; it is an integral part of the political message of the verse. Economic relations between the classes, between "the high and low," have been deliberately mystified, Elliott suggests, and what is required to reveal their true basis is plainly spoken mockery. In that mockery as a dominant tone lies the crucial generic difference between, say, the *Lyrical Ballads* and the *Corn Law Rhymes*.

There are important differences in subject matter as well. As all these poems and his nickname indicate, Elliott is primarily a satirist of basic economic conditions. (Even the Miltonic prophecy-curse quoted above prays, "Whip them, oh Lord! with *poverty!*" [my emphasis].) He actually wrote epigrams in the voices of famous political economists: "Adam Smith 1766":

> Wealth is not only coin or gold,
> But beef, cloth, brandy, rye;
> And all that can be bought or sold
> Is property.

And "Thomas Hobbes in 1651":

> The labour that but stirs the earth
> Imparts to worthless matter worth.

More than mere schoolbook exercises, as they may at first appear to be, these epigrams indicate a serious interest by the autodidact Elliott in theories of economic social structure—and in learning to boil them down to memorable public rhymes. The wordplay here is deliberately "reductive" in the sense that it is meant to reveal underlying utilitarian structural realities rather than to generate fruitful indeterminacies and rich ambiguities. Elliott even went so far as to dedicate a later edition of the *Corn Law Rhymes* to "All who revere the Memory of / OUR SECOND LOCKE, JEREMY BENTHAM." He always returns to the question of basic economies in songs like "The Four Dears" (quoted above) and in "The Taxed Cake":

> GIVE, give, they cry—and take!
> For willful men are they
> Who tax'd our cake, and took our cake,
> To throw our cake away.
> The cake grows less and less,
> For profits lessen, too;
> But land will pay, at last, I guess,

For land-won Waterloo.
They mix our bread with bran,
And call potatoes bread;
And, get who may, or keep who can,
The starved, they say, are fed.
Our rivals fatten fast,
But we are free to pay;
And dearly they shall pay, at last,
Who threw our cakes away.
Lend, lend thy wing, oh, steam,
And bear me to some clime
Where splendid beggars dare not dream
That law's best fruit is crime!
Oh, Landlord's Devil, take
Thy own elect, I pray,
That tax'd our cake, and took our cake,
To throw our cake away.

(62–63)

As I explained in chapter 3, using examples from Hone and Wooler, the potato possessed a disproportionate symbolic significance in postwar radical discourse, a material sign of the differences between high and low and of the natural tendency of the poor to revolt. The taxed cake also ultimately alludes to previous rebellions, both the American and the French. All this brings a larger political tradition to bear on the specific issues of the Corn Laws.

Elliott's poem is of its nineteenth-century moment, however. He represents a direct link between wartime radicalism and the Manchester School of Richard Cobden and John Bright, and the Free Trade movement in general. This is a utilitarian and progressive outlook, but one especially at home in the realm of technology. Perhaps the strangest passage in the poem is the apostrophe to "steam," the technology of industrial-age transportation, asking it to rescue the speaker from the economic evils of English industrial society. Wordsworth's notoriously celebratory sonnet on "Steamboats, Viaducts, and Railway" idealizes material technology in Romantic fashion ("Nature doth embrace / Her lawful offspring in Man's art"). In contrast, Elliott's poem is matter-of-factly at ease with technology as a tool for doing work, and with material stuff in general. Elsewhere in his poetry, economic lessons and prophetic exhortations are mixed in the same poem, as in the lines, "Hopeless trader, answer me! / What hath bread-tax done for thee?" (which can readily be compared to Shelley's "Men of England, wherefore plow").

Elliott's work is full of sentiment, even within his satires, but it is always nonetheless unblinkingly materialist, sometimes brutally pragmatic or even reductive in taking on precisely limited targets. In this way it is perfectly in sync with the utilitarian strain of the political mainstream on the eve of the Reform Bill of 1832. E. P. Thompson has asserted that by 1832, "there were *two* Radical publics: the middle-class, which looked forward to the Anti–Corn Law League, and the working-class, whose journalists . . . were already maturing the Chartist movement"; he goes on to suggest that the "dividing-line came to be, increasingly, not alternative 'reform' strategies . . . but alternative notions political economy."[11] In situating Elliott's political verse, it is important to measure the significant distance he has traveled by 1828 from Thomas Wooler's threatening radical satire. Still, his example challenges the clear distinction between ameliorative reformers and revolutionary Chartists. His class background, as well as his temperament, affiliated him with the radicals leading up to Chartism, while his fundamental lived experience in trade and his tendency to utilitarianism allied him with the middle-class reformers of the Anti–Corn Law League. From a radical family himself and considered a "working class" poet, self-educated rather than "uneducated," Elliott's interests were from 1815–32 aligned with the Sheffield manufacturers; but, as Elie Halévy explains, the protests leading up to the Corn Law of 1815 and the riots afterwards "proved that on the question of Free Trade the manufacturers had working-class opinion on their side, despite the conflict of interests between employers and employed, and could therefore organize against a small group of agriculturalists a large popular opposition party truly representative of the will of the nation."[12] Elliott performed the *Rhymes* as the respectable spokesman for the Anti–Corn Law League, which, as Nigel Cross observes, "was essentially a manufacturer's pressure group," so "it was not surprising that *Corn Law Rhymes* should have proved an instant success with progressive middle-class readers, quite apart from their evident literary merit."[13] Though he retained a legacy of radicalism from the 1790s and the war, his political appeal was to a broad, middle-class audience.

This appeal is the reason his literary defenders were often so concerned and yet so hard pressed to separate Elliott's poetry from his politics. The *New Monthly Magazine* claimed to be the first to notice Elliott, printing his "Byron and Napoleon" in 1831 and claiming that it demonstrated "the same nerve, vigour, and originality on the one hand—the same roughness and obscurity on the other."[14] In 1831, the *New Monthly* published a "Letter to Doctor Southey . . . Respecting a Remarkable Poem by a Mechanic," which invoked Southey's own book on the *Uneducated Poets*.

You have therein expressed a doubt, scarce seriously perhaps, whether, indeed, the "March of Intellect," bannered by tracts and hydrostatics, with steam-carriages for its cavalry, and the Mechanics' Institute for its camp, will

allow persons of lowly rank to cultivate gardens so lovely as those of poetry—
but you imagine the Utilitarians will add, also, so useless. (289)

As evidence to the contrary, the writer presents Elliott, of whose politics he
knows Southey will not approve, but whose aesthetic merits he hopes the
laureate will recognize. The reviewer assumes that the poetic efforts of men
like Elliott must be depoliticized, walled around, and reduced to decorative
"gardens."

Southey was also the author of the essay on the "Popular Disaffection"
of writers, in which he seemed to blame much of the political turmoil of
the times on writers like "the notorious Junius" who first demonstrated in
their "Jacobin" satire the power of insubordinate and subversive publications. Ironically, as the piratical radical publishers were well aware, the
young Southey, the author of *Wat Tyler,* could himself be counted among
these writers. The *New Monthly* reviewer is at pains to praise the aesthetic
qualities and feeling of Elliott's verse ("gardens so lovely as those of poetry") but then moves into a reading of the Ranter's sermon, which is the
most obviously satiric portion of the poem. This passage, the reviewer says,
is "dark, menacing, and stern; a vein of fierce and coarse, but never vulgar
sarcasm, wanders through the whole, and makes, at times, some of the
most effective parts of the poem"(291). The specific power of Elliott's poetry is herein recognized—contrary to the larger rhetorical purpose of the
reviewer—as fundamentally satiric. This stands in contradiction to the
overall plea to Southey to consider Elliott's aesthetic merits apart from his
politics. Indeed, the *New Monthly* under Henry Colburn continued to try
to shape Elliott's identity, to depoliticize his poetry by publishing (and
publicizing) his nonsatirical, sentimental verses, prefacing one such contribution, a sublime prophetic vision of Byron and Napoleon in heaven,
with this earnest indirect exhortation to the poet himself:

> We are sure that every man of pure and genuine knowledge of criticism will
> unite with us in hailing the rise of a Poet of so great promise, from the lower
> ranks of life and the heart of a manufacturing town—and in trusting that
> powers of so high an order will be exerted in a flight more lofty and sustained,
> than those in which they have, as yet, toyed with their own strength. (*New
> Monthly Magazine,* 1831, pt. II, p. 552)

The critics' pressure toward greater sincerity and sublimity, away from
popular satire and toward more "serious" kinds of poetry, is an attempt to
save Elliott from his own ephemerality, to rescue him for posterity and the
canon. As Joseph Warton had argued long ago, "WIT and SATIRE and
transitory and perishable, but NATURE and PASSION are eternal."[15] If

such rescue attempts ultimately failed, this was not because they misjudged public taste or because Elliott lacked poetic ambition. It was because his sentimental side was too weak to stand once the satire was discarded. This despite the fact that Elliott's anger was increasingly construed as something like a post-Romantic Dickensian gesture of honest indignation in the face of suffering, the mark of the enlightened, middle-class, Victorian-era reformer. Elliott's anger *can* be read as essentially unsatiric, and so his defenders chose to read it. Elliott's ire is construable as a kind of "radical" anger potentially adoptable by a wide spectrum of the nascent middle-class audience at the advent of the age of Reform. If only he had written more sincerely, less satirically, as in this "Song":

> CHILD, is thy father dead?
> Father is gone!
> Why did they tax his bread?
> God's will be done!
> Mother has sold her bed;
> Better to die than wed!
> Where shall she lay her head?
> Home we have none! . . .

(60–61)

Even Elliott's early satire was often combined with sentimental modes, sometimes in the same poem. The overall effect encouraged his supporters to offset his reputation for radical satire and "sarcasm" with the sanction of his virtuous sincerity.

Elliott's satire echoes earlier radicalism, but it displays and demands of its readers sincerity of feeling. His precarious survival for a time at the margin of the canon seems to have depended on just this construction of his work as, underneath, a sincere expression of natural, deep feeling, which could be seen as outweighing his satiric tendencies. Witness the rhetorical emphasis of Margaret Oliphant's encapsulation of Elliott in a paragraph on "minor" writers for her important 1882 *Literary History of England:* "In hardheaded Yorkshire, the rude and fervent spirit—usually inspired with political themes, but sometimes dropping into unexpected strains of tenderness—of Ebenezer Elliot [*sic*]."[16] The implied opposition is between Elliott's satire and his sentiment: "usually . . . political . . . but sometimes . . . unexpected strains of tenderness." By splitting in two what are so frequently combined in Elliott's work—the "political themes" (nearly coextensive with his satire) from the supposedly rarer ("unexpected") "tenderness"—Oliphant elevates the latter at the expense of the former, preserving the sentimental portrait of the working-class poet, though not very prominently and not for long. For Oliphant this is primarily a way to affiliate Elliott with what appeared from her vantage as the dominant modes of his era, modes of Romantic sensibility. But Elliott's identity as a political satirist always stubbornly remains in the mix to set him apart from the Romantics. An 1853 American edition of his *Poems* opens with a telling memoir of Elliott, its bibliographic codes (the text is framed by vinous decorations on every page) reinforcing the stately memorial effect. The essay moves from acknowledging Elliott's power as a political satirist to praising his humanitarian qualities:

> His stern and indignant attacks on the Corn-laws are well known to the world. The vigorous strains of his poetry had a great influence in producing the state of public opinion that led to their repeal. His weapons were composed of "songs, sarcasms, curses, and battle-cries." His verses had the best qualities of his own Sheffield steel—strong, keen, pointed, armed with a murderous edge, and flashing torrent of sun at the slightest friction. His muse was inspired with a genuine sympathy with the people, and an indignant horror or every from of social oppression. In many respects, he is entitled to the blessed and venerable name of Poet of Humanity.[17]

In a gradual transition, here Elliott's poetic muse, "genuine sympathy," leads to the transcendent naming of him as "blessed" and as a universal "Poet."

This sort of attempted apotheosis was reiterated many times in Victorian-period literary history, and not only on behalf of Elliott: Percy Shelley's reputation underwent a similar process of revisionist canonization as his heirs selected his works, protected his manuscripts, and screened visitors and scholars, choosing those who would pay suitable tribute to the spiritualized, monumentalized poet. Even more than in Shelley's case, with Elliott this process depended on suppressing his (politically) irreverent satiric tendencies. This happened while the popular taste in satire moved away from Hone's scurrilous pamphlets and closer to "Boz's" parlor-humor, resulting eventually in the respectable satires of *Punch*.[18] In 1854 William Thackeray wrote of the distance traveled from the Regency to his own mid-Victorian era, saying that though society would wish to preserve "Satyr with his pipe and dances and gambols,"

> we have washed, combed, clothed, and taught the rogue good manners: or rather, let us say, he has learned them himself; for he is of nature soft and kindly, and he has put aside his mad pranks and tipsy habits; and, frolicsome always, has become gentle and harmless, smitten into shame by the pure presence of our women and the sweet confiding smiles of our children.[19]

In numerous critical defenses, Elliott was presented to the public similarly "cleaned up" and his satire—never "soft and kindly"—was relegated to a subordinate place. Eventually, the satire would be underplayed even further in favor of the late Romantic elements in Elliott's verse.[20] By the time Arthur Symons writes his history of the Romantic movement in 1909, for example, Elliott appears as a minor Crabbe, related to Thomas Hood and (distantly) to Wordsworth, and, with only a brief mention of his "labour poetry," treated with almost no acknowledgment of the dominant satiric tendencies of his work.[21]

The Corn Law Rhymer as a Sign of the Times

At the height of his short day of fame, Elliott looked to some like a healthy alternative to the established forms of sentimental Romantic poetry, namely Thomas Carlyle, whose 1832 review of the 1831 third edition of *Corn Law Rhymes* asks "What such a one, so gifted and so placed, shall say to a Time like ours" (131), and then sketches out his own idea of an answer. Carlyle's early Victorian view of this working-class poet and angry satirist is especially interesting because it praises Elliott by attacking Romantic modes.

> Poetry having ceased to be read, or published, or written, how can it continue to be reviewed? With your Lake Schools, and Border-Thief Schools, and Cockney and Satanic Schools, there has been enough to do; and now, all these Schools having burnt or smouldered themselves out, and left nothing behind but a wide-spread wreck of ashes, dust and cinders,—or perhaps dying embers, kicked to and fro under the feet of innumerable women and children in the Magazines, and at best blown here and there into transient sputters, with vapor enough, so as to form what you might name a boundless Green-sick, or New-Sentimental, or Sleep-Awake School,—what remains but to adjust ourselves to circumstances?[22]

This is in the voice of the editorial persona, "Smelfungus Redivivus." As he does in *Sartor Resartus,* here Carlyle uses a form of Romantic irony to frame his "prophetico-satiric" pronouncements. In his own more detached and ironic voice, but still in a mood of belatedness, Carlyle reports that he has been watching the skies for changes in the literary weather, and has recently spotted Elliott's work, which he nearly damns with condescendingly faint praise as appearing on the horizon like "some little fraction of a rainbow; hues of joy and harmony, painted out of troublous tears."

> No round full bow, indeed; gloriously spanning the heavens; shone on by the full sun; ad with seven-striped, gold-crimson border (as is in some sort the office of Poetry) dividing Black from Brilliant: not such; alas! Far from it! Yet in

> very truth, a little prismatic blush, glowing genuine among the wet clouds;
> which proceeds, if you will, from a sun cloud-hidden, yet indicates that a sun
> does shine, and above those vapors, a whole azure vault and celestial firma-
> ment stretch serene. (121).

But having set this limit to its praise, the review goes on to celebrate Elliott
as "genuine," sincere, and original—all qualities set by Carlyle in salutary
contrast to gloomy, overimaginative Romantic intensity—especially as it is
exemplified in Byron.

These very terms of praise are themselves recognizably Romantic. Carlyle's point is to associate Elliott in this way with what the times consider
valuable in poetry (and these are Romantic values). Moreover, this is part of
his own program to negotiate a space for his own creative genius in the wake
of Romanticism, an attempt to pit a positive version of Romanticism against
its negation, what he would call "the everlasting no" but might also be called
the Romantic Agony.

> Be of what class he may, the man is provided, as we can perceive, with a ra-
> tional god-created soul; which too has fashioned itself into some clearness,
> some self-subsistence, and can actually see and know with its own organs; and
> in rugged substantial English, nay with tones of poetic melody, utter forth
> what it has seen. (122)

Elliott is represented as a man speaking to men, in language really used by
men, writing a poetry of experience; but his rugged, working-class background and clear-eyed self-sufficiency set him apart from the darker side of
the Romantics themselves—"consider what advantage those same uneducated Working classes have over the educated Unworking classes, in one particular; herein, namely, that they must *work*. To work! What incalculable
sources of cultivation lie in that process . . ." (126). For Carlyle, Elliott represents a bridge to his desired post-Romantic ideal of healthy action, which
he will express more fully in *Sartor Resartus* ("Produce!"): "*Do* one thing, for
the first time in thy life do a thing!" (127).

Ultimately, though he wishes to stress Elliott's background, Carlyle also
questions the whole popular cliché of the "uneducated" poet: "For a generation that reads Cobbett's Prose, and Burns's Poetry, it need be no miracle that
here is also a man who can handle both pen and hammer like a man" (123).
Moreover, he asks, "what, after all, is meant by uneducated, in a time when
Books have come into the world; come to be household furniture in every
habitation of the civilized world? In the poorest cottage are Books . . ." (125).
Elliott serves as the type of the modern autodidact poet who seeks no patronage and needs none, Carlyle claims, but presents himself as "sturdy, defiant, al-

most menacing;" he is a poet of "Sincerity" and "Originality," and though too practical and manly to be a "sentimentalizer," he is a man of feeling (128–29).

In keeping with this line of praise, Carlyle says in one passage that Elliott's genuineness and realism remind him of George Crabbe. Carlyle seems in the same passage somewhat embarrassed by some of the results of Elliott's self-education, which has left something of "a tang of the Circulating Libraries":

> To be reminded of Crabbe, with his truthful severity of style, in such a place, we cannot object; but what if there were a slight bravura dash of the fair tuneful Hemans? Still more, what have we to do with Byron, and his fierce vociferous mouthings, whether "passionate," or not passionate and only theatrical? . . . Strength, if that be the thing aimed at, does not manifest itself in spasms, but in stout bearing of burdens. (136)

In this context Felicia Hemans, one of the best-selling poets of her age, stands for overly popular sentimentality, the "feminized" verse then dominating the magazines and gift-book annuals. Despite his dismissive language, Carlyle knows very well that it is from Hemans's strengths that he must distinguish Elliott.[23] But Byron stands for the darkest negations of passionate Romanticism, the Romantic Agony itself. In this company, the un-Romantic Crabbe stands out as a positive, healthy alternative, a realist and moralist, and one in touch with the salt-of-the-earth existence Carlyle idealizes. He cites an exemplary Crabbean portrait by Elliott, the story of Jem the Poacher, which he says represents a "rustic, rude existence; barren moors, with the smoke of Forges rising over the waste expanse. Alas, no Arcadia; but the actual dwelling-place of actual toil-grimed sons of Tubalcain . . ." (139). Though there are "blossoms" to be found in this counter-pastoral world, a modest natural "inheritance" for the "Craftsman" when he "pauses in his toil," this is mostly the realm of satiric truth rather than Romantic fantasy, and for this Carlyle values Elliott's poetry, almost against the grain of his larger program of celebrating Elliott's positive Romantic qualities.

At the time he was writing this review, Carlyle had just completed but not yet published *Sartor Resartus,* a Romantic-ironic satire in pursuit of self-transcendence, which he called a "kind of 'Satirical Extravaganza on Things in general,'" This same "prophetico-satiric" style is reflected in the Elliott review, the same stylistic medley and the same plot of the casting out of the Romantic skepticism—the product of the "Satanic School" at the Center of Indifference—and redemptive turn towards an affirmation of life and productive activity. At this point in his own literary career, therefore, it is no surprise that Carlyle would find Elliott a useful example of a poetry and authorial outlook based on work and faith (he spends several paragraphs on Elliott's religious themes). But the most recognizably satiric qualities of Elliott's writing (which even his son-in-law saw the need to defend) are downplayed or ignored by Carlyle, replaced with a certified genuineness and sincerity, just as Crabbe is represented as "truthful and severe" rather than satiric or judgmental. Crabbe is in this way Romanticized in order to make him a suitable scourge for the Romantics, in order to allow Carlyle to declare the affiliated Romantic schools (Laker, Satanic, Cockney) old hat.

A similar yet even more severe fate awaits Elliott, it is clear. His rhymes are posed as a healthy alternative to the poetry of the Romantics, but they must nonetheless be canonized, if they are to be canonized, along the same lines as Romantic writing, his sarcasms more or less purged in favor of his sincerities. Where Elliott displeases Carlyle, it is because he tries to imitate from an inferior position (including, it is clear, his inferior class position) the satiric Byron, with the result an unfortunate "pert snappishness"—"In his vituperative prose Notes, he seems embarrassed; and but ill hides his embarrassment, under an air of predetermined sarcasm; of knowing briskness, almost of vulgar pertness" (137). This echoes Elliott's own description of his "feelings," quoted above, when they are "*hammered* till they are 'cold-short'—habit can no longer bend them to courtesy; they snap—and fly off in a sarcasm." But Carlyle's additional qualifiers and modifications—"pertness" and "pert snappishness"—are telling choices of words, invoking the very class codes from which he had earlier claimed Elliott was free.

> He says, he cannot help it; he is poor, hard-worked, and "soot is soot." True, indeed; yet there is no connection between Poverty and Discourtesy; which latter originates in Dulness alone. Courtesy is the due of man to man; not of suit-of-clothes to suit-of-clothes. He who could master so many things, and make even Corn-Laws rhyme, we require of him this further thing: a bearing worthy of himself, and of the order he belongs to,—the highest and most ancient of all orders, that of Manhood. A pert snappishness is no manner for a brave man . . . (137)

It is difficult to escape the conclusion that direct satire in the dialect of the working class is simply a generic and social affront to Carlyle, despite his overall preference for Elliott's Crabbean perspective over stereotypical Romanticism. Elliott must become classless and sincere if he is to ascend to the canon. Though he lectures aristocratic readers, as well, urging them through *noblesse oblige* to learn from Elliott's representations of working life a certain sympathetic compassion, he finds himself ambivalently using Elliott as a lesson and giving lessons to Elliott. But Carlyle is caught in a contradiction:

despite his patronizing dehortation against the "snappish dialect," he seems to believe that it is primarily Elliott's humble origins that can save him from falling into Byron's everlasting no:

> In good truth, if many a sickly and sulky Byron, or Byronlet, glooming over the woes of existence, and how unworthy God's Universe is to have so distinguished a resident, could transport himself into the patched coat and sooty apron of a Sheffield Blacksmith, made with a strange faculties and feelings as he, made by God Almighty all one as he was,—it would throw a light on much for him. (141)

On such grounds, Carlyle insists, Elliott might theoretically build a serious poetry of *moral* reform.

> For is has been often said, and must often be said again, that all Reform except a moral one will prove unavailing. Political Reform, pressingly enough wanted, can indeed root out the weeds . . . but it leaves the ground *empty*,— neither ready for noble fruits, or for new worse tares." (143)

Elliott's choice of the mode of popular satire proves problematic, so Carlyle handles it by elevating Elliott's countersatiric qualities, his genuineness, religion, and heartfelt earnestness.

By the time he has finished, Carlyle has reconstructed Elliott—at least potentially—as something of a post-Crabbean realist *and* a sub-Carlylean prophet, a universal Man telling God's truth. He says he will not admonish Elliott to quit politics (though he hints he might wish to) but will exhort him to engage his mind in "rather considering what, in his own sphere, could be *done,* than what, in his own or other spheres, out to be *destroyed*"(148). Carlyle even counsels the Corn Law Rhymer to take up prose, his own preferred mode of public address: "Will our Rhymer consider himself, then; and decide for what is actually best. Rhyme, up to this hour, never seems altogether obedient to him; and disobedient Rhyme,—who would ride on *it* that had once leaned walking!" (148). Thus imagined as depoliticized, "depoeticized," and to some degree desatirized—or at least with his satire leavened with prophetic sincerity—Elliott seems to be made to stand as an exemplary figure of the future of public discourse for Carlyle, a writer fitted to his own program for moral and spiritual (rather than political) reform. What is most remarkable about the essay is the extent to which Carlyle is willing to go in order to remake Elliott as anything but what he was: a satirist.

John Rosenberg has said of *Sartor Resartus* that through the Romantic-ironic character of Herr Teufelsdröckh, Carlyle manages both to be himself and to mock himself, to be poet and anti-poet. Beneath Teufelsdröckh's outlandish dress and speech we recognize the soul of a Romantic poet, and in Carlyle's ambivalence toward his hero we detect his deeper ambivalences toward Romanticism. . . . *Sartor Resartus* may be read as Romanticism half-way down the road to renouncing itself. . . .[24]

The review of Elliott's *Corn Law Rhymes,* using the same Romantic-ironic devices and tones as *Sartor Resartus,* betrays an even more Romantic leaning in Carlyle's ambivalence. But both Carlyle's achieved distance from Romanticism and the need for that distance—due to the cultural power of the "New-Sentimental" and other post-Romantic schools—bespeak a significant moment in the canonization of Romantic modes. It is this same moment at which Elliott appears on the scene and fairly quickly fades away. Elliott is presented to the public in an elegiac tone in Carlyle's essay, since the point is in a limited way to canonize him and the canonical is always already passed away, into the timeless past of historical transcendence.[25] But at least immediately after the establishment of the touchstones of Romanticism, topical, political satire—and especially of the "low" or "laboring" variety, the "pert" discourteous vein of "sarcasm"—simply cannot be admitted to the canon on its own. In reading the review, it is difficult to avoid the conclusion that Carlyle is in part concerned to justify his own "higher" satire and is thus attempting to differentiate Elliott's brand of satiric prophecy from his own in order to assure his own ultimate dominance. Carlyle reduces Elliott to a minor Romantic in order supposedly to praise him but in reality to trap him in the realm of his own precursors. In this way, Carlyle's essay would turn the Corn Law Rhymer into a doomed harbinger of a new species of active, affirming, prophetico-satiric writing: his own.

Any sincere attempt by Carlyle to instruct and reconstruct Elliott for canonization would have been doomed at any rate, as subsequent history has verified. Any cursory reading of the *Corn Law Rhymes* themselves reveals how far Carlyle's wishfully projected image of Elliott as a pious and industrious model has diverged from the surface qualities of the voice of Elliott's characteristic sentimental-sarcastic satire:

> DRONE v. WORKER
> How God speeds the tax-bribed plough,
>   Fen and moor declare, man;
> Where once fed the poor man's cow,
>   ACRES drives his share, man.
> But he did not steal the fen,
>   Did not steal the moor, man;
> If he feeds on starving men,
>   Still he loves the poor, man.

Hush! he bullies state and throne,
　　Quids them in his jaw, man;
Thine and mine he calls his own;
　　Acres' lie is law, man.
Acres eats his tax on bread,
　　Acres loves the plough, man;
Acres' dogs are better fed,
　　Beggar's slave! than thou, man.
Acres' feeder pays his debts,
　　Waxes thin and pale, man,
Harder works, and poorer gets,
　　Pays his debts in jail, man.

Like much satire, this poem traffics in allegorical types and masks. And yet,
the allegory here is deliberately transparent, the types based on observed
ways of living. "Acres" the landowner is the target, and the snarling repeti-
tion of "man" reminds us of our speaker's station and also indirectly addresses us, the reader, in a tone of fraternal equality. The lines grow
increasingly spare, almost encrypted in their telegraphic simplicity, as the
satiric chant extends itself:

Acres in a palace lives,
　　While his feeder pines, man;
Palaced beggar ne'er forgives
　　Dog on whom he dines, man.
Acres' feeder, beggar'd, begs,
　　Treadmill'd rogue is he, man;
Scamp! he deals in pheasants' eggs,—
　　Hangs on gallows tree, man!
Who would be an useful man?
　　Who sell cloth, or hats, man?
Who make boiler, or mend pan?
　　Who keep Acres' brats, man?
Better ride, and represent—
　　Better borough tools, man;
Better sit in pauperment—
　　Better corn-law fools, man.

Then, as in so many Romantic and radical satires of the period, Elliott's attack turns into a rousing exhortation, a call to the action of resistance:

Why not right the plunder'd poor?
　　Why not use our own, man?

Plough the seas, and not the moor?
    Why not pick a bone, man?
Lo, the merchant builds huge mills,—
    Bread-tax'd thinks, and sighs, man!
Thousand mouths and bellies fills,—
    Bread-tax'd breaks, and dies, man!
Thousand mouths and bellies, then,
    Bread-tax'd, writhe and swear, man:
England once bred honest men,
    Bread-tax'd, Burke and Hare, man!
Hark ye! millions soon may pine,
    Starving millions curse, man,
Desperate millions long to dine
    A-la-Burke, and worse, man!
What will then remain to eat?
    Who be eaten then, man?
"Few may part, though many meet,"
    At Famine's Feast, ye ken, man.

                                                            (87–89)

"A-la-Burke and worse" is an open threat with a dense and loaded history, a promise of apocalyptic mob violence, should reform fail. The bloody Feast of Famine—at this distance and with a canonical context unavailable to Elliott—recalls the line running from Charles Churchill to Percy Bysshe Shelley, whose suppressed and virtually unknown *Swellfoot the Tyrant* earlier imagined such a feast as the turning point for English society after Peterloo. Elliott's is a body of work belonging to that line of Romantic-period radical satire, but it was produced at a moment when such satire was expected to make itself more presentable to a middle-class audience and was being pressed by intellectual social critics like Carlyle to strike less confrontational and discourteous stances, to blend itself with prophetic and spiritual modes toward the higher goal of a natural supernaturalism. Nevertheless, as this study has been intent to demonstrate, the subtradition of radical satire, with the related satiric traditions running throughout the Romantic period, had already helped to define and shape, bound and set off from without and within what would by the Victorian period become solidified as the dominant modes of the time, the unsatiric, even countersatiric modes of Romanticism.

Notes

Introduction

1. Robert Southey, "On the Rise and Progress of Popular Disaffection," in *Essays, Moral and Political,* 2 vols. (1817; London: John Murray, 1832), II, 82. The identity of Junius remained a mystery, and even Edmund Burke was suspected. For an argument that he was Sir Philip Francis, see Alvar Ellegård, *Who Was Junius?* (The Hague, 1962).

2. Byron, "The Vision of Judgment" in *Lord Byron: The Complete Poetical Works,* ed. Jerome J. McGann and Barry Weller, 7 vols. (Oxford: Clarendon Press, 1980–92), VI, 309–45.

3. M. H. Abrams, *Natural Supernaturalism: Tradition and Revolution in Romantic Literature* (New York: W. W. Norton, 1971), p. 13.

4. See Anne K. Mellor, *English Romantic Irony* (Cambridge: Harvard University Press, 1980).

5. Jerome J. McGann, *The Romantic Ideology: A Critical Investigation* (Chicago and London: University of Chicago Press, 1983), pp. 23–24.

6. Jerome J. McGann, *Towards a Literature of Knowledge* (Oxford: Clarendon Press, 1989), p. 39.

7. McGann, *Towards a Literature of Knowledge,* p. 39.

8. McGann, "Literary Pragmatics and the Editorial Horizon," in *Devils and Angels: Textual Editing and Literary Theory,* ed. Philip Cohen (Charlottesville and London: University Press of Virginia, 1991), pp. 1–21 (13).

9. Marilyn Butler, "Satire and the Images of Self in the Romantic Period: The Long Tradition of Hazlitt's *Liber Amoris,*" in *English Satire and the Satiric Tradition,* ed. Claude Rawson (Oxford: Basil Blackwell, 1984), 209–25 (209).

10. Stuart Curran, *Poetic Form and British Romanticism* (New York and Oxford: Oxford University Press, 1986), pp. 12–13.

11. Gary Dyer, *British Satire and the Politics of Style, 1789–1832* (Cambridge: Cambridge University Press, 1997). Treatments of Romantic-period satire before this tend to be uneven and burdened with a lack of information on the primary texts, which often accompanies an assumption that there is no significant satire after Pope. Perhaps the clearest example is Thomas Lockwood's *Post–Augustan Satire: Charles Churchill and Satirical Poetry, 1750–1800* (Seattle and London: University of Washington Press, 1979),

which contains some useful information on poets and their works but whose bias is revealed in the admission that Lockwood views his study as "something in the way of an autopsy" (p. 3). One recent helpful study is Claude Rawson's *Satire and Sentiment, 1660–1830* (Cambridge: Cambridge University Press, 1994). Rawson places his key terms in narrative sequence, "a patrician culture in decline" being reflected in the decline of satire and its displacement by sentimental modes (xi). As this implies, Rawson is interested in strong canonical works, and accepts as given the opposition of satiric and sentimental modes it is my purpose to challenge.

12. The importance of Romantic-period parody, precisely defined, is also beginning to become apparent, beginning with a collection edited by David A. Kent and D. R. Ewen, *Romantic Parodies 1797–1831* (London and Toronto: Associated University Presses, 1992), and culminating in the more complete anthology edited by Graeme Stones and John Strachan, *Parodies of the Romantic Age*, 5 vols. (London: Pickering & Chatto, 1999).

13. Marilyn Butler, *Romantics, Rebels and Reactionaries* (New York and Oxford: Oxford University Press, 1982), p. 2.

14. For a summary of precisely how this shift in critical opinion was effected, see Upali Amarasinghe, *Dryden and Pope in the Early Nineteenth Century: A Study of Changing Literary Taste, 1800–1830* (Cambridge: Cambridge University Press, 1962).

15. Joseph Warton, *Essay on Pope*, 2 vols. (London: 1756–82), I, 344; the importance of Warton's judgments is discussed by Amarasinghe, esp. pp. 27–51.

16. David Perkins, "The Construction of 'The Romantic Movement' as a Literary Classification," *Nineteenth-Century Literature* (1990), 129–43.

17. M. M. Bakhtin, *The Dialogic Imagination*, ed. Michael Holquist, trans. Caryl Emerson and Michael Holquist (Austin: University of Texas Press, 1981); Peter Stallybrass and Allon White, *The Politics and Poetics of Transgression* (Ithaca: Cornell University Press, 1986).

18. I take the example of the contextualized wink from Gilbert Ryle, as cited in Clifford Geertz's "Thick Description: Toward an Interpretive Theory of Culture," in *The Interpretation of Cultures* (New York: Harper Collins/Basic Books, 1973), pp. 3–30.

19. Aubrey Beardsley's illustrations to *The Rape of the Lock* first appeared in an 1896 edition (London: Leonard Smithers), which was reprinted by Dover Publications in 1968.

20. Gary Taylor, *Cultural Selection: Why Some Achievements Survive the Test of Time—and Others Don't* (New York: Basic Books/Harper Collins, 1996).

21. Pierre Bourdieu, *Distinction: A Social Critique of the Judgement of Taste*, trans. Richard Nice (Cambridge, Mass.: Harvard University Press, 1984), p. 511. For a useful sample of relevant applications of Bourdieu's theory to literary studies, see the special issue of *Modern Language Quarterly* 58.4 (December 1997), especially articles by John Guillory, William Paulson, Trevor Ross, and Marilyn Butler.

22. Pierre Bourdieu, "The Field of Cultural Production, or: the Economic World Reversed," *Poetics* 12 (1983), 311–56 (315).

Chapter 1

1. Letter to Samuel Rogers, 29 September 1808, *The Letters of William and Dorothy Wordsworth: The Middle Years,* ed. Ernest de Selincourt, 6 vols. (Oxford: Clarendon Press, 1935–39; 1937), I, 243–45.

2. As Frank Whitehead puts it in *George Crabbe: A Reappraisal* (Selingsgrove: Susquehanna University Press; London: Associated University Presses, 1995),"in 1807, in his fifty-third year, [Crabbe] launched into a new writing career . . ." (p. 15).

3. Robert L. Chamberlain, *George Crabbe* (New York: Twayne, 1965), p. 102.

4. William Hazlitt, *The Spirit of the Age* (1825) in *The Complete Works of William Hazlitt,* ed. P. P. Howe, 21 vols. (London: J. M. Dent and Sons, 1930–34; 1932), XI, 164.

5. Arthur O. Lovejoy, "On Discriminations of Romanticisms," *PMLA* 39 (1924), 229–53; Jerome J. McGann, "Rethinking Romanticism," *ELH* 59 (1992), 735–54; Raymond Williams, *The Country and the City* (New York: Oxford University Press, 1973), esp. pp. 90–95; René Huchéns, *George Crabbe and His Times 1754–1832* (New York: E. P. Dutton, 1907), p. 255. Some other notable treatments include that of Roger Sales, *English Literature in History 1780–1830: Pastoral and Politics* (New York: St. Martin's, 1983), who cuts through critical pieties in his assessment of Crabbe as an apologist for "officialdom," a perspective I find helpful even if it sometimes verges on reductionism. One widespread twentieth-century reading of Crabbe is expressed in an essay by L. J. Swingle, "Late Crabbe in Relation to the Augustans and Romantics: The Temporal Labyrinth of his Tales in Verse, 1812," *ELH* 42 (1975), 580–94, which argues that late Crabbe, at least, looks more like modernism than either "Augustanism" or "Romanticism." It may be that Crabbe's Romantic-period *satire* is what looks to us more like modernism than anything usually called "Romantic."

6. *Byron's Letters and Journals,* ed. Leslie Marchand, 12 vols. (Cambridge: Harvard University Press, 1973–82), V, 265 (15 September 1817). Those going the wrong way, according to Byron, included those now recognized as Romantic: Scott, Southey, Wordsworth, Moore, Campbell, and Byron himself.

7. Leslie Stephen, *Cornhill Magazine* XXX (1874), 454–73, in *Crabbe: The Critical Heritage,* ed. Arthur Pollard (London and Boston: Routledge & Kegan Paul, 1972), pp. 437–50 (447–48). Despite this opposition of Crabbe and Keats, Stephen means to preserve Crabbe's reputation against the most "bigoted" Keatsians. Coventry Patmore compares Crabbe and Shelley in the *St. James Gazette,* 16 February 1887, in Pollard, pp. 465–67.

8. Byron, *English Bards and Scotch Reviewers,* l. 858, *Lord Byron: The Complete Poetical Works,* ed. Jerome J. McGann and Barry Weller, 7 vols. (Oxford:

Clarendon Press, 1980–92; 1980), I, 256; Francis Jeffrey, writing in the *Edinburgh Review* (November 1812), 277–305; (April 1810), 30–55.

9. Jerome J. McGann, "The Anachronism of George Crabbe," in *The Beauty of Inflections: Literary Investigations in Historical Method and Theory* (Oxford: Clarendon Press, 1988), pp. 294–312 (p. 294). McGann anticipates some of my arguments, here, beginning with his assertion that the Romantic judgments against Crabbe were "part of a polemic on behalf of certain poetical criteria" (p. 295), and his recognition that Jeffrey's critical response is "one of the most important local manifestations of the various cultural struggles which marked the entire period" (p. 295). I intend, however, to shift the emphasis to genre, and to take the *differences* between Crabbe and the Romantics as the starting place for examining how those differences themselves get constructed in terms of genre and mode.

10. *Edinburgh Review,* July 1819, 118–48.

11. Fenwick note to "Lucy Gray," *The Poetical Works of William Wordsworth,* ed. Ernest de Selincourt and Helen Darbishire, 5 vols. (Oxford: Clarendon Press, 1940–49; 1940), I, 360.

12. Pierre Bourdieu, *Distinction: A Social Critique of the Judgment of Taste,* trans. Richard Nice (Cambridge, Mass.: Harvard University Press, 1984), p. 511. The remark in this case is made in the context of Bourdieu's recognition that sociological analysis of aesthetics is itself open to charges of "terroristic" leveling. On the contrary, he replies, it is the process of taste-making itself that exercises the truly terrorizing "symbolic violence" of exclusion and denigration. He goes on to cite modern French magazines as the best examples of such symbolic violence. It is intriguing to consider that it was late eighteenth-century "magazines" of a different sort, also aimed at what was then a new "middle-brow" audience, were one important venue for the kind of rural poetry both Wordsworth and Crabbe produced, in their different ways.

13. See Toril Moi, "Appropriating Bourdieu," *NLH* 22 (1991), 1017–1049.

14. Duncan Wu, *Wordsworth's Reading, 1770–1799;* and *1800–1815* (Cambridge; New York: Cambridge University Press, 1993; 1995).

15. *The Life of George Crabbe, by his son,* [George Crabbe], intro. E. M. Forster (London: Oxford University Press and Humphrey Milford, 1932), p. 164; Crabbe's letter to Scott, in Scott's *Letters,* ed. H. J. C. Grierson, 3 vols. (London: Constable, 1937), III, 279n.

16. *The Village* in George Crabbe, *The Complete Poetical Works,* 3 vols., ed. Norman Dalrymple-Champneys and Arthur Pollard (Oxford: Clarendon Press, 1988-), I, 155–74.

17. Raymond Williams, *The Country and the City,* p. 91.

18. John Guillory, *Cultural Capital: The Problem of Literary Canon Formation* (Chicago: University of Chicago Press, 1993), p. 107.

19. Whitehead, p. 222.

20. Wordsworth, "Extempore Effusion upon the Death of James Hogg," in *The Poetical Works of William Wordsworth,* ed. Ernest DeSelincourt and

Helen Darbishire, 5 vols. (Oxford: Clarendon Press, 1940–49; 1947), IV, 276–78.

21. Wordsworth to Henry Crabb Robinson, 3 January 1839, quoted in Mary Moorman, *Wordsworth, A Biography,* 2 vols. (Oxford: Clarendon Press, 1957–65), II *(The Later Years, 1803–1850),* 572.

22. Robert J. Griffin, *Wordsworth's Pope: A Study in Literary Historiography* (Cambridge: Cambridge University Press, 1995).

23. Paul de Man, "Autobiography As De-facement," in *The Rhetoric of Romanticism* (New York: Columbia University Press, 1984), pp. 67–81 (pp. 78–79). See also the related reading of these essays and Wordsworth's poetics by Frances Ferguson, *Wordsworth: Language as Counter-Spirit* (New Haven: Yale University Press, 1977).

24. Wordsworth, *Essays on Epitaphs,* in *The Prose Works of William Wordsworth,* ed. W. J. B. Owen and Jane Worthington Smyser, 3 vols. (Oxford: Clarendon Press, 1974), II, 49–96 (64).

25. Others have noticed a connection between the *Essays on Epitaphs* and Crabbe's "matter-of-fact" treatment of the rural poor. One who makes the connection explicit in passing is D. D. Devlin, in *Wordsworth and the Poetry of Epitaphs* (Totowa, N.J.: Barnes & Noble, 1981), p. 70, who notes that for Wordsworth, "Telling the facts is not the same as telling the truth," as the poet's judgment of Crabbe makes clear. For the *Essays* and *The Excursion* as responses to Crabbe, I have also benefited from discussions at the Wordsworth Summer Conference in Grasmere, and in particular, both there and in subsequent correspondence, with Sally Bushell, Queen's College, Cambridge University, whose thesis is on "Narrative and the Boundaries of Genre in *The Excursion.*"

26. *The Deserted Village* in *Collected Works of Oliver Goldsmith,* ed. Arthur Friedman, 5 vols. (Oxford: Clarendon Press, 1966), IV, 273–304, ll. 159–62.

27. Samuel Taylor Coleridge, *Table Talk* (1834) in *The Collected Works of Samuel Taylor Coleridge,* ed. Carl Woodring, 2 vols. (Princeton: Princeton University Press; London: Routledge, 1990) I, 465–66.

28. William Hazlitt, *The Spirit of the Age,* in *The Complete Works,* XI, 164–65.

29. Leigh Hunt, *The Feast of the Poets, 1814* (Oxford: Woodstock Books, 1989), "Notes," pp. 47–48.

30. *Edinburgh Review,* September 1819.

31. On the extensive special effects employed by magic lantern slides, see Steve Humphries, *Victorian Britain Through the Magic Lantern* (London: Sidgwick & Jackson, 1989). And compare science-fiction author Bruce Sterling's notes, based on period advertisements, on the *Dead Media Project* Website, Internet <http://www.well.com/mirrorshades/deadmed.html>.

32. William Hazlitt, "On Thomson and Cowper," in *Lectures on the English Poets* (1818) in *The Complete Works,* XI, 85–104 (97).

33. Mary Moorman, *Wordsworth, A Biography,* 2 vols. (Oxford: Clarendon Press, 1957–65), vol. 2 : *The Later Years, 1803–1850.* Moorman remarks: "it may be in telling these stories Wordsworth was making a deliberate answer to

Crabbe's *Parish Register,* which he had read and criticized in 1808" (p. 173). Sally Bushell (see n. 24 above) has called to my attention to the fact that Judson Stanley Lion says much the same in *The Excursion: A Study* (New Haven: Yale University Press, 1950), also suggesting that Wordsworth is attempting in Books VI and VII to "meet Crabbe on his own ground and to vindicate himself from the charges of Jeffrey" (p. 39).

34. Karl Kroeber, *Romantic Narrative Art* (Madison: University of Wisconsin Press, 1966), pp. 118–19.

35. Wordsworth, "Simon Lee, the Old Huntsman," in *Lyrical Ballads, 1798,* facs. rpt. (Oxford and New York: Woodstock Books, 1990).

36. "Simon Lee" can also be read as a parody of mock elegies such as Robert Burns's "Tam Samson's Elegy" (1787). Again the lyrical ballad defines its mode as counter-satiric. I am grateful to Carol McGuirk for this suggestion, made on a NASSR-L discussion, Internet, 28 September 1999.

37. The strongest articulation of this dialogic perspective is Don H. Bialostosky's *Making Tales: The Poetics of Wordsworth's Narrative Experiments* (Chicago: University of Chicago Press, 1984). For a different treatment of the Romantics' idea of the reader, one following the poets' own formulations of the relationship, see John R. Nabholtz, *"My Reader My Fellow-Labourer": A Study of English Romantic Prose* (Columbia: University of Missouri Press, 1986).

38. Wordsworth, "Andrew Jones," in *Lyrical Ballads* (1800), ed. R. L. Brett and A. R. Jones (London and New York: Methuen, 1963), pp. 174–75.

39. Wordsworth, *Peter Bell,* ed. John E. Jordan (Ithaca: Cornell University Press, 1985), Appendix I, pp. 627–28.

40. Wordsworth, *Peter Bell,* Appendix I.

41. See Alan Bewell, *Wordsworth and the Enlightenment: Nature, Man, Society in the Experimental Poetry* (New Haven and London: Yale University Press, 1989), pp. 154–57.

42. Alan Liu, *Wordsworth: The Sense of History* (Stanford: Stanford University Press, 1989), pp. 296, 603n.

43. Leslie Stephen, *Cornhill Magazine* XXX (1874), 453–73, in *Crabbe: The Critical Heritage,* ed. Arthur Pollard, pp. 447–48.

44. William Godwin, *The Adventures of Caleb Williams or Things As They Are* (New York and Toronto: Rinehart & Co., 1960), pp. 53–54.

45. Crabbe, "The Convert," *Tales, 1812,* in *The Complete Works,* II, 249–61.

46. Steven E. Jones, *Shelley's Satire: Violence, Exhortation, and Authority* (DeKalb: Northern Illinois University Press, 1994), pp. 50–51.

47. Ronald B. Hatch, *Crabbe's Arabesque: Social Drama in the Poetry of George Crabbe* (Montreal: McGill–Queen's University Press, 1976), points out that the laws sanction Grimes's murders, and in revealing this Crabbe points the finger at the community (pp. 105–106).

48. Crabbe, "The Poor of the Borough—Peter Grimes," first pub. in *The Borough* (1810); *The Complete Works,* I, 564ff. (749n).

49. Roy Porter, *English Society in the Eighteenth Century* (London: Penguin Books, 1982), p. 101.

50. "Inscription for the Door of a Cell in Newgate, where Mrs. Brownrigg, the Prentice-cide, was confined previous to her execution," in *Poetry of the Anti-Jacobin* (1799), facs. rept. (Oxford: Woodstock Books, 1991), p. 6.
51. William Blackstone, *Commentaries on the Laws of England,* adapted by Robert Malcom Kerr, 4 vols. (1773; Boston: Beacon Press, 1962), IV, 245.
52. Stuart Curran, *Poetic Form and British Romanticism* (New York and Oxford: Oxford University Press, 1986), pp. 87–89.
53. John Wilson (anon.), *Blackwood's Edinburgh Magazine,* V, July 1819, 469–83; and xxii, November 1827, 537–40.
54. Anon., "Lyrical Ballad," in *The Country Constitutional Guardian and Literary Magazine* (Liverpool), April 1822, 367–68; rept. in David A. Kent and D. R. Ewen, eds., *Romantic Parodies, 1797–1831* (London and Toronto: Associated University Presses, 1992), pp. 299–301.
55. Raymond Williams, *The Country and the City,* pp. 87–88.
56. John Goodridge, *Rural Life in Eighteenth-Century English Poetry* (Cambridge: Cambridge University Press, 1995), part I.
57. Stuart Curran, *Poetic Form and British Romanticism,* pp. 87–99.
58. Pope to John Gay, 1730, *The Correspondence of Alexander Pope,* ed. G. Sherburn, 5 vols. (Oxford: Clarendon Press, 1956), III, 143.
59. *The Thresher's Labour (1736) and The Woman's Labour (1739),* ed. Moira Ferguson, Augustan Reprint Society pub. No. 230 (Los Angeles: Clark Memorial Library, UCLA, 1985).
60. Moira Ferguson, introduction, *The Thresher's Labour (1736) and The Woman's Labour (1739),* p. iii.

Chapter 2

1. Marilyn Gaull, "Romantic Humor: The Horse of Knowledge and the Learned Pig," *Mosaic* 9.4 (1976), 43–64 (43).
2. *Romantic Parodies, 1797–1831,* ed. David A. Kent and D. R. Ewen (London and Toronto: Associated University Presses, 1992); and *Parodies of the Romantic Age,* ed. Graeme Stones and John Strachan, 5 vols. (London: Pickering & Chatto, 1999).
3. Linda Hutcheon, Foreword to *Romantic Parodies,* ed. Kent and Ewen, pp. 7–8.
4. Linda Hutcheon, *A Theory of Parody: The Teachings of Twentieth-Century Art Forms* (New York: Methuen, 1985), p. 37.
5. Southey's literary miscellany, the *Omniana,* was first published in the *Athenaeum* but was then collected, with the addition of items by Coleridge, in 2 volumes in 1812. See the *Collected Coleridge: Shorter Works and Fragments,* ed. H. J. Jackson and J. R. de J. Jackson, and 2 vols. (London: Routledge & Kegan Paul; Princeton: Princeton University Press, 1995), I, 305.
6. Coleridge, *Biographia Literaria,* in *Collected Coleridge,* ed. James Engell and W. Jackson Bate, 2 vols., II, 6 (chapter 14).

7. Anon., review of *Sibylline leaves* in *Monthly Review* (January 1819), 24–38; rept. *Coleridge: The Critical Heritage,* ed. J. R. de J. Jackson (New York: Barnes & Noble, 1970), pp. 399–412.

8. Though he is interested primarily in Coleridge's use of vampirism, James B. Twitchell, in *The Living Dead: A Study of the Vampire in Romantic Literature* (Durham: Duke University Press, 1981), pp. 142–60, generally emphasizes the origins of the *Mariner* in the gothic milieu and also sees Coleridge as revising away from his original conception of the poem. On the particulars of those revisions, see Jack Stillinger, *Coleridge and Textual Instability: The Multiple Versions of the Major Poems* (New York and Oxford: Oxford University Press, 1994), pp. 70–73.

9. Wordsworth to Cottle, 24 June 1799, in *The Early Letters of William and Dorothy Wordsworth (1787–1805),* ed. Ernest de Selincourt (Oxford: Clarendon Press, 1935), 226–27.

10. Robert Southey, review of *Lyrical Ballads,* in *Critical Review* (October 1798), 197–204; rept. in *The Critical Heritage,* pp. 53–54 ; Lamb to Southey, 8 November 1798, in *The Letters of Charles and Mary Anne Lamb,* ed. Edwin W. Marrs, Jr., 3 vols. (Ithaca and London: Cornell University Press, 197⁵), I, 142; Lamb to Wordsworth, 30 January 1801, *Letters,* I, 266. Interestingly enough in light of what I will argue below, Lamb disliked the supernatural ("miraculous") parts of the poem but was attracted to its representation of the "feelings" of the narrator.

11. J. G. Lockhart, "Essays on the Lake School," *Blackwood's Edinburgh Magazine* (October 1819), 3–12; rept. in *The Critical Heritage,* 436–51.

12. William Hazlitt, *The Spirit of the Age: or, Contemporary Portraits,* in *The Complete Works of William Hazlitt,* ed. P. P. Howe, 21 vols. (J. M. Dent & Sons, 1930–34; 1932), XI, 28–38 (34–35).

13. Michel Foucault, "What is an Author?" in *Language, Counter-Memory, Practice* (Ithaca: Cornell University Press, 1977), pp. 113–38: "unlike a proper name, which moves from the interior of a discourse to the real person outside who produced it, the name of the author remains at the contours of texts—separating one from the other, defining their form, and characterizing their mode of existence" (p. 123). Cases such as Coleridge's, however, point to the role of the author as a "real person" with real agency who performs these shaping and defining functions.

14. *Table Talk* in the *Collected Coleridge,* ed. Carl Woodring, 2 vols. (1990), I, 149.

15. For a comparative perspective, see Lawrence Lipking, "The Marginal Gloss: Notes and Asides on Poe, Valéry, 'The Ancient Mariner,' the Ordeal of the Margin, Storiella as She is Sung, Versions of Leonardo, and the Plight of Modern Criticism," *Critical Inquiry* 3 (1977), 609–55.

16. Huntington Brown, "The Gloss to the *Ancient Mariner,*" *Studies in Philology* 61 (1964), 669–88; Lawrence Lipking, "The Marginal Gloss"; Tilottama Rajan, *Dark Interpreter: The Discourse of Romanticism* (Ithaca: Cornell University Press, 1980), pp. 22–23; David Simpson, *Irony and Authority in Eng-*

lish Romantic Poetry (London: Macmillan, 1979), pp. 98–101; Kathleen M. Wheeler, *The Creative Mind in Coleridge's Poetry* (Cambridge: Harvard University Press, 1981), pp. 42–64; Jerome J. McGann, *The Beauty of Inflections: Literary Investigations in Historical Method and Theory* (Oxford: Clarendon Press, 1985), pp. 135–72.

17. Coleridge, *The Rime of Ancient Mariner* in *Sibylline leaves,* ed. Jonathan Wordsworth (Oxford and New York: Woodstock Books, 1990), pp. 1–39.

18. D. M. Moir, "The Rime of the Auncient Waggonere," in *Romantic Parodies,* ed. Kent and Ewen, pp. 163–68 (p. 163).

19. For a collection of nineteenth-century examples, see *Parodies of the Romantic Age,* ed. Stones and Strachan, vol. 2.

20. Hunt Emerson, *The Rime of the Ancient Mariner,* Crack Comics version, reprinted, colored by Carol Bennett (London: Knockabout Comics, 1989). In a 1997 exhibit of illustrations of the poem mounted by the Wordsworth Trust, this version was included along with other examples, such as the engravings by Gustave Doré. Emerson's initial inspiration for this parody, interestingly enough, was a *MAD* magazine parody of Longfellow's *Wreck of the Hesperus.* My thanks to the artist for permission to reproduce the images in figures 2.1–2.3 below, and for his helpful e-mails about his artwork.

21. I quote this deleted passage in *Lyrical Ballads, 1798,* ed. Jonathan Wordsworth, facsim. (New York and Oxford: Woodstock Books, 1990), p. 40.

22. *Frankenstein* is an interesting example of another kind, a work whose popularity and authorship by a young woman worked to keep it at the margins of the canon—in that honorary space reserved for "minor" but "significant" works—until recently, when developments in feminist studies, New Historicism, and canon revision, along with new versions of Mary Shelley's texts, worked together to increase its canonical status. On the use of vernacular literature, beginning in the eighteenth century, as alternative routes to the canonical authority and cultural capital once provided by classical languages and texts, see John Guillory, *Cultural Capital: The Problem of Literary Canon Formation* (Chicago and London: University of Chicago Press, 1993).

23. On the craze for Kotzebue and German melodrama in general, see David Simpson, *Romanticism, Nationalism, and the Revolt Against Theory* (Chicago and London: University of Chicago Press, 1993).

24. Jonathan Livingston Lowes, *The Road to Xanadu: A Study in the Ways of the Imagination* (London: Constable, 1927).

25. Marilyn Gaull, *English Romanticism: The Human Context* (New York: Norton, 1988), p. 269. Taylor's "Lenora" appeared in the "Original Poetry" section, pp. 135–37.

26. Lamb's letter is quoted and Lamb's and Coleridge's interest in "Lenore" is pointed out by Jonathan Wordsworth, as are the Nehemiah Higginbottom parodies, which I discuss below, in his introduction to the purported target

of those parodies, *Samuel Taylor Coleridge, Charles Lamb, Charles Lloyd, Poems 1797* (Poole, Washington D.C.: Woodstock Books, 1997).

27. *Critical Review,* February 1797, 194–200.

28. Letter to Bowles, 16 March 1797, in *Collected Letters of Samuel Taylor Coleridge,* ed. Earl Leslie Griggs, 6 vols. (Oxford: Clarendon Press, 1956–71), I, 317–19.

29. Letter to Cottle, ca. 20 November 1797, *Collected Letters,* I, 356–58.

30. David V. Erdman, "Coleridge as Nehemiah Higginbottom," *Modern Language Notes* 73 (December 1958), 569–80. The sonnets appeared in the *Monthly Magazine,* November 1797; I quote them, however, in the more accessible text found in *Collected Verse Parody,* ed. John Strachan, vol. II of *Parodies of the Romantic Age,* ed. Stones and Strachan, 51. Strachan's and Stones's introductory note cites many of the same primary sources and makes the same general point I am making here, that these sonnets reveal Coleridge "demonstrating a desire to put away childish things, or at least manifesting an anxiety about his poetic style" (47)

31. Erdman, "Coleridge as Nehemiah Higginbottom," 578–79.

32. *Biographia Literaria,* chapter 1, pp. 170–71.

33. Headnote to "Christabel, Part Third" in *Romantic Parodies,* ed. Kent and Ewen, p. 185.

34. Anon., review in *Edinburgh Magazine* (October 1817), 245–50; rept. in *The Critical Heritage,* 392–99.

35. On this topic in general, the best treatment remains Carl R. Woodring, *Politics in the Poetry of Coleridge* (Madison: University of Wisconsin Press, 1961).

36. Coleridge, "Monody on the Death of Chatterton," in *Poems on Various Subjects 1796,* ed. Jonathan Wordsworth, facsim. (Oxford and New York: Woodstock Books, 1990), pp. 1–11.

37. This way of viewing the revisionism of Romanticism offers a slight modification of the usual way of treating the "Romantic Ideology," which is as a displacement of politics by transcendent aesthetics. I agree that this is a dominant pattern, but wish to emphasize a subtle difference within aesthetic modes, in which sentimental and gothic writing accompanies political radicalism, and a hermeneutically dense symbolist poetry develops along with the displacement of political hopes. Coleridge's self-parody in this case extends itself to the straightforward "Monody on a Tea-Kettle."

38. I cite "Fire, Famine, and Slaughter" and the "Apologetic Preface" in *Sibylline leaves,* ed. Jonathan Wordsworth, facsim. (Oxford: Woodstock Books, 1990), pp. 87–116 (p. 90).

39. Woodring, *Politics in the Poetry of Coleridge,* p. 129.

40. Shelley not only wrote his own *Devil's Walk* in imitation of Coleridge and Southey's *Devil's Thoughts,* he directly imitated "Fire, Famine, and Slaughter" in his own "Falshood and Vice." "Fire, Famine, and Slaughter" and "France: an Ode" are copied together in a single manuscript in Mary Shel-

ley's hand (*Shelley and His Circle, 1773–1822,* vol. VII, ed. Donald H. Reiman [Cambridge: Harvard University Press, 1986], pp. 1–12).

Chapter 3

1. The historical narrative here and in what follows is based on Elie Halévy, *The Liberal Awakening 1815–1830,* trans. E. I. Watkin (New York: Peter Smith, 1949), pp. 22–34; and E. P. Thompson, *The Making of the English Working Class* (New York: Vintage Books, 1966), pp. 631–69.
2. Richard D. Altick, *The English Common Reader* (Chicago: University of Chicago Press, 1957), p. 326. Circulation for such publications, however, is notoriously difficult to determine, since copies were shared, read aloud in pubs and at public meetings.
3. Thompson, *The Making of the English Working Class,* pp. 674–75.
4. Jon P. Klancher, *The Making of English Reading Audiences, 1790–1832* (Madison: University of Wisconsin Press, 1987), p. 119. Klancher's reading of Wooler is indispensable. Other important sources for my thinking about Wooler's work are cited below, but the most lucid analysis of its stylistic vectors remains an article to which I am indebted, Richard Hendrix's "Popular Humor in 'The Black Dwarf'," *Journal of British Studies* 16 (Fall 1976), 108–28. Hendrix recognizes the same basic factors I cover here as setting the stage for what Wooler does: economic controversies, theatricality in Wooler's writing, and the general context of popular fairs and carnivals. More recently, Michael Scrivener has shed further light on Wooler's discourse in "The *Black Dwarf* Review of Byron's *The Age of Bronze,*" *Keats-Shelley Journal* 41 (1992), 42–48. For a rich sense of the larger overlapping contexts in which to understand Wooler, see both Marcus Wood, *Radical Satire and Print Culture, 1790–1822* (Oxford: Clarendon Press, 1994); and Kevin Gilmartin, *Print Politics: The Press and Radical Opposition in Early Nineteenth-Century England* (Cambridge: Cambridge University Press, 1996). Gilmartin specifically treats of Wooler's use of satire, pp. 94–96. For many teachers and scholars of Romantic period literature, such excellent work in the radical culture offers a fresh perspective not available from within conventional definitions of the canon or of literature.
5. See Sir Walter Scott, *The Black Dwarf,* ed. P. D. Garside (Edinburgh: Edinburgh University Press; New York: Columbia University Press, 1993), pp. 132–33, including helpful notes on the genesis and production of the novel. (Quotations from the novel are from this edition.)
6. Interestingly enough, the *Quarterly Review* for January 1817 (published April) contains a review of *Tales of My Landlord* that recognizes the Dwarf as a type of Scottish outcast attached to landowning families, like Shakespeare's fools (the reviewer suggests). This review in effect anticipates part of my analysis, suggesting that the northern superstitions about such outcast figures acts as a displacement or cover-up of endemic social violence—dueling, revenge, and so on.

7. Robert C. Elliott, *The Power of Satire: Magic, Ritual, Art* (Princeton: Princeton University Press, 1960).

8. The significance of Wooler's satiric exploitation of the potato as a symbol is noted by Marcus Wood, *Radical Satire*, pp. 1–2.

9. R. N. Salaman, *The History and Social Influence of the Potato* (Cambridge: Cambridge University Press, 1949), pp. 480, 495, 506, 541–42 (quoted in Thompson, p. 315).

10. Iain McCalman, *Radical Underworld: Prophets, Revolutionaries and Pornographers in London, 1795–1840* (Cambridge: Cambridge University Press, 1988). See as well his valuable collection, *The Horrors of Slavery and Other Writings by Robert Wedderburn* (New York and Princeton: Markus Wiener, 1991).

11. McCalman, *Radical Underworld*, p. 149.

12. Klancher, *Reading Audiences*, p. 114.

13. M. M. Bakhtin, *The Dialogic Imagination*, ed. Michael Holquist, trans. Caryl Emerson and Michael Holquist (Austin: University of Texas Press, 1982), pp. 158–224.

14. This and the other examples in the following paragraphs are taken from Henry Morley, *Memoirs of Bartholomew Fair* (London: Chatto and Windus, 1880).

15. Bakhtin, *The Dialogic Imagination*, pp. 159–60.

16. Peter Stallybrass and Allon White, *The Politics and Poetics of Transgression* (Ithaca: Cornell University Press, 1989), pp. 16, 14.

17. Wordsworth, *The Prelude: 1799, 1805, 1850*, ed. Jonathan Wordsworth, M. H. Abrams, and Stephen Gill (New York and London: W.W. Norton, 1979), ll. 686–87; 672–708.

18. On the role of journalism in the Romantic period and the plural alternatives to Jürgen Habermas's hegemonic "public sphere," see Kevin Gilmartin's contribution to a forum, "Popular Radicalism and the Public Sphere," *Studies in Romanticism* 33.4 (Winter 1994), 549–57. My reading of Wooler's work suggests that he consciously exploited the class and cultural heterogeneity among his readers and potential readers.

19. Published in *Farrago or Miscellanies in Verse and Prose*, quoted in Sybil Rosenfeld, *The Theatre of the London Fairs in the Eighteenth Century* (Cambridge: Cambridge University Press, 1960), p. 46.

20. Rosenfeld, *The Theatre of London Fairs*, pp. 46–47, 150–51.

21. Bakhtin, *Rabelais and His World*, p. 7; and *The Dialogic Imagination*, p. 163.

22. James Anderson, *The Bee* (1790); cited in Klancher, pp. 22–23.

23. Klancher, p. 116. Both Hendrix and McCalman note the performative qualities of radical oratory, which is a discourse often very little removed from radical journalism.

24. Wooler, *A Verbatim Report of the Two Trials of Mr. T. J. Wooler* . . . (London: Wooler, 1817).

25. Marcus Wood, *Radical Satire and Print Culture*, pp. 155–214.

26. On the material textuality at the level of what he calls the "bibliographic code," see Jerome J. McGann, *Black Riders: The Visible Language of Mod-*

ernism (Princeton: Princeton University Press, 1993). For various pertinent discussions of graphical features of textuality and the "textuality" of images, see a number of contributions to *Reimagining Textuality: Textual Studies in the Late Age of Print,* ed. Neil Fraistat and Elizabeth Loizeaux (Madison: University of Wisconsin Press, forthcoming).

27. On *The Political House That Jack Built,* see Robert L. Patten, *George Cruikshank's Life, Times, and Art,* Vol. 1: 1792–1835 (London: Lutterworth Press, 1992), p. 157; Marcus Wood (*Radical Satire and Print Culture*) devotes the central portion of his impressive study to this most influential of the Hone-Cruikshank collaborations.

28. Carl R. Woodring, *Politics in the Poetry of Coleridge* (Madison: University of Wisconsin Press, 1961), p. 235, calls our attention to various analogous examples of verbal picture-making—"For coronations, victories, and similar events public spirit required those who wrote letters to the press to describe emblematic transparencies for artists to carry out"—including Coleridge's verbal "design" in for an emblematic print celebrating Napoleon's defeat, to be executed by his friend, the artist Washington Allston.

29. Aileen Ward, "Keats's Sonnet 'Nebuchadnezzar's Dream'," *Philological Quarterly,* 34.2 (April 1955), 177–88 (183).

30. Aileen Ward, 187. For the text of the sonnet and its composition, see *John Keats: Complete Poems,* ed. Jack Stillinger (Cambridge, Mass.: Belknap Press of Harvard University Press, 1982).

31. Aileen Ward, 181.

32. I treat at greater length these works by Shelley in *Shelley's Satire: Violence, Exhortation, and Authority* (DeKalb: Northern Illinois University Press, 1994).

33. Letter of John Grove, February 1857, quoted in Hogg, *Life of Shelley,* I, 196–97.

34. Iain McCalman, in *Radical Underworld,* pp. 241–42, n. 50.

35. Stephen C. Behrendt, *Shelley and His Audiences* (Lincoln and London: University of Nebraska Press, 1989).

36. Donald H. Reiman, "Shelley as Agrarian Reactionary," in *Romantic Texts and Contexts* (Columbia: University of Missouri Press, 1987), pp. 262–74.

37. Shelley, "Song: To the Men of England," in *Poetical Works,* ed. Hutchinson, pp. 572–73.

38. Shelley, *Oedipus Tyrannus; or, Swellfoot the Tyrant,* in *Poetical Works,* ed. Hutchinson, pp. 389–410.

39. In a letter to Byron, Shelley asks, more than half seriously, whether the famous lord would return to England if the government were to fall: "Shall you or not return as a candidate for any part in the power they will lose?" *The Letters of Percy Bysshe Shelley,* ed. Frederick L. Jones, 2 vols. (Oxford: Clarendon Press, 1964), II, 236.

40. *Letters of Percy Bysshe Shelley,* II, 207.

41. *Letters of Percy Bysshe Shelley,* II, 207, 212–13.

42. Jones, *Shelley's Satire,* p. 189, n. 10.

43. Marcus Wood, *Radical Satire and Print Culture,* p. 266.

44. Michael Scrivener, "The *Black Dwarf* Review of Byron's *The Age of Bronze*," *Keats-Shelley Journal,* 41 (1992), 42–48 (44).

45. See note 4 above for examples of such revisionists.

Chapter 4

1. Marilyn Butler, *Romantics, Rebels and Reactionaries: English Literature and its Background 1760–1830* (New York and Oxford: Oxford University Press, 1982), p. 2.

2. Such is the effect of Marilyn Butler's notion, the "Cult of the South," for example, as a way to redefine and recontextualize the Hunt-Shelley circle (pp. 113–37). The symbolic regionalism of that category works to force an attention to shared material contexts as helping to define a "family resemblance" more than a "movement" per se. For one application of the metaphor of the constellation to the theory of literary history, see Thomas McFarland, "Field, Constellation, and Aesthetic Object," in *Romantic Poetry: Recent Revisionary Criticism,* ed. Karl Kroeber and Gene W. Ruoff (New Brunswick: Rutgers University Press, 1993), pp. 15–37.

3. Marjorie Levinson, *Keats's Life of Allegory: The Origins of a Style* (Oxford: Basil Blackwell, 1988); Susan Wolfson, "Feminizing Keats," in *Critical Essays on John Keats,* ed. Hermione de Almeida (Boston: G. K. Hall, 1990), 317–56; Nicholas Roe, *John Keats and the Culture of Dissent* (Oxford: Clarendon Press, 1997); Alan Bewell, "Keats's Realm of Flora," *Studies in Romanticism* 31 (Spring 1992), 71–98; Anne K. Mellor, *Romanticism and Gender* (New York and London: Routledge, 1993), pp. 171–86; Elizabeth Jones, "Keats in the Suburbs," *Keats-Shelley Journal* 45 (1996), 23–43; Jeffrey N. Cox, *Poetry and Politics in the Cockney School: Keats, Shelley, Hunt and their Circle* (Cambridge: Cambridge University Press, 1998).

4. Jerome J. McGann, ed., *The New Oxford Book of Romantic Period Verse* (Oxford and New York: Oxford University Press, 1994), introduction, p. xx.

5. Jerome J. McGann, *The Poetics of Sensibility* (Oxford: Clarendon Press, 1996), p. 74. The best and most thorough recent discussion of the Della Cruscans is in Judith Pascoe, *Romantic Theatricality: Gender, Poetry, and Spectatorship* (Ithaca and London: Cornell University Press, 1997), pp. 68–94.

6. William Maginn, review in *Blackwood's Edinburgh Magazine,* December 1821, 696–700; rept. Donald H. Reiman, ed. *The Romantics Reviewed* C.1 (New York: Garland, 1972), 147–51. Reiman attributes the anonymous review to George Croly, and this remains a viable possibility, though the review was later reprinted in a Victorian collection of Maginn's writings. In the absence of other evidence, I attribute it to Maginn.

7. Jeffrey N. Cox, *Poetry and Politics in the Cockney School,* p. 4. Cox's first chapter, entitled, "The Cockney School Attacks; or, the Antiromantic Ideology," is in many ways consonant with my arguments here.

8. *Scots Magazine* (October 1817), 257; Lockhart (with John Wilson), as "Z," "On the Cockney School of Poetry," nos. I-VI, *Blackwood's Edinburgh Mag-*

azine (November 1817, July 1818, August 1818, April 1819, and October 1819). These reviews are discussed by Alan Bewell, "Keats's 'Realm of Flora'," 94, in the context of the feminized "realm of flora" with which Keats identified. The contextual gendering of modes like satire and lyric is a complex subject; I address one side of it in chapter 5 below, but the topic of gender and genre deserves further discussion.

9. Review of *Lamia, Monthly Magazine,* July 1820.

10. William Hazlitt, "On Mr. Coleridge's Christabel," in *The Complete Works of William Hazlitt,* ed. P. P. Howe, 21 vols. (London and Toronto: J. M. Dent & Sons, 1930–34), XIX, 34.

11. William Hazlitt, *On the Living Poets,* in *The Complete Works of William Hazlitt,* ed. P. P. Howe, V, 143–168 (148).

12. Percy Bysshe Shelley, *Adonais* in *Shelley's Poetry and Prose,* ed. Donald H. Reiman and Sharon B. Powers (New York and London: Norton, 1977), pp. 390–406; all citations of this poem are from this edition.

13. Mary Shelley to Maria Gisborne, 15 August 1822, in *The Letters of Mary Wollstonecraft Shelley,* ed. Betty T. Bennett, 3 vols. (Baltimore: Johns Hopkins University Press, 1980–88), I, 249. On this statue and other Shelleyana in relation to Mary Shelley, see Bette London, "Mary Shelley, *Frankenstein,* and the Spectacle of Masculinity, PMLA 108.2 (March 1993), 253–67. I am also indebted to Karen Swann's presentation at a 1995 MLA conference session in Chicago, "The Construction of Romanticism," on the aesthetics of the beautiful corpses of the male Romantic poets; and to the remarks of Hugh Roberts, NASSR-L online discussion, Internet, 22 September 1997.

14. Cox, *Poetry and Politics in the Cockney School,* p. 21.

15. See Edward Bostetter, "The Original Della Cruscans and the Florence Miscellany," *Huntington Library Quarterly* 19.3 (May 1956), 277–300. Bostetter argues as well for a poetic lineage connecting the Della Cruscans and the Romantics. For an excellent treatment of the Della Cruscans and their relation to the Romantics, but with a special emphasis on the crucial role of gender, see Judith Pascoe, *Romantic Theatricality,* pp. 68–94.

16. James L. Clifford, "Robert Merry—A Pre-Byronic Hero," *Bulletin of the John Rylands Library* 27 (1942–43), 74–96 (93–94).

17. William Gifford, *The Baviad and The Maeviad,* London 1797 (originally published 1791, 1795).

18. *The Letters of Percy Bysshe Shelley,* ed. Frederick L. Jones, 2 vols. (Oxford: Clarendon Press, 1964), II, 382–83; Shelley, "Letter to Maria Gisborne," in *Shelley's Poetry and Prose,* pp. 313–21 (ll. 240–42).

19. *Blackwood's Edinburgh Magazine,* June 1829, p. 732.

20. *Lycidas,* in *The Works of John Milton,* ed. Frank Allen Patterson, 18 vols. (New York: Columbia University Press, 1931), I, 76–83.

21. Byron, "Prometheus," in *Lord Byron: The Complete Poetical Works,* ed. Jerome J. McGann and Barry Weller, 7 vols. (Oxford: Clarendon Press, 1980–92), IV, 31–33.

22. Alan Bewell, "Keats's 'Realm of Flora'," 72–79, and Elizabeth Jones, "Keats in the Suburbs," 31–34.

23. Jerome J. McGann, *The Textual Condition* (Princeton: Princeton University Press, 1991), p. 35.

24. *The Florence Miscellany* (Florence: G. Cam, 1785).

25. These terms summarizing Bourdieu's theory are from Jonathan Brody Kramnick, *Making the English Canon: Print Capitalism and the Cultural Past, 1700–1770* (Cambridge: Cambridge University Press, 1998), p. 34. The theory is best encapsulated in Bourdieu's "The Field of Cultural Production, or: the Economic World Reversed," *Poetics* 12 (1983), 311–56.

26. *Endymion* is quoted in Jack Stillinger, ed., *The Poems of John Keats* (London: Heinemann, 1978), 102–220.

27. Roe, *John Keats and the Culture of Dissent*, p. 218.

28. Carl R. Woodring, *Politics in English Romantic Poetry* (Cambridge, Mass.: Harvard University Press, 1970), p. 78.

29. Robert Gittings, *The Mask of Keats: A Study of Problems* (Cambridge, Mass.: Harvard University Press, 1956), p. 141.

30. James Chandler extends the allusions beyond merely national Cockney politics, pointing out that "The Jealousies" and *Otho the Great* show signs of Keats's larger ambition, that they are about "emperors and empires" at a time the poet was considering a post with the East India Company. See *England in 1819: The Politics of Literary Culture and the Case of Romantic Historicism* (Chicago: University of Chicago Press, 1998), pp. 432–35.

31. *The Letters of John Keats,* ed. Hyder Edward Rollins, 2 vols. (Cambridge: Harvard University Press, 1958), II, 179. Though he figures journalism as cockfighting, Keats also immediately compares it to prostitution; then, he says that he will "be able to cheat as well as any literary Jew of the Market and shine up an article on any thing without much knowledge of the subject, aye like an orange." In another letter on Hazlitt (I, 152), Keats had begun by lamenting that people should "damn" or spoil "the fin[est] things" by associating themselves with them. As examples, he lists Wordsworth and the Lakes and Peacock and satire. The remark about Hazlitt comes as a qualification in his favor and turns the word "damner" into a backhanded compliment. Alan Bewell similarly sees Keats as responding to the negative reviews by "trying to write like a man" after 1817 ("Keats's 'Realm of Flora'," 94).

32. "The Jealousies," in *John Keats: Complete Poems,* ed. Jack Stillinger (Cambridge, Mass.: Belknap Press of Harvard University Press, 1982).

33. "Biaco-pany" is a comic Italianism for "White-bread" or Whitbread. This and other topical names are decoded by Gittings, pp. 116–17. Among some of the other possibilities he suggests: Hum=Hunt (pp. 128–130) or Lamb; Crafticant=Wordsworth or Southey (p. 131).

34. Keats, *Letters,* ed. Hyder Rollins, II, 327–28.

35. On Tipu's man-tiger organ, see Phyllis G. Mann, "Keats's Indian Allegory," *Keats-Shelley Journal* 6 (1957), 4–9.

36. Jerome McGann remarks that the correspondence of Merry and Cowley amounted to "sentimental love-dialogue, carried out in public," *New Oxford Book of Romantic-Period Literature*, p. 786n.

37. Roe, *John Keats and the Culture of Dissent*, p. 221, and chapter 8.

38. Thomas Campbell, *Life of Mrs. Siddons* (London, 1834; rept. New York: Benjamin Blom, 1972), pp. 39–40.

39. *The Autobiography of Leigh Hunt with Reminiscences of Friends and Contemporaries,* 3 vols. (London: Smith, Elder & Co., 1850), vol. II, pp. 87–88.

40. Sir Walter Scott, "Death of Lord Byron," *Edinburgh Weekly Journal,* 1824.

41. Letter dated 4 July 1834, quoted in H. F. Chorley, *Memorials of Mrs. Hemans, with Illustrations of her Literary Character from Private Correspondence,* 2 vols. (London: Saunders and Otley, 1836), II, 262.

42. Leigh Hunt, *Ultra-Crepidarius: A Satire on William Gifford* (London: John Hunt, 1823); rept. in *The Poetical Works of Leigh Hunt*, ed. H. S. Milford (London: Oxford University Press, 1923), pp. 161–67.

43. See Judith Pascoe, pp. 70, 91. Earlier, Edward Bostetter observed that "the Victorians were more than ready "to sacrifice the Della Cruscans in order to strengthen their defense of Keats and Shelley" (p. 298).

44. Alfred, Lord Tennyson, "A Character," in *Tennyson: A Selected Edition,* ed. Christopher Ricks (Berkeley and Los Angeles: University of California Press, 1989), no. 88, p. 14.

45. Leigh Hunt, "The Modern School of Poetry," first publ. October 1842; in *Leigh Hunt's Literary Criticism,* ed. Lawrence Huston Houchens and Carolyn Washburn Houchens (New York: Columbia University Press, 1956), pp. 509–27 (517–18).

Chapter 5

1. William Gifford, Introduction to *The Baviad and the Maeviad* (London: 1797).

2. As pointed out by Jonathan Brody Kramnick, *The Making of the English Canon: Print Capitalism and the Cultural Past, 1700–1770* (Cambridge: Cambridge University Press, 1998), the eighteenth century saw the emergence of an idea of English "antiquity," including "national" authors, such as Chaucer and Shakespeare. It was not until the Romantic period that a comparable canon of "moderns" began to be established, elevating Wordsworth and other Romantics.

3. Pierre Bourdieu, *Distinction: A Social Critique of the Judgement of Taste,* trans. Richard Nice (Cambridge, Mass.: Harvard University Press, 1984), p. 511.

4. Virginia Woolf, *Orlando* (New York and London: Harvest/Harcourt Brace Jovanovich, 1928; 1956), pp. 202–203.

5. Robert C. Elliott, *The Power of Satire: Magic, Ritual, Art* (Princeton: Princeton University Press, 1960).

6. My suggestion that the "antisocial" forces of satire are necessary to the self-definition and cohesion of society, in which the satirist appears as a scapegoat,

draws upon the general speculative anthropology of René Girard. See for example, *Violence and the Sacred,* trans. Patrick Gregory (Baltimore and London: Johns Hopkins University Press, 1972). A Girardian reading of satire informs in part Michael Seidel's *Satiric Inheritance: Rabelais to Sterne* (Princeton: Princeton University Press, 1979).

7. Chauncey Brewster Tinker, *The Salon and English Letters* (New York: Gordian Press, 1967), p. 31. Tinker makes the comparison between salon and review, and points out that both were a modern form of patronage.

8. Pierre Bourdieu, "The Market of Symbolic Goods," in *The Field of Cultural Production: Essays on Art and Literature,* ed. Randal Johnson (New York: Columbia University Press, 1993), p. 113.

9. Sylvia Harcstark Myers, *The Bluestocking Circle: Women, Friendship, and the Life of the Mind in Eighteenth-Century England* (Oxford: Clarendon Press, 1990; rept. 1992), p. 9.

10. See Tinker, p. 136, on Montagu's visits to Mme. Geoffrin and Mme. Deffand, in particular, the chief hostesses of the earlier era in France.

11. Tinker articulates the shift in style from French wit to English common sense (p. 125).

12. Hannah More, *Florio: A Tale, for Fine Gentlemen and Fine Ladies: and, The Bas Bleu; or, Conversation: Two Poems* (London: T. Cadell, 1786).

13. Richard Polwhele, *The Unsex'd Females* (London: Cadell & Davies, 1798).

14. On the spatially and socially structured interiors where the salons were laid out, see Elizabeth Fay, "The Bluestocking Archive: Constructivism and Salon Theory Revisited," *Romanticism on the Net* 10 (May 1998), Internet <http://users.ox.ac.uk/~scat0385/fay.html>

15. *The Journal of Sir Walter Scott,* ed. W. E. K. Anderson (Oxford: Clarendon Press, 1972), 10 August 1826 (cited in Myers, pp. 290–91).

16. For readings of these satirists in the context of the larger political climate, see Gary Dyer, *British Satire and the Politics of Style, 1789–1832* (Cambridge: Cambridge University Press, 1997).

17. Marguerite (Countess of) Blessington, *Conversations of Lord Byron,* ed. Ernest J. Lovell, Jr. (Princeton: Princeton University Press, 1969), p. 33. On Byron's mobility of character as a shift away from depth and toward a surface self, see Jean Hall, "The Evolution of the Surface Self: Byron's Poetic Career," *Keats-Shelley Journal* 36 (1987), 134–57.

18. Byron, *English Bards and Scotch Reviewers,* in *Lord Byron: The Complete Poetical Works,* ed. Jerome J. McGann and Barry Weller, 7 vols. (Oxford: Clarendon Press, 1980–92), I, 227–64 (288).

19. Roy Benjamin Clark, *William Gifford: Tory Satirist, Critic, and Editor* (New York: Columbia University Press, 1930), p. 112.

20. Gifford's "Essay" makes use of a long extract from a previous translator, the Girondist Jean Dusaulx, which emphasizes political constancy and sincere passion as the standards of satiric virtue.

21. Mary Clearman, "A Blueprint for *English Bards and Scotch Reviewers:* The First Satire of Juvenal," *Keats-Shelley Journal* 19 (1970), 87–99.

22. *Byron's Letters and Journals,* ed. Leslie Marchand, 12 vols. (Cambridge, Mass.: Belknap Press of Harvard University Press, 1973–82), 8, 172; hereafter cited as *BLJ.*

23. *BLJ,* 8, 216; for the publication of the skit, see *Lord Byron: The Complete Poetical Works,* 7 vols. (Oxford: Clarendon Press, 1980–92), VI, 1991, esp. commentary and notes, pp. 664ff. McGann's edition is the text cited in the present chapter. On the publication of the third number of *The Liberal* and the immediate reception of "The Blues" in that context, see William H. Marshall, *Byron, Shelley, Hunt and* The Liberal (Philadelphia: University of Pennsylvania Press, 1960), pp. 164–84.

24. As one index of the persistence of its minor status, "The Blues" is not included in Jerome McGann's shorter, one-volume Oxford edition. Nor is it readily found in anthologies of Romantic literature. Criticism on it has been limited. It is briefly treated with intelligence in Frederick L. Beaty's *Byron the Satirist* (DeKalb: Northern Illinois University Press, 1985), pp. 177–80.

25. *Complete Poetical Works,* VI, 664–65.

26. On *Blackwood's* use of violent satiric devices, beast imagery, ad hominem physical attacks, and the like, see Emily Lorraine de Montluzin, "Killing the Cockneys: *Blackwood's* Weapons of Choice Against Hunt, Hazlitt, and Keats," *Keats-Shelley Journal* 47 (1998), 87–107.

27. *Complete Poetical Works,* VI, 664.

28. *Lady Blessington's Conversations of Lord Byron,* ed. Ernest J. Lovell, Jr. (Princeton: Princeton University Press, 1969). The conversations held in spring 1823 were recorded in Lady Blessington's diary, then published in several forms over the coming years, first in the *New Monthly Magazine,* 1832–33, then in book form in 1834. On this publishing history, see James Soderholm, *Fantasy, Forgery, and the Byron Legend* (Lexington: University of Kentucky Press, 1996), p. 134.

29. Soderholm, *Fantasy, Forgery, and the Byron Legend,* p. 12, chapter 5 (passim). Citing Teresa Guiccoli, Soderholm suggests that Byron was studying Lady Blessington as a model for Lady Adeline in the English cantos of *Don Juan* (p. 149).

30. Leigh Hunt, *Blue-Stocking Revelries; or, The Feast of the Violets* (1837); rept. in *The Poetical Works of Leigh Hunt,* ed. H. S. Milford (London: Oxford University Press, 1923), pp. 176–92.

31. For understanding Byron's "bisexuality" in a larger sociological context, see Louis Crompton, *Byron and Greek Love: Homophobia in Nineteenth-Century England* (Berkeley: University of California Press, 1985).

32. On such triangular desire, see Eve Kosofsky Sedgwick, *Between Men: English Literature and Male Homosocial Desire* (New York: Columbia University Press, 1985).

33. "Beppo," in *Lord Byron: The Complete Poetical Works,* IV, 129–60.

34. See, for example, *BLJ,* 3, 216.

35. Quoted in Joyce Hemlow, *The History of Fanny Burney* (Oxford: Clarendon Press, 1958), p. 135.

36. *Lady Blessington's Conversations,* p. 13. This is one of the passages in Blessington that Byron's mistress, Teresa Guiccoli, marked in the margin, seemingly to indicate her agreement or approval.

37. These influences are noted by McGann, *Complete Poetical Works,* VI, 766, 214n.

38. Byron, *Letter to [John Murray] on the Rev. W. L. Bowles' Strictures on The Life and Writings of Pope* [1821], in Rowland Prothero, ed., *The Works of Lord Byron,* 6 vols. (London: 1898–1901), V, appendix III (201). For discussions of the Pope controversy in light of the larger question of the emergence of Romanticism, see Upali Amarasinghe, *Dryden and Pope in the Early Nineteenth Century: A Study of Changing Literary Taste, 1800–1830* (Cambridge: Cambridge University Press, 1962), pp. 130–34; and Robert J. Griffin, *Wordsworth's Pope: A Study in Literary Historiography* (Cambridge, Cambridge University Press, 1995), pp. 24–63.

39. Paul Graham Trueblood, *The Flowering of Byron's Genius: Studies in Byron's Don Juan* (Stanford: Stanford University Press, 1945), pp. 24–25. Trueblood sees in this phase of Byron's spiritual and creative maturity" an inclination toward "revolutionary indoctrination" that I prefer to read as general re-engagement in the world, including politics. Jean Hall, in "The Evolution of the Surface Self," personalizes this shift as from the (Romantic) idea of a deep self toward the (Byronic) idea of the surface self, which also includes a turn toward the world of action.

Chapter 6

1. *Byron's Letters and Journals,* ed. Leslie Marchand, 12 vols. (Cambridge, Mass.: Harvard University Press, 1973–82), VIII, 90 (22 January 1821); hereafter cited as *BLJ.*

2. *English Bards and Scotch Reviewers,* in *Lord Byron: The Complete Poetical Works,* ed. Jerome McGann and Barry Weller, 7 vols. (Oxford: Clarendon Press, 1980–92), I, 227–64.

3. *BLJ,* IX, 36–37; cited in Peter W. Graham, *"Don Juan" and Regency England* (Charlottesville and London: University Press of Virginia, 1990), pp. 74–76. Graham reads the remembered incident as an example of the blurring of the distinction between life and art in Byron—of his theatricality. He also usefully points out that this pantomime thematizes authorship as a mock-Hamlet's dilemma (p. 76), whether to write or make a pantomime.

4. That the mask might possibly represent a pirate was first suggested by Catherine Payling, Curator, Keats House, Rome. (I am very grateful to her for coordinating the photography of the mask for figure 6.1, and for permission to reproduce the image here and on the cover.) The identity of the mask is unknown. It could also be a Bacchus or some other mythological figure.

5. The connection has been noticed by others; I am preceded in my comparison of *Don Juan* to pantomime by several excellent critical treatments, my debt to which should become clear in what follows. Among these are Freder-

ick Beaty, "Harlequin Don Juan," *JEGP* 67.3 (1968), 395–405; Peter W. Graham, *"Don Juan" and Regency England* (Charlottesville and London: University of Virginia Press, 1990), pp. 62–88; and Moyra Haslett, *Byron, 'Don Juan' and the Don Juan Legend* (Oxford: Clarendon Press, 1997), esp. pp. 39–40, 59–60.

6. Pierre Bourdieu, "The Market of Symbolic Goods," in *The Field of Cultural Production: Essays on Art and Literature,* ed. Randal Johnson (New York: Columbia University Press, 1993), p. 113.

7. William Makepeace Thackeray, *The Four Georges: Sketches of Manners, Morals, and Court, and Town Life* (New York: Harper and Brothers, 1863), p. 69.

8. David Mayer, *Harlequin in His Element: The English Pantomime, 1806–1836* (Cambridge: Harvard University Press, 1969), p. 54.

9. Mayer, pp. 9–10.

10. Gerald Frow, *"Oh, Yes It Is!" A History of Pantomime* (London: BBC, 1985), pp. 57–58.

11. Frow, p. 58.

12. Dibdin cited in Frow, p. 148.

13. Review of *Harlequin's Vision,* in *The Theatrical Inquisitor and Monthly Mirror* (January 1818), 51.

14. Isaac Disraeli, "The Pantomimical Characters," in *Curiosities of Literature,* ed. Earl of Beaconsfield, 3 vols. (London: Frederick Warne and Co., 1881), II, 117. Disraeli compares the English pantomime characters unfavorably with their Italian sources, who were, he says, "the grotesque children of wit, and whim, and satire."

15. Paula R. Backscheider, *Spectacular Politics: Theatrical Power and Mass Culture in Early Modern England* (Baltimore: Johns Hopkins University Press, 1993), pp. 155, 175–76.

16. *A Satirical View of London at the Commencement of the Nineteenth Century* (London, 1801), p. 238.

17. *Leigh Hunt's Literary Criticism,* ed. Lawrence Huston Houtchens and Carolyn Washburn Houtchens (New York: Columbia University Press, 1956), pp. 7–8.

18. W. N. Hargreaves-Mawdsley, *The English Della Cruscans in their Time, 1783–1828* (The Hague: Martinus Nijhoff, 1967), chapter 7. My text of the pantomime is the copy in the Library of Congress, *Sketch of the Pantomime, Entitled The Picture of Paris. Taken in The Year 1790* (London: T. Cadell, 1790 [1791?]).

19. Marilyn Gaull, *English Romanticism: The Human Context* (New York: W. W. Norton, 1988), p. 91.

20. On piracies and the publication of *Don Juan,* see McGann's notes to the *Complete Poetical Works;* see also Peter J. Manning, "The Hone-ing of Byron's Corsair," in *Textual Criticism and Literary Interpretation,* ed. Jerome J. McGann (Chicago and London: University of Chicago Press, 1985), 107–26; and William St. Clair, "The Impact of Byron's Writings:

An Evaluative Approach," in Andrew Rutherford, ed., *Byron: Augustan and Romantic* (London: Macmillan, 1990), 1–25.

21. Specifically, on Larpent's chilling effect, see Mayer, pp. 240–44; Terence Allan Hoagwood, *Politics, Philosophy, and the Production of Romantic Texts* (DeKalb: Northern Illinois University Press, 1996).

22. This satire survives only in fragmentary form in Shelley's rough-draft notebooks. See Steven E. Jones, "Shelley's 'Satire upon Satire': A Complete Transcription of the Text with Commentary, *Keats-Shelley Journal* 37 (1988), 136–63; and see Donald H. Reiman's text and notes in *Shelley adds. E. 15, adds e. 20, and adds. c. 4, folios 212–245,* volume 7 of *The Bodleian Shelley Manuscripts* (New York: Garland Publishing, 1986). In the lines quoted above, square brackets represent canceled words in Shelley's manuscript.

23. Shelley, *A Defence of Poetry,* in *Shelley's Poetry and Prose,* ed. Donald H. Reiman and Sharon B. Powers (New York and London: W.W. Norton, 1977), p. 487.

24. Leigh Hunt, *Tatler,* 28 December 1831, III, 613.

25. Steven E. Jones, *Shelley's Satire: Violence, Exhortation, and Authority* (DeKalb: Northern Illinois University Press, 1994), pp. 124–48.

26. *Oedipus Tyrannus; or, Swellfoot The Tyrant,* in *Shelley: Poetical Works,* ed. Thomas Hutchinson, corrected G. M. Matthews (London: Oxford University Press, 1970).

27. Ralph M. Rosen, *Old Comedy and the Iambographic Tradition* (Atlanta: Scholars Press, 1988), p. 21, n. 46.

28. Mayer, pp. 103–104.

29. David Simpson, *Irony and Authority in Romantic Poetry* (London: Macmillan, 1979), p. 190; Anne K. Mellor, *English Romantic Irony* (Cambridge, Mass.: Harvard University Press, 1980), pp. 5–8.

30. Jerome J. McGann, *The Romantic Ideology: A Critical Investigation* (Chicago and London: University of Chicago Press, 1983), pp. 23–24.

31. Irving Babbitt, *Rousseau and Romanticism* (New York: Meridan Books, 1957), p. 191.

32. Friedrich Schlegel, *Atheneum Fragments* (no. 244; hereafter *AF*) in *Friedrich Schlegel's Lucinde and the Fragments,* trans. Peter Firchow (Minneapolis: University of Minnesota Press, 1971), p. 196.

33. On Gozzi, see John Louis DiGaetani, introduction to *Carlo Gozzi: Translations of "The Love of Three Oranges," "Turandot," and "The Snake Lady"* (New York, Westport, London: Greenwood Press, 1988); and Hedwig Hoffmann Rusack, *Gozzi in Germany* (New York: AMS Press, 1966).

34. Rusack, *Gozzi in Germany,* pp. 56–71, and passim.

35. The usage of "Romantic" among the Jena group surrounding Friedrich Schlegel is noted by Mariyln Butler, *Romantics, Rebels and Reactionaries: English Literature and its Background 1760–1830* (New York and Oxford: Oxford University Press, 1982), p. 4.

36. Marguerite (Countess of) Blessington, *Conversations of Lord Byron,* ed. Ernest J. Lovell, Jr. (Princeton: Princeton University Press, 1969), p. 33.

37. On the character of the Don himself, see Frederick Beaty, "Harlequin Don Juan"; Peter W. Graham, in *"Don Juan" and Regency England,* argues convincingly that English pantomime and Italian *commedia dell'arte* at least parallel and "may have influenced" Byron's poem (p. 63); and Moyra Haslett, in *Byron, 'Don Juan' and the Don Juan Legend* (Oxford: Clarendon Press, 1997), pp. 39–40, 59–60, goes further to establish many specific opportunities for influence.

38. Moyra Haslett, p. 59.

39. James Chandler, *England in 1819: The Politics of Literary Culture and the Case of Romantic Historicism* (Chicago and London: University of Chicago Press, 1998), p. 363.

40. Haslett, p. 94, cites Gendarme de Bévotte (1906) for this claim about the traditional Don Juan story.

41. Friedrich Schlegel, *Critical Fragments,* no. 42, in Firchow, p. 148.

42. Friedrich Schlegel, *Ideas,* no. 69, in Firchow, p. 247.

43. Mellor, *English Romantic Irony,* pp. 49–50.

44. *The Letters of John Keats,* ed. Hyder Edward Rollins, 2 vols. (Cambridge, Mass.: Harvard University Press, 1958), I, 191–94. Keats had been to see *Harlequin's Vision, or, The Feast of the Statue* at Drury Lane (193 n. 6).

45. *The Letters of John Keats,* I, 395

Chapter 7

1. The satiric tradition I am sketching is more literary and cross-canonical (that is, it includes canonical with non-canonical authors) than his, but I have in mind the alternative or underground tradition represented by Marcus Wood in *Radical Satire and Print Culture, 1790–1822* (Oxford: Clarendon Press, 1994).

2. Jerome J. McGann, *The Romantic Ideology: A Critical Investigation* (Chicago: University of Chicago Press, 1983).

3. As cited in Thomas Carlyle's review of the *Corn Law Rhymes* (discussed below), in the *Edinburgh Review,* July 1832.

4. T. S. Ashton, *The Industrial Revolution, 1760–1830* (New York: Oxford University Press, 1964), pp. 105–106.

5. E. P. Thompson, *The Making of the English Working Class* (New York: Vintage Books, 1963), p. 315.

6. John Watkins, ed. *The Life, Poetry, and Letters of Ebenezer Elliott, the Corn Law Rhymer* (London: John Mortimer, 1850), p. 114.

7. Mary Moorman, *Wordsworth, A Biography,* 2 vols. (Oxford: Clarendon Press, 1957; 1965), II, 572.

8. Ebenezer Elliott, "The Four Dears," in John Watkins, ed., *The Life, Poetry, and Letters of Ebenezer Elliott,* pp. 61–62. All quotations of Elliott's work are from this edition.

9. Quoted in Watkins, Introduction.

10. Robert Burns, "Song—For a' that and a' that—," in *Burns: Poems and Songs,* ed. James Kinsley (Oxford, New York, Toronto, Melbourne: Oxford University Press, 1969), p. 602 (#482).

11. E. P. Thompson, *The Making of the English Working Class,* p. 727.

12. Elie Halévy, *England in 1815,* trans. E. I. Watkin and D. A. Barker (London: Ernest Benn, Ltd., 1949), pp. 105–106.

13. Nigel Cross, *The Common Writer: Life in Nineteenth-Century Grub Street* (Cambridge: Cambridge University Press, 1985), p. 149.

14. *New Monthly Magazine,* 32 (1831), pt. II, 552.

15. Joseph Warton, *Essay on Pope,* I, 344.

16. Margaret Oliphant, *Literary History of England,* 2 vols. (1882; rept. New York: AMS Press, 1970), II, 384.

17. *Poems of Ebenezer Elliott,* intro. Rufus W. Griswold (New York: Leavitt & Allen, 1853), pp. 5–9.

18. On the readership and generic makeup of *Punch,* see Richard D. Altick, *Punch: The Lively Youth of a British Institution 1841–1851* (Columbus: Ohio State University Press, 1997). Altick suggests that the magazine was born during a "reformation of manners," the transition from the Regency to the more middle-class early Victorian Reform period. Elliott's acceptance serves as a portent of these changes, I would suggest.

19. William Makepeace Thackeray, "John Leech's Pictures of Life and Character," *The Works of William Makepeace Thackeray,* 26 vols. (London: Smith, Elder and Co., 1910–11), XXIII, 460; cited and discussed in Gary Dyer, *British Satire and the Politics of Style,* p. 167. With Dyer's concluding chapter I share the general thesis that the Victorian era saw a domestication or displacement of satiric tendencies, though for me this is a function of the blindnesses and insights of canon formation and of shifts to popular forms more than any actual decline in satire itself, which Dyer claims "largely disappeared as a distinct literary form or distinct group of forms" in the 1820s and 1830s (p. 139).

20. John Stuart Mill, for example, cites Elliott with approval but, as Anne Janowitz has shown, quotes him selectively in order to depoliticize his theory of poetry as "impassioned truth." As Janowitz writes, "Mill recasts both Elliott and Shelley . . . in the image of the [Romantic] lyric poet he wishes to encourage, and dispossess each of their claim to a robust social and political poetic intervention" (*Lyric and Labour in the Romantic Tradition* [New York and Cambridge: Cambridge University Press, 1998], pp. 59–60).

21. Arthur Symons, *The Romantic Movement in English Poetry* (London: Constable, 1909), pp. 209–12.

22. Thomas Carlyle, review of Ebenezer Elliott's *Corn Law Rhymes, Edinburgh Review* 110 (July 1832).

23. On Hemans's success in the poetry market in the second two decades of the nineteenth century, see Paula R. Feldman, "The Poet and the Profits: Felicia Hemans and the Literary Marketplace," *Keats-Shelley Journal* 46 (1997), 148–76.

24. John D. Rosenberg, *Carlyle and the Burden of History* (Oxford: Clarendon Press, 1985), p. 10.

25. Gary Taylor, "The Rhetoric of Textual Criticism," in *TEXT: Transactions of the Society for Textual Scholarship* 4 (New York: AMS Press, 1988), 39–57, applies these terms to the editorially posited author, who "has passed away. The Author is always in the past" (44).

Bibliography

Abrams, M. H. *Natural Supernaturalism: Tradition and Revolution in Romantic Literature.* New York: W. W. Norton, 1971.

Altick, Richard D. *The English Common Reader.* Chicago: University of Chicago Press, 1957.

Babbitt, Irving. *Rousseau and Romanticism.* New York: Meridan Books, 1957.

Backscheider, Paula R. *Spectacular Politics: Theatrical Power and Mass Culture in Early Modern England.* Baltimore: Johns Hopkins University Press, 1993

Bakhtin, M. M. *The Dialogic Imagination.* Ed. Michael Holquist. Trans. Caryl Emerson and Michael Holquist. Austin: University of Texas Press, 1981.

Beaty, Frederick L. *Byron the Satirist.* DeKalb: Northern Illinois University Press, 1985.

———. "Harlequin Don Juan." *JEGP* 67.3 (1968), 395–405.

Behrendt, Stephen C. *Shelley and His Audiences.* Lincoln and London: University of Nebraska Press, 1989.

Benjamin, Walter. *Illuminations.* Ed. Hannah Arendt. Trans. Harry Zohn. New York: Schocken Books, 1969.

Bewell, Alan. "Keats's Realm of Flora." *Studies in Romanticism* 31 (Spring 1992), 71–98.

———. *Wordsworth and the Enlightenment: Nature, Man, Society in the Experimental Poetry.* New Haven and London: Yale University Press, 1989.

Bialostosky, Don H. *Making Tales: The Poetics of Wordsworth's Narrative Experiments.* Chicago: University of Chicago Press, 1984.

The Black Dwarf. Ed. T. J. Wooler. London, 1817–24.

Blackstone, William. *Commentaries on the Laws of England.* Adapted by Robert Malcolm Kerr. 4 vols. London: 1773; Boston: Beacon Press, 1962.

Blackwood's Edinburgh Magazine. Edinburgh, W. Blackwood; London, T. Cadell and W. Davies.

Blessington, Marguerite (Countess of). *Conversations of Lord Byron.* Ed. Ernest J. Lovell, Jr. Princeton: Princeton University Press, 1969.

Bostetter, Edward. "The Original Della Cruscans and the Florence Miscellany." *Huntington Library Quarterly* 19.3 (May 1956), 277–300.

Bourdieu, Pierre. *Distinction: A Social Critique of the Judgement of Taste.* Trans. Richard Nice. Cambridge, Mass.: Harvard University Press, 1984.

———. "The Market of Symbolic Goods." In *The Field of Cultural Production: Essays on Art and Literature.* Ed. Randal Johnson. New York: Columbia University Press, 1993.

Brown, Huntington. "The Gloss to the *Ancient Mariner.*" *Studies in Philology* 61 (1964), 669–88.

Bushell, Sally. "Narrative and the Boundaries of Genre in *The Excursion.*" D. Phil. thesis (in progress), Cambridge University.

Butler, Marilyn. *Romantics, Rebels and Reactionaries.* New York and Oxford: Oxford University Press, 1982.

———. "Satire and the Images of Self in the Romantic Period: The Long Tradition of Hazlitt's *Liber Amoris.*" In *English Satire and the Satiric Tradition,* ed. Claude Rawson. Oxford: Basil Blackwell, 1984, 153–69.

Byron, George Gordon, Lord. *Byron's Letters and Journals.* Ed. Leslie Marchand, 12 vols. Cambridge, Mass.: Harvard University Press, 1973–82.

———. *Lord Byron: The Complete Poetical Works.* Ed. Jerome J. McGann and Barry Weller. 7 vols. Oxford: Clarendon Press, 1980–92.

Campbell, Thomas. *Life of Mrs. Siddons.* London, 1834. Rept. New York: Benjamin Blom, 1972.

Chamberlain, Robert L. *George Crabbe.* New York: Twayne, 1965.

Chandler, James. *England in 1819: The Politics of Literary Culture and the Case of Romantic Historicism.* Chicago: University of Chicago Press, 1998.

Clifford, James L. "Robert Merry—A Pre-Byronic Hero." *Bulletin of the John Rylands Library* 27 (1942–43), 74–96.

Coleridge, Samuel Taylor. *The Collected Works of Samuel Taylor Coleridge.* Gen. ed. Kathleen Coburn. London: Routledge & Kegan Paul; Princeton, Princeton University Press, 1969-.

———. *Poems 1796.* Ed. Jonathan Wordsworth. Facsim. Oxford and New York: Woodstock Books, 1990.

———. *Samuel Taylor Coleridge, Charles Lamb, Charles Lloyd, Poems 1797.* Ed. Jonathan Wordsworth. Facsim. Poole, Washington D.C.: Woodstock Books, 1997.

———. *Sibylline leaves.* Ed. Jonathan Wordsworth. Facsim. Oxford: Woodstock Books, 1990.

Collier, Mary, and Stephen Duck. *The Thresher's Labour (1736) and The Woman's Labour (1739).* Ed. Moira Ferguson. Augustan Reprint Society Pub. No. 230. Los Angeles: Clark Memorial Library, UCLA, 1985.

Cox, Jeffrey N. *Poetry and Politics in the Cockney School: Keats, Shelley, Hunt and Their Circle.* Cambridge: Cambridge University Press, 1998.

Crabbe, George. *The Complete Poetical Works.* 3 vols. Ed. Norman Dalrymple-Champneys and Arthur Pollard. Oxford: Clarendon Press, 1988.

Crabbe. *The Life of George Crabbe by His Son.* Intro. E. M. Forster. London: Oxford University Press and Humphrey Milford, 1932.

Critical Review. London.

Crompton, Louis. *Byron and Greek Love: Homophobia in Nineteenth-Century England.* Berkeley: University of California Press, 1985.

Curran, Stuart. *Poetic Form and British Romanticism.* New York and Oxford: Oxford University Press, 1986.

de Man, Paul. "Autobiography As De-facement." In *The Rhetoric of Romanticism.* New York: Columbia University Press, 1984, pp. 67–81.

de Montluzin, Emily Lorraine. "Killing the Cockneys: *Blackwood's* Weapons of Choice Against Hunt, Hazlitt, and Keats," *Keats-Shelley Journal* 47 (1998), 87-107.

Devlin, D. D. *Wordsworth and the Poetry of Epitaphs.* Totowa, N. J.: Barnes & Noble, 1981.

DiGaetani, John Louis. *Carlo Gozzi: Translations of "The Love of Three Oranges," "Turandot," and "The Snake Lady."* New York, Westport, London: Greenwood Press, 1988.

Disraeli, Isaac. *Curiosities of Literature.* Ed. Earl of Beaconsfield. 3 vols. London: Frederick Warne and Co., 1881.

Duck, Stephen, and Mary Collier. *The Thresher's Labour (1736) and The Woman's Labour (1739).* Ed. Moira Ferguson. Augustan Reprint Society Pub. No. 230. Los Angeles: Clark Memorial Library, UCLA, 1985.

Dyer, Gary. *British Satire and the Politics of Style, 1789–1832.* Cambridge: Cambridge University Press, 1997.

Edinburgh Review. Edinburgh, A Constable; London, Longmans, Greene, & Co.

Elliott, Ebenezer. *Corn Law Rhymes.* London, 1831.

———. John Watkins, ed. *The Life, Poetry, and Letters of Ebenezer Elliot, the Corn Law Rhymer.* London: John Mortimer, 1850.

———. *The Poems of Ebenezer Elliott.* Intro. Rufus W. Griswold. New York: Leavitt & Allen, 1853.

Elliott, Robert C. *The Power of Satire: Magic, Ritual, Art.* Princeton: Princeton University Press, 1960.

Emerson, Hunt [and Samuel Taylor Coleridge]. *The Rime of the Ancient Mariner.* Crack Comics version. Reprinted, colored by Carol Bennett. London: Knockabout Comics, 1989.

Erdman, David V. "Coleridge as Nehemiah Higginbottom." *Modern Language Notes* 73 (December 1958), 569–80.

Ferguson, Frances. *Wordsworth: Language as Counter-Spirit.* New Haven: Yale University Press, 1977.

The Florence Miscellany. Florence: G. Cam, 1785.

Foucault, Michel. "What is an Author?" *Language Counter-Memory, Practice.* Ithaca, N.Y.: Cornell University Press, 1977, 113–38.

Frow, Gerald. *"Oh Yes it Is!" A History of Pantomime.* London: BBC, 1985.

Gaull, Marilyn. *English Romanticism: The Human Context.* New York: W. W. Norton and Co., 1988.

———. "Romantic Humor: The Horse of Knowledge and the Learned Pig." *Mosaic* 9.4 (1976), 43–64.

Geertz, Clifford. *The Interpretation of Cultures.* New York: Harper Collins/Basic Books, 1973.

Gifford, William. *The Baviad and The Maeviad.* London, 1797.

Gilmartin, Kevin. "Popular Radicalism and the Public Sphere" ("Forum"). *Studies in Romanticism* 33.4 (Winter 1994), 549–57.

———. *Print Politics: The Press and Radical Opposition in Early Nineteenth-Century England.* Cambridge: Cambridge University Press, 1996.

Girard, René. *Violence and the Sacred.* Trans. Patrick Gregory. Baltimore and London: Johns Hopkins University Press, 1972

Gittings, Robert. *The Mask of Keats: A Study of Problems.* Cambridge, Mass.: Harvard University Press, 1956.

Godwin, William. *The Adventures of Caleb Williams: Or Things as they Are.* New York and Toronto: Rinehart & Co., 1960.

Goldsmith, Oliver. *Collected Works of Oliver Goldsmith.* Ed. Arthur Friedman. 5 vols. Oxford: Clarendon Press, 1966.

Goodridge, John. *Rural Life in Eighteenth-Century English Poetry.* Cambridge: Cambridge University Press, 1995.

Graham, Peter W. *"Don Juan" and Regency England.* Charlottesville and London: University Press of Virginia, 1990.

Griffin, Robert J. *Wordsworth's Pope: A Study in Literary Historiography.* Cambridge: Cambridge University Press, 1995.

Guillory, John. *Cultural Capital: The Problem of Literary Canon Formation.* Chicago: University of Chicago Press, 1993.

Halévy, Elie. *The Liberal Awakening 1815–1830.* Trans. E. I. Watkin. New York: Peter Smith, 1949.

Hall, Jean. "The Evolution of the Surface Self: Byron's Poetic Career." *Keats-Shelley Journal* 36 (1987), 134–57.

Hargreaves-Mawdsley, W. N. *The English Della Cruscans in Their Time, 1783–1828.* The Hague: Martinus Nijhoff, 1967.

Haslett, Moyra. *Byron, 'Don Juan' and the Don Juan Legend.* Oxford: Clarendon Press, 1997.

Hatch, Ronald B. *Crabbe's Arabesque: Social Drama in the Poetry of George Crabbe.* Montreal: McGill-Queen's University Press, 1976.

Hazlitt, William. *The Complete Works of William Hazlitt.* Ed. P. P. Howe. 21 vols. London: J. M. Dent & Sons, 1930–34.

Hemlow, Joyce. *The History of Fanny Burney.* Oxford: Clarendon Press, 1958.

Hendrix, Richard. "Popular Humor in 'The Black Dwarf'," *Journal of British Studies* 16 (Fall 1976), 108–28.

Hoagwood, Terence Allan. *Politics, Philosophy, and the Production of Romantic Texts.* DeKalb: Northern Illinois University Press, 1996.

Hogg, Thomas Jefferson. *The Life of Percy Bysshe Shelley.* 2 vols. London and Toronto: J. M. Dent & Sons, 1933.

Hone, William, and George Cruikshank. *The Political House That Jack Built.* 1819.

Huchens, René. *George Crabbe and His Times 1754–1832.* New York: E. P. Dutton, 1907.

Humphries, Steve. *Victorian Britain Through the Magic Lantern.* London: Sidgwick & Jackson, 1989.

Hunt, Leigh. *The Autobiography of Leigh Hunt with Reminiscences of Friends and Contemporaries.* 3 vols. London: Smith, Elder & Co., 1850.

———. *Leigh Hunt's Literary Criticism.* Ed. Lawrence Huston Houtchens and Carolyn Washburn Houtchens. New York: Columbia University Press, 1956.

———. *The Poetical Works of Leigh Hunt.* Ed. H. S. Milford. London: Oxford University Press, 1923.

Hutcheon, Linda. *A Theory of Parody: The Teachings of Twentieth-Century Art Forms.* New York: Methuen, 1985.

Janowitz, Anne F. *Lyric and Labour in the Romantic Tradition.* New York and Cambridge: Cambridge University Press, 1998.

Jones, Elizabeth. "Keats in the Suburbs." *Keats-Shelley Journal* 45 (1996), 23–43.

Jones, Steven E. "Shelley's 'Satire upon Satire': A Complete Transcription of the Text with Commentary." *Keats-Shelley Journal* 37 (1988), 136–63.

———. *Shelley's Satire: Violence, Exhortation, and Authority.* DeKalb: Northern Illinois University Press, 1994.

Keats. *John Keats: Complete Poems.* Ed. Jack Stillinger. Cambridge, Mass.: Belknap Press of Harvard University Press, 1982.

———. *The Letters of John Keats.* Ed. Hyder Edward Rollins. 2 vols. Cambridge, Mass.: Harvard University Press, 1958.

Kent, David A., and D. R. Ewen, eds. *Romantic Parodies 1797–1831.* London and Toronto: Associated University Presses, 1992.

Klancher, Jon P. *The Making of English Reading Audiences, 1790–1832.* Madison: University of Wisconsin Press, 1987.

Kroeber, Karl. *Romantic Narrative Art.* Madison: University of Wisconsin Press, 1966.

———, and Gene W. Ruoff, eds. *Romantic Poetry: Recent Revisionary Criticism.* New Brunswick: Rutgers University Press, 1993.

Levinson, Marjorie. *Keats's Life of Allegory: The Origins of a Style.* Oxford: Basil Blackwell, 1988.

Lion, Judson Stanley. *The Excursion: A Study.* New Haven: Yale University Press, 1950.

Lipking, Lawrence. "The Marginal Gloss: Notes and Asides on Poe, Valéry, 'The Ancient Mariner,' the Ordeal of the Margin, Storiella as She is Sung, Versions of Leonardo, and the Plight of Modern Criticism." *Critical Inquiry* 3 (1977), 609–55.

Liu, Alan. *Wordsworth: The Sense of History.* Stanford: Stanford University Press, 1989.

Lockwood, Thomas. *Post-Augustan Satire: Charles Churchill and Satirical Poetry, 1750–1800.* Seattle and London: University of Washington Press, 1979.

London, Bette. "Mary Shelley, *Frankenstein,* and the Spectacle of Masculinity." *PMLA* 108.2 (March 1993), 253–67.

Lovejoy, Arthur O. "On Discriminations of Romanticisms." *PMLA* 39 (1924), 229–53.

Lowes, Jonathan Livingston. *The Road to Xanadu: A Study in the Ways of the Imagination* London: Constable, 1927.

McCalman, Iain. *Radical Underworld: Prophets, Revolutionaries and Pornographers in London, 1795–1840.* Cambridge: Cambridge University Press, 1988.

———, ed. *The Horrors of Slavery and Other Writings by Robert Wedderburn.* New York and Princeton: Markus Wiener, 1991.

McGann, Jerome J. *The Beauty of Inflections: Literary Investigations in Historical Method and Theory.* Oxford: Clarendon Press, 1988.

———. *Black Riders: The Visible Language of Modernism.* Princeton: Princeton University Press, 1993.

———. "Literary Pragmatics and the Editorial Horizon." In *Devils and Angels: Textual Editing and Literary Theory.* Ed. Philip Cohen. Charlottesville and London: University Press of Virginia, 1991, pp. 1–21.

———, ed. *The New Oxford Book of Romantic Period Verse.* Oxford and New York: Oxford University Press, 1994.

———. *The Poetics of Sensibility.* Oxford: Clarendon Press, 1996.

———. "Rethinking Romanticism." *ELH* 59 (1992), 735–54.

———. *The Romantic Ideology: A Critical Investigation.* Chicago and London: University of Chicago Press, 1983.

———. *The Textual Condition.* Princeton: Princeton University Press, 1991.

———. *Towards a Literature of Knowledge.* Oxford: Clarendon Press, 1989.

Mann, Phyllis G. "Keats's Indian Allegory." *Keats-Shelley Journal* 6 (1957), 4–9.

Manning, Peter. "The 'Hone-ing' of Byron's Corsair." In *Textual Criticism and Literary Interpretation,* ed. Jerome J. McGann. Chicago and London: University of Chicago Press, 1985, 107–26.

Marshall, William H. *Byron, Shelley, Hunt and 'The Liberal'.* Philadelphia: University of Pennsylvania Press, 1960.

Mayer, David. *Harlequin in His Element: The English Pantomime, 1806–1836.* Cambridge, Mass.: Harvard University Press, 1969.

Mellor, Anne K. *English Romantic Irony.* Cambridge, Mass.: Harvard University Press, 1980.

———. *Romanticism and Gender.* New York and London: Routledge, 1993.

Merry, Robert. *Sketch of the Pantomime, Entitled The Picture of Paris. Taken in The Year 1790.* London: T. Cadell, 1790 [1791].

Milton, John. *The Works of John Milton.* Ed. Frank Allen Patterson. 18 vols. New York: Columbia University Press, 1931.

Modern Language Quarterly 58.4 (December 1997).

Moi, Toril. "Appropriating Bourdieu." *NLH* 22 (1991), 1017–49.

Monthly Magazine. London, R. Phillips.

Monthly Review. London, Griffiths.

Moorman, Mary. *Wordsworth, A Biography.* 2 vols. Oxford: Clarendon Press, 1957–65.

More, Hannah. *Florio: A Tale, for Fine Gentlemen and Fine Ladies: and, The Bas Bleu; or, Conversation: Two Poems.* London: T. Cadell, 1786.

Morley, Henry. *Memoirs of Bartholomew Fair.* London: Chatto and Windus, 1880.

Myers, Sylvia Harcstark. *The Bluestocking Circle: Women, Friendship, and the Life of the Mind in Eighteenth-Century England.* Oxford: Clarendon Press, 1990; rept. 1992.

Nabholtz, John R. *"My Reader My Fellow-Labourer": A Study of English Romantic Prose.* Columbia: University of Missouri Press, 1986.

New Monthly Magazine. London, H. Colburn.

Pascoe, Judith. *Romantic Theatricality: Gender, Poetry, and Spectatorship.* Ithaca and London: Cornell University Press, 1997.

Patten, Robert L. *George Cruikshank's Life, Times, and Art. Vol. 1: 1792–1835.* London: Lutterworth Press, 1992.

Perkins, David. "The Construction of 'The Romantic Movement' as a Literary Classification." *Nineteenth-Century Literature* (1990), 129–43.

Poetry of the Anti-Jacobin (1799). Facs. rept. Oxford: Woodstock Books, 1991.

Pollard, Arthur, ed. *Crabbe: The Critical Heritage.* London and Boston: Routledge & Kegan Paul, 1972.

Pope, Alexander. *The Correspondence of Alexander Pope.* Ed. G. Sherburn. 5 vols. Oxford: Clarendon Press, 1956.

Porter, Roy. *English Society in the Eighteenth Century.* London: Penguin Books, 1982.

Quarterly Review. London, John Murray.

Rajan, Tilottama. *Dark Interpreter: The Discourse of Romanticism.* Ithaca, N. Y.: Cornell University Press, 1980.

Rawson, Claude. *Satire and Sentiment: 1660–1830.* Cambridge: Cambridge University Press, 1994.

Reiman, Donald H., ed. *Bodleian Shelley Manuscripts.* Vol. 7 (New York: Garland Publishing, 1986).

———, ed. *The Romantics Reviewed, C.1.* New York: Garland, 1972.

———. "Shelley as Agrarian Reactionary." In *Romantic Texts and Contexts.* Columbia: University of Missouri Press, 1987.

Roe, Nicholas. *John Keats and the Culture of Dissent.* Oxford: Clarendon Press, 1997.

Rosen, Ralph M. *Old Comedy and the Iambographic Tradition.* Atlanta: Scholars Press, 1988.

Rosenfeld, Sybil. *The Theatre of the London Fairs in the Eighteenth Century.* Cambridge: Cambridge University Press, 1960.

Rusack, Hedwig Hoffmann. *Gozzi in Germany.* New York: AMS Press, 1966.

St. Clair, William. "The Impact of Byron's Writings: An Evaluative Approach." In Andrew Rutherford, ed. *Byron: Augustan and Romantic.* London: Macmillan, 1990, 1–25.

Salaman, R. N. *The History and Social Influence of the Potato.* Cambridge: Cambridge University Press, 1949.

Sales, Roger. *English Literature in History 1780–1830: Pastoral and Politics.* New York: St. Martin's, 1983.

A Satirical View of London at the Commencement of the Nineteenth Century. London, 1801.

Schlegel, Friedrich. *Friedrich Schlegel's Lucinde and the Fragments.* Trans. Peter Firchow. Minneapolis: University of Minnesota Press, 1971.

Scots Magazine. Edinburgh, Sands, Brymer, Murray, & Cochran.

Scott, Sir Walter. *The Black Dwarf.* Ed. P. D. Garside. Edinburgh: Edinburgh University Press; New York: Columbia University Press, 1993.

———. *The Journal of Sir Walter Scott.* Ed. W. E. K. Anderson. Oxford: Clarendon Press, 1972.

———. *Letters.* Ed. H. J. C. Grierson. 3 vols. London: Constable, 1937.

Scrivener, Michael. "The Black Dwarf Review of Byron's The Age of Bronze." *Keats-Shelley Journal* 41 (1992), 42–48.

Sedgwick, Eve Kosofsky. *Between Men: English Literature and Male Homosocial Desire.* New York: Columbia University Press, 1985.

Seidel, Michael. *Satiric Inheritance: Rabelais to Sterne.* Princeton: Princeton University Press, 1979.

Shelley, Percy Bysshe. *The Complete Poetical Works of Shelley.* Ed. Thomas Hutchinson (1904). Corrected ed. G. M. Matthews. London: Oxford University Press, 1970.

———. *The Letters of Percy Bysshe Shelley.* Ed. Frederick L. Jones. 2 vols. Oxford: Clarendon Press, 1964.

———. *Shelley's Poetry and Prose.* Ed. Donald H. Reiman and Sharon B. Powers. New York and London: Norton, 1977.

Simpson, David. *Irony and Authority in Romantic Poetry.* London: Macmillan, 1979.

———. *Romanticism, Nationalism, and the Revolt Against Theory* (Chicago and London: University of Chicago Press, 1993.

Soderholm, James. *Fantasy, Forgery, and the Byron Legend.* Lexington: University of Kentucky Press, 1996.

Southey, Robert. *Essays, Moral and Political.* 2 vols. London: John Murray, 1832.

Stallybrass, Peter, and Allon White. *The Politics and Poetics of Transgression.* Ithaca, N.Y.: Cornell University Press, 1986.

Sterling, Bruce. *Dead Media Project* Website. Internet. <http://www.well.com/mirrorshades/deadmed.html>.

Stillinger, Jack. *Coleridge and Textual Instability: The Multiple Versions of the Major Poems.* New York and Oxford: Oxford University Press, 1994.

Stones, Graeme and John Strachan, eds. *Parodies of the Romantic Age.* 5 vols. London: Pickering & Chatto, 1999.

Swingle, L. J. "Late Crabbe in Relation to the Augustans and Romantics: The Temporal Labyrinth of his Tales in Verse, 1812." *ELH* 42 (1975), 580–94.

Taylor, Gary. *Cultural Selection: Why Some Achievements Survive the Test of Time—and Others Don't.* New York: Basic Books/Harper Collins, 1996.

———. "The Rhetoric of Textual Criticism." *TEXT: Transactions of the Society for Textual Scholarship* 4. New York: AMS Press, 1988.

Tennyson, Alfred, Lord. *Tennyson: A Selected Edition.* Ed. Christopher Ricks. Berkeley and Los Angeles: University of California Press, 1989.

Thackeray, William Mackepeace. *The Four Georges: Sketches of Manners, Morals, and Court, and Town Life.* New York: Harper and Brothers, 1863.

The Theatrical Inquisitor and Monthly Mirror.

Thompson, E. P. *The Making of the English Working Class.* New York: Vintage Books, 1966.

Tinker, Chauncey Brewster. *The Salon and English Letters.* New York: Gordian Press, 1967.

Trueblood, Paul Graham. *The Flowering of Byron's Genius: Studies in Byron's Don Juan.* Stanford: Stanford University Press, 1945.

Twitchell, James B. *The Living Dead: A Study of the Vampire in Romantic Literature.* Durham: Duke University Press, 1981.

Ward, Aileen. "Keats's Sonnet 'Nebuchadnezzar's Dream'." *Philological Quarterly* 34.2 (April 1955), 177–88.

Wheeler, Kathleen M. *The Creative Mind in Coleridge's Poetry.* Cambridge: Harvard University Press, 1981.

Whitehead, Frank. *George Crabbe: A Reappraisal.* Selingsgrove: Susquehanna University Press; London: Associated University Presses, 1995.

Williams, Raymond. *The Country and the City.* New York: Oxford University Press, 1973.

Wolfson, Susan. "Feminizing Keats." In *Critical Essays on John Keats.* Ed. Hermione de Almeida. Boston: G. K. Hall, 1990, 317–56.

Wood, Marcus. *Radical Satire and Print Culture, 1790–1822.* Oxford: Clarendon Press, 1994.

Woodring, Carl. *Politics in English Romantic Poetry.* Cambridge, Mass.: Harvard University Press, 1970.

———. *Politics in the Poetry of Coleridge.* Madison: University of Wisconsin Press, 1961.

Woolf, Virginia. *Orlando.* New York and London: Harvest/Harcourt Brace Jovanovich, 1956.

Wordsworth, William. *The Letters of William and Dorothy Wordsworth: The Middle Years.* Ed., Ernest de Selincourt. 6 vols. Oxford: Clarendon Press, 1935–39; 1937.

———. *Peter Bell.* Ed. John E. Jordan. Ithaca, N.Y.: Cornell University Press, 1985.

———. *The Poetical Works of William Wordsworth.* Ed. Ernest de Selincourt and Helen Darbishire. 5 vols. Oxford: Clarendon Press, 1940–49.

———. *The Prelude: 1799, 1805, 1850.* Ed. Jonathan Wordsworth, M. H. Abrams, and Stephen Gill. New York and London: W. W. Norton, 1979.

———. *The Prose Works of William Wordsworth.* Ed. W. J. B. Owen and Jane Worthington Smyser. 3 vols. Oxford: Clarendon Press, 1974.

Wordsworth, William, and S. T. Coleridge. *Lyrical Ballads, 1798.* Facs. rept. Oxford and New York: Woodstock Books, 1990.

———. *Lyrical Ballads* (1800). Ed. R. L. Brett and A. R. Jones. London and New York: Methuen, 1963.

Wu, Duncan. *Wordsworth's Reading, 1770–1799; and 1800–1815.* 2 vols. Cambridge and New York: Cambridge University Press, 1993; 1995.

Index